JON STEWART

JON STEWART

A Biography

Michael Blitz

GREENWOOD BIOGRAPHIES

 GREENWOOD

AN IMPRINT OF ABC-CLIO, LLC
Santa Barbara, California • Denver, Colorado • Oxford, England

Library of Congress Cataloging-in-Publication Data

Blitz, Michael.
  Jon Stewart : a biography / Michael Blitz.
    pages cm — (Greenwood biographies)
  Includes index.
  ISBN 978-0-313-35828-9 (hardback) — ISBN 978-0-313-35829-6 (ebook)
  1. Stewart, Jon, 1962– 2. Comedians—United States—Biography.
3. Actors—United States—Biography. 4. Television personalities—
United States—Biography. I. Title.
  PN2287.S683B55 2014
  792.702'8092—dc23
  [B]   2014005303

ISBN: 978-0-313-35828-9
EISBN: 978-0-313-35829-6

18 17 16 15 14   1 2 3 4 5

This book is also available on the World Wide Web as an eBook.
Visit www.abc-clio.com for details.

Greenwood
An Imprint of ABC-CLIO, LLC

ABC-CLIO, LLC
130 Cremona Drive, P.O. Box 1911
Santa Barbara, California 93116-1911

This book is printed on acid-free paper ∞

Manufactured in the United States of America

CONTENTS

Series Foreword   vii

Preface and Acknowledgments   ix

Introduction   xi

Timeline: Events in the Life of Jon Stewart   xvii

Chapter 1   The (Hairy) Backstory   1

Chapter 2   Before Jon Stewart Was Jon Stewart   13

Chatper 3   "Leibo"   25

Chapter 4   The Bitter End and a New Beginning   37

Chapter 5   A Show of His Own—Part I   49

Chapter 6   A Show of His Own—Part II   59

Chapter 7   A Show of His Own—Part III   67

Chapter 8   The Daily Show with Jon Stewart   85

Chapter 9   Exceeding His Own Track Record   103

Chapter 10   Kill or Be Killed   121

CONTENTS

Chapter 11   Jon, Judaism, and Jewish Humor   135
Chapter 12   A Long Moment of Zen   147
Appendix: My Guest Tonight . . .   157
Notes   171
Further Reading   197
Index   199

SERIES FOREWORD

In response to school and library needs, ABC-CLIO publishes this distinguished series of full-length biographies specifically for student use. Prepared by field experts and professionals, these engaging biographies are tailored for students who need challenging yet accessible biographies. Ideal for school assignments and student research, the length, format, and subject areas are designed to meet educators' requirements and students' interests.

ABC-CLIO offers an extensive selection of biographies spanning all curriculum-related subject areas including social studies, the sciences, literature and the arts, history and politics, and popular culture, covering public figures and famous personalities from all time periods and backgrounds, both historic and contemporary, who have made an impact on American and/or world culture. The subjects of these biographies were chosen based on comprehensive feedback from librarians and educators. Consideration was given to both curriculum relevance and inherent interest. Readers will find a wide array of subject choices from fascinating entertainers like Miley Cyrus and Lady Gaga to inspiring leaders like John F. Kennedy and Nelson Mandela, from the greatest athletes of our time like Michael Jordan and Muhammad Ali to the most amazing success stories of our day like J. K. Rowling and Oprah Winfrey.

While the emphasis is on fact, not glorification, the books are meant to be fun to read. Each volume provides in-depth information about the subject's life from birth through childhood, the teen years, and adulthood. A thorough account relates family background and education, traces personal and professional influences, and explores struggles, accomplishments, and contributions. A timeline highlights the most significant life events against an historical perspective. Bibliographies supplement the reference value of each volume.

PREFACE AND
ACKNOWLEDGMENTS

Jon Stewart is, quite simply, a cultural force to be reckoned with. As host of Comedy Central's *The Daily Show with Jon Stewart*, he has created a complex theatrical stage on which the "actors" are comedians, politicians, authors, athletes, scientists, actors and actresses, legal scholars, and, above all, the network news media themselves. With Stewart as the conductor of each night's performance, audiences are treated to a kind of controlled chaos in which real information is combined with comic bits, fake "news" commentaries, video clips of public figures contradicting themselves, and more. Stewart likes to remind viewers that he is just a comedian on a cable television channel, but his career trajectory tells a different story. He is a big—possibly the *biggest* voice on a small channel whose popularity has exploded largely as a result of *The Daily Show*'s appeal and influence. Jon Stewart's story is about a man who has worked incredibly hard at a craft designed to seem so easy: comedy. He has said, of his career, that there is no magical moment of having "made it" in the business. Rather, he has told virtually anyone who asks, finding—and making—humor from the raw material of the world around us is a day-to-day labor of love: a *daily* show.

Many thanks to the people who have been supportive in a variety of creative ways. My editor George Butler deserves a prize for patience and kindness. Lydia Shinoj and Michelle Scott made the revising and editing processes relatively painless. Greenwood Press/ABC-CLIO publishes wonderful books, and I am honored to be a Greenwood author. To Victor Marchese, I owe a debt of gratitude beyond words for working miracles and restoring me to myself. To Maureen Tita, my thanks for her wisdom, insight, and medical science. My friend and brother-in-spirit, Jim DeFelice has been an inspiration and role model for over 35 years. Louise Krasniewicz's remarkable imagination continues to inform me in all my research and writing. For a long list of reasons, thank you to dear friends Claude Mark Hurlbert, Debra Scacciafero, Derek Owens, Teresa Hewitt, Mark Dalton, Joyce Rambo, Kevin and Suzanne Reid, and Don Byrd who taught me how to learn. I am deeply grateful for my extended family—Michael, Barbara, and Alli (my LBFF) Cohen, my "parental units" Anne & Nat Director, and for Marcy & Izzy Peter, Jody Eisner, and Jed and Sheryl Woelfle. Thanks also to the fantastic BLITZ Krav Maga gang—Ena Jain, Dean Angel, Paul Benincasa, MC, John Coughlin, Fran Faustino, Flash Flashner, TJ Flynn, Craig Handyside, Todd Kettler, Angel Lorente, Tim Marinace, Amy Morgenstern, Vinny and Kim Paolella, Frank Pomara, KR, Chris Zaleski, Sheri Schlicher, Knuckles Rosenberg, and Matt Roman.

My Interdisciplinary Studies colleagues and friends at John Jay College of Criminal Justice have been enormously supportive, especially Jerry Markowitz, Shirley Sarna, Susannah Crowder, Priscila Acuna, Dennis Sherman, Mary Ann McClure, Abby Stein, and Andrea Balis.

And most profoundly, my love and gratitude to my wife, soulmate, and LOML, Mozelle, and to our children Daina "Dab" Blitz, Cory "Bud" Blitz, Celine "Bean" Dayan-Bonilla, and Rene "The Bundle" Dayan-Bonilla.

INTRODUCTION

Jon Stewart is "an intense Manhattan smarty-pants who has the style and air of a man perpetually slouching toward adulthood."[1]

—Maureen Dowd, 2006

I am a tiny, neurotic man, standing in the back of the room, throwing tomatoes at the chalkboard.[2]

A life is made of a million moments, events, ideas, actions, and if we are honest with ourselves, we forget most of them. It turns out that this is probably a good thing. If we could remember everything about our lives, we might feel as though we have to take a "time out" from living, just to let our memories catch up with us.

Writing the biography of a living person poses similarly unique challenges. For one thing, the subject's life is always far ahead of any attempt to capture it in a narrative. There are no time outs. By the time the biographer finishes a chapter, or even a sentence, about the subject—Jon Stewart, for example—Stewart will have already lived many additional minutes, hours, and days. The public Jon will have interviewed dozens of new guests, made perhaps hundreds of newsworthy remarks, won still more awards, been quoted in another dozen publications, perhaps written one more himself, and on and on. The behind-the-scenes-of-*The-Daily-Show* Jon would have met again and again with his top-notch team of writers to discuss a few hundred potential ideas for the show or to watch hours upon hours of video clips, newscasts, campaign ads and speeches, and election results. The private Jon would have seen his kids grow and change, his marriage evolve, his relationship with his mother, father, brother, and half-brothers shift with time. It's a little like trying to take a still photograph of someone sprinting past the camera's lens with no intention of stopping long enough to be "captured" by the photographer. And few subjects move as rapidly as Jon Stewart does.

Traditional biographies often begin at "the beginning." The subject is born, grows up, passes through a variety of milestones on the way to adulthood, ages, winds down, and so on. Sometimes the story begins a generation or two before the birth of the biographical subject. But no matter how the biography is structured, it is always, in essence, a set of answers to hundreds of questions—asked and unasked—about the subject's life. The answers may not always be definitive. There are bound to be discrepancies among sources of information. For example, in most of the biographical material already out there about Jon Stewart's life, his father is identified as a physicist and a physics teacher. But in the program on Jon Stewart's life featured on The Biography Channel, Stewart's father is described as a "psychiatrist."[3] In this case, it's easy enough to verify that Stewart's father, Don Leibowitz, was a physicist and a physics professor, a far cry from psychiatry. Some biographical websites say that Jon's parents divorced when he was 11 years old, but other sites suggest that Jon was 9 or 10 years old[4] when Marian and Donald Leibowitz divorced. Jon himself can be evasive about his personal life. Interviews with him yield a wide variety of anecdotes that may or may not be true; they may even simply be jokes that serve to deflect attention from the personal to the comedic. Interestingly enough, when Jon is at home, he and his wife Tracey and their kids, Nathan and Maggie, are not terribly interested in *The Daily Show*. He told an interviewer, "We don't watch the show. We don't watch the news. We don't do any of that stuff." Of course, Jon Stewart wouldn't be Jon Stewart if he didn't add, "I sit down, I play with Barbies. And sometimes the kids will come home and play with me."[5]

Writing the story of a life that is, at that moment, still being lived—dynamically, energetically, imaginatively, and to a great extent, publicly—also entails accepting that the individual's defining moments must be continuously updated and re-understood. One way to do this is to try to talk to those close to the subject. In this case, an initially promising contact and brief e-mail exchange with one of Stewart's half-brothers led only to silence thereafter. Attempts to speak to, or correspond with, Stewart's father, Don Leibowitz, his mother Marian Leibowitz, or his brother, Larry Leibowitz, were all to no avail. One of Stewart's half-brothers had explained that he would first need to consult with one of the family's attorneys before consenting to be interviewed. It's possible that that consultation resulted in his being told *not* to speak to Jon Stewart's biographer. Efforts to speak with Jon himself, including contacting his publicity manager, members of *Daily Show* executive staff, and a high-ranking employee of Comedy Central's owner, ViaCom, all proved fruitless. Or perhaps not. As will be illustrated throughout this biography, despite a viral popularity and notoriety, Jon Stewart has managed to insulate his personal life in a way that few super-celebrities can do. Remarks made by Stewart's friends and associates have yielded mostly fleeting glimpses into the life and work of *The Daily Show* host. And the relative silence of family members attests to Stewart's intention to protect his family from as much of the media clamor as possible.

One of the most interesting, and challenging, aspects of writing Jon Stewart's biography is weighing and interpreting an enormous number of quotable remarks Stewart himself has made about his *"own"* life. In most cases, it's evident that Stewart is joking—exaggerating, poking fun at himself, deflecting personal questions with humor. But such deflections often hint, for example, at important truths about Stewart's childhood. When asked about lessons he'd learned from his mother, he replied, "Always refer to my father sarcastically as Mr. Wonderful."[6] Despite the obvious sarcastic humor in it, Stewart's response points to a conflict not only between his parents, but also between Jon and his father, a tension that persisted through Jon's adulthood.

Described as "a workaholic, an insomniac and thoroughly addicted to the news,"[7] equally "addicted" to crossword puzzles,[8] "America's Most Trusted Newsman,"[9] "The Most Trusted Man in Fake News,"[10] a "man many consider to be the preeminent political analyst of our time,"[11] even the "Most Powerful Economic Force in the U.S.,"[12] it would be absurd to write the biography of Jon Stewart without devoting a substantial portion of it to a "biography" of one of the country's most well-known late-night talk shows, Comedy Central's *The Daily Show with Jon Stewart*. For over 15 years, Jon Stewart and *The Daily Show* have been synonymous in the public consciousness. At 52, Stewart has spent more than 20 percent of his life in front of Comedy Central audiences, telling them, "Welcome to the Daily Show! My name is Jon Stewart." It's an exciting moment for viewers because "Jon Stewart" has come to represent more than just the name of *The Daily Show*'s host; it represents, as philosophy professor Terrance MacMullan puts it, "a public intellectual who fosters critical thinking across an enormous audience and who defends democratic principles from erosion by partisan punditry and the government's apparent disregard for genuine debate."[13] That's quite a mouthful, and it's likely that Jon Stewart would make a joke about such a wordy (or as Stewart's former *Daily Show* colleague Stephen Colbert might have said, "truthy") description of himself. But there is no denying that Stewart has a uniquely sharp-witted point of view on politics and politicians, pundits and news media, language, and daily life in New York City (and, frequently, New Jersey). At times, he seems like the voice of reason amid the clamor of political rhetoric—he once said, "Don't you see the problem our country is having? I'm making sense and the President isn't."[14] But Stewart manages to keep a level head and a sense of humor about his own ever-growing significance to a generation raised on television "news." When long-time CNN talk-show host Larry King tells Stewart, "You're an American fixture," Stewart replies by saying remarks like that "make me sound like a toilet."[15]

It's easy, however, to agree with King. Whether through his work as one of America's most insightful political media analysts (Stewart always argues "I'm a comedian!"), or as best-selling author (Stewart said of his hugely successful book, *Earth: (The Book)*, "It's mostly false. But there are a lot of funny pictures. And isn't that the important thing?"),[16] viewers across America experience Jon Stewart and *The Daily Show* as culturally and socially important. Stewart's keen understanding of local, national, and global politics and events is matched by his daily consternation about mass media's typical coverage of them. His viewers are provoked to think more creatively, to watch and listen to "news" sources more critically, and, of course, to appreciate the comedy inherent in much of what Americans, often, take too seriously. About his show, Stewart says, "I love it. I feel it's the one job I've ever had that feels like I'm able to completely immerse myself in it."[17] Others go much farther, suggesting that Stewart and the *Daily Show* have morphed into something much more influential in American culture. Political scientists Jody Baumgartner and Jonathan S. Morris have dubbed this influence "*The Daily Show* Effect" and discuss the ways in which Stewart has reshaped the dialogue about political candidates and the ways in which they are elected.[18] How did a kid from Jersey named Jon Stuart Leibowitz come to be the kind of public figure that has politicians, journalists, celebrities, and scholars scrambling for his attention or, at times, scrambling to avoid a confrontation with him? How does someone who describes himself first and foremost as "a comedian who has the pleasure of writing jokes about things that I actually care about"[19] come to be mentioned in the same context as the author of *Moby Dick*, Herman Melville?[20] How does the self-proclaimed *fake* newscaster of *fake* news win multiple *real* Peabody Awards, one of the most prestigious acknowledgments that can be bestowed upon *real* professional journalists? The story of Jon Stewart is the story of both a journey and a set of arrivals, each richer and more remarkable than the last.

TIMELINE: EVENTS IN
THE LIFE OF JON STEWART

1962   November 28, Jon Stuart Leibowitz born to Marian and Donald Leibowitz.

1963   The Leibowitz family moves to Lawrenceville, New Jersey.

1967   Attends Yeshiva Kindergarten. Thereafter in public schools.

1971   Marian and Donald Stewart divorce. Jon and his brother Larry remain living with their mother.

1975   Jon has his Bar Mitzvah at Princeton Jewish Center, New Jersey.

1976   Fired from job at Woolworth's by his brother, Larry, who was assistant manager.

1980   Graduates from Lawrenceville High School, Lawrenceville, New Jersey.
Accepted to University of Virginia (UVA).

1981   Leaves UVA after a semester, transferring to the College of William and Mary (Williamsburg, Virginia).
Meets and becomes friends with the future congressman Anthony Weiner (many years later, Stewart contributed to Weiner's campaign—one of the only times Stewart donated money to a political campaign).
Joins the soccer team at William and Mary and moves up to varsity in 1982.

1983 Recruited by the College of William and Mary's head soccer coach, Al Albert, to play soccer for the first Pan American Maccabi Games in São Paolo, Brazil.

1984 Has an annual award named after him by the College of William and Mary's soccer team: the "Leibo."
Graduates from the College of William and Mary with a degree in psychology.
Gets a job as a contingency planner for the New Jersey Department of Human Services.

1986 Moves to New York City to pursue a career in stand-up comedy.

1987 First stand-up gig at New York City's club, The Bitter End.
Changes name from Jon Stuart Leibowitz to "Jon Stewart."

1989 Hired as writer for *Caroline's Comedy Hour*, which was broadcast from Caroline's (comedy club) in New York City.

1990 Opens several times for singer Sheena Easton's concerts.[21]

1991 Hired to host Comedy Central's *Short Attention Span Theater*.

1992 Hired to host MTV's *You Wrote It, You Watch It*, which featured the comedy troupe, "The State." The show is canceled after one season.

1993 Finalist to replace David Letterman when Letterman leaves NBC. (Conan O'Brien is ultimately hired.)
Hired to host his own MTV talk show, *The Jon Stewart Show*. The show is canceled in 1995.

1996 Signs a three-year contract with Miramax Films to star in, write, and produce two movies each year. Also signs a contract with David Letterman's production company World Wide Pants for future projects.
Co–executive producer of TV movie *Jon Stewart: Unleavened*.
Appears in the movie *Wishful Thinking*.
Introduced to Tracey McShane by a production assistant on sets of the movie, *Wishful Thinking*.

1997 Appears on TV show *News Radio*, plays Andrew, fake twin brother of Matt (Andy Dick).

1998 Publishes his first book, a collection of short essays, entitled *Naked Pictures of Famous People*, which becomes a *New York Times* best-seller.
Appears in the movie *Since You've Been Gone*.

1999   Hired to replace Craig Kilborne on Comedy Central's *The Daily Show*. The show is renamed *The Daily Show with Jon Stewart*.

Chosen by *People* magazine as one of 1999's 50 Most Beautiful People in the World.

Co–executive producer of the TV movies *The Daily Show Third Anniversary Special, In Search of the Unsolved, The Daily View, The Daily Show Summer Spectacular*, and *The Greatest Millennium*.

2000   *The Daily Show* wins a Peabody Award for coverage of the presidential election.

Jon wins $125,000 for Alzheimer's disease research during an appearance on a celebrity episode of *Who Wants to Be a Millionaire*.

Jon proposes to Tracy McShane through a crossword puzzle created for him by Will Shortz.

Jon marries Tracy.

Jon quits smoking.

Appears in the movies *Committed* and *Office Party*.

Co–executive producer of the TV movies *Wrinkled Nuts, The Daily Show Fourth Anniversary Special, The Out at the Movies Fabulous Big 'O' Special: Being Frank DeCaro, The Campaign Trail to the Road to the Whitehouse: Storytellers*, and *Tales of Survival*.

Co–executive producer of Comedy Central's *Indecision 2000: Election Night—Choose and Lose*.

2001   Nominated for the American Comedy Award for Funniest Male Performer in a TV Special for *Indecision 2000: Election Night—Choose and Lose* (2000).

The Daily Show with Jon Stewart wins the Emmy Award for Outstanding Writing for a Variety, Music, or Comedy Program and is nominated for the Emmy Award for Outstanding Variety, Music, or Comedy Series.

Time magazine calls Jon Stewart America's best talk show host.

Appears in the movie *Jay and Silent Bob Strike Back*.

Executive producer of the TV movies *Steve Carell Salutes Steve Carell, The Daily Show Fifth Anniversary Special, The Out at the Movies Fabulous Big 'O' Special: Miscast Away, Mo Rocca's Back to School Special*, and *Stephen Colbert Again: A Look Back*.

2002   Writer and co–executive producer of Comedy Central's *Indecision 2002: Election Night.*
        The Daily Show with Jon Stewart is nominated for two Emmy Awards for Outstanding Variety, Music, or Comedy Series and for Outstanding Writing for a Variety, Music, or Comedy Program.
        Hosts *The Grammy Awards* (CBS).
        Nominated by The Television Critics Association for Outstanding Individual Performance in a Variety or Music Program.
        Nominated for Teen Choice Award for TV-Choice Personality.
        Hosts *Saturday Night Live.*
        Moderates a panel called "September 11th: How It Changed Us" at the Michael Schimmel Center for the Arts, Pace University, New York.
        Executive producer (and star) of *Indecision 2002: Election Night.*
        Plays the voice of Godfrey in the movie *The Adventures of Tom Thumb and Thumbelina.*
        Co–executive producer of the TV movies *The Road to Washington, The Big O! True West Hollywood Story, On the Air: An On Air Guide to Getting on the Air,* and *Matt Walsh Goes to Hawaii.*
        Appears in the movie *Death to Smoochy.*
        September 21, *The Daily Show with Jon Stewart: Global Edition* debuts worldwide on CNNi (CNN International).
        Jon does a Q&A session at his alma mater, the College of William & Mary.
        Speaks at Harvard's Kennedy School of Government at the ARCO Forum, Boston, Massachusetts.

2003   *The Daily Show with Jon Stewart* wins two Emmy Awards for Outstanding Variety, Music, or Comedy Series and for Outstanding Writing for a Variety, Music, or Comedy Program.
        Nominated for the Emmy Award for Outstanding Individual Performance in a Variety or Music Program.
        Appears on a panel with *The Daily Show* producers, writers, and correspondents at John Jay College Theater, New York, for a program, "Behind the Scenes of The Daily Show with Jon Stewart."
        With Patti LaBelle, appears at the United Jewish Appeal Federation's J. Ross Humanitarian Award Dinner to honor Ralph J. Robert and Brian L. Roberts (owners of the Philadelphia 76ers), at the Waldorf Astoria Hotel in New York City.

Wins the Television Critics Association Award for Individual Achievement in Comedy as host of *The Daily Show with Jon Stewart*.

One of the Man of the Year winners in the special "Man of the Year awards" issue by *GQ* magazine.

On September 15, Senator John Edwards (D-NC) formally announces his candidacy for the U.S. presidency on *The Daily Show*.

On October 31, Jon appears on the cover of *Entertainment Weekly* and featured in the cover story.

Executive producer (and star) of *Re-Decision 2003: The California Recall*.

Executive producer (and star) of *Iraq: A Look Baq (Or, How We Learned to Stop Reporting and Love the War)*.

Executive producer of the TV movies *I'm a Correspondent, Please Don't Fire Me*; *The Frank DeCaro Big 'O' Special: A Fable*; and *Who Are the Daily Show?*

2004   On July 3, Jon's wife Tracey gives birth to their first child, Nathan Thomas Stewart, named for Jon's maternal grandfather, Nathan Laskin.

With *The Daily Show* cast and staff members, publishes *America: The Book*, a mock textbook. The book becomes one of the best-selling books of the year.

The Daily Show again wins a Peabody Award for coverage of the presidential election.

Voted second funniest person in America (behind Chris Rock) by *Entertainment Weekly*.

On August 9, former president Bill Clinton appears on *The Daily Show*, the first of six appearances between 2004 and 2010.

Executive producer (and star) of *Indecision 2004: Prelude to a Recount*.

The Daily Show with Jon Stewart wins two Emmy Awards for Outstanding Variety, Music, or Comedy Series and for Outstanding Writing for a Variety, Music, or Comedy Program.

Nominated for the Television Critics Association Award for Individual Achievement in Comedy as host of *The Daily Show with Jon Stewart*.

Featured on the cover of *TV Guide*.

Executive producer of the TV movie *The Race from the White House 2004.*

2005 The audio edition of *America: The Book* wins a Grammy Award for Best Comedy Album.

On December 5, former president Jimmy Carter appears on *The Daily Show*, the first of four appearances between 2005 and 2010.

The Daily Show with Jon Stewart wins two Emmy Awards for Outstanding Variety, Music, or Comedy Series and for Outstanding Writing for a Variety, Music, or Comedy Program.

Nominated for the Emmy Award for Outstanding Individual Performance in a Variety or Music Program.

Wins the Television Critics Association Award for Individual Achievement in Comedy as host of *The Daily Show with Jon Stewart.*

Nominated for the People's Choice Award for Favorite Funny Male Star and Favorite Late Night Talk Show Host.

Featured on the cover of *Wired* magazine.

Executive producer of the Comedy Central *Daily Show* spinoff, *The Colbert Report.*

2006 On February 4, Stewart's wife Tracey gives birth to their second child, Maggie Rose Stewart.

Hosts *The 78th Annual Academy Awards.*

Executive producer (and star) of *Indecision 2006: Midterm Midtacular.*

On June 16, appears with David Steinberg on *Sit Down Comedy with David Steinberg,* at John Jay College Theater, John Jay College, New York.

The Daily Show with Jon Stewart wins two Emmy Awards for Outstanding Variety, Music, or Comedy Series and Outstanding Writing for a Variety, Music, or Comedy Program.

Nominated for the Television Critics Association Award for Individual Achievement in Comedy as host of *The Daily Show with Jon Stewart.*

Executive producer of *Night of Too Many Stars: An Overbooked Event for Autism Education.*

Executive producer of the TV movie *Three Strikes.*

Appears in the documentary film *Wordplay*.

Plays the voice of Zeebad in the movie *Doogal*.

Executive producer of TV documentary *Sportsfan*.

Appears as himself (voice) in episode "Irregarding Steve," in TV series *American Dad*.

Appears as himself in TV special *Comic Relief*.

Appears as himself in *The 58th Annual Prime Time Emmy Awards*.

Appears as himself in Al Franken's TV documentary *Al Franken: God Spoke*.

Appears as himself on TV series *Howard Stern on Demand*.

Appears as himself on TV series *Corazon de . . .* (March 6 episode).

Appears as himself on TV series *Film '72* (February 20 episode).

Appears as himself (guest) on *Ellen: The Ellen DeGeneres Show* (March 3 episode).

2007   Appears as himself in the movie *Evan Almighty*.

Renews his contract with Comedy Central, agreeing to host *The Daily Show* through 2010.

The Daily Show with Jon Stewart wins the Emmy Award for Outstanding Variety, Music, or Comedy Series and is also nominated for Outstanding Writing for a Variety, Music, or Comedy Program.

Nominated for the Emmy Award for Outstanding Individual Performance in a Variety or Music Program.

Nominated for the Television Critics Association Award for Individual Achievement in Comedy as host of *The Daily Show with Jon Stewart*.

The Daily Show throws its "support" behind Stephen Colbert's run for U.S. president in 2008.

Narrator (voice) for documentary *Twisted: A Balloonamentary*.

Appears as himself on the TV documentary *1968 with Tom Brokaw*.

Appears as himself on the video documentary *The Making of the "Larry Sanders Show."*

Appears as himself on *The 59th Primetime Emmy Awards*.

2008   *The Daily Show with Jon Stewart* is nominated for the Emmy Award for Outstanding Writing for a Variety, Music, or Comedy Series.

Hosts *The 80th Annual Academy Awards*.

Nominated for the Emmy Award for Outstanding Individual Performance in a Variety or Music Program for his role as Host of the *80th Annual Academy Awards* (2008).

On October 3, Jon Stewart and Steven Colbert are featured on the cover of *Entertainment Weekly*.

Executive producer of *A Colbert Christmas: The Greatest Gift of All!* and *Night of Too Many Stars: An Overbooked Event for Autism Education*.

Executive producer (and star) of *Indecision 2008: Election Night—America's Choice*.

2009   Nominated for BAFTA TV Award for Best International Show (for *The Daily Show with Jon Stewart*).

The Daily Show with Jon Stewart wins the Emmy Award for Outstanding Writing for a Variety, Music, or Comedy Series.

Executive producer of 17 episodes of TV series *Important Things with Demetri Martin*.

Executive producer of TV movie *Changefest '09" Rebirth of a Nation—A Night of History & Balls*.

2010   On October 30, organizes *Rally to Restore Sanity and/or Fear* in Washington, D.C., coproduced with Stephen Colbert.

President Barack Obama appears as a guest on *The Daily Show*, the first time Jon Stewart hosts an incumbent U.S. president.

The Daily Show with Jon Stewart is nominated for the Emmy Award for Outstanding Writing for a Variety, Music, or Comedy Series.

Publishes *Earth (The Book): A Visitor's Guide to the Human Race*, becomes a best-seller.

Executive producer of the documentary *Naturalized*.

2011   Appears in the movie *The Adjustment Bureau*.

Awarded the Emmy for Best Writing for a Variety, Music, or Comedy Series at *The 63rd Primetime Emmy Awards* (Fox).

Appears as himself in the TV documentary *When Pop Culture Saved America: A 9-11 Story* (Biography Channel).

Appears in the movie *The Beaver*.

2012   On October 17, interviews President Obama during presidential campaign.

Co-hosts Hurricane Sandy Telethon (raised money to provide relief after Hurricane Sandy devastated large areas of Long Island, New York City, and New Jersey).

2013   Goes on hiatus from *The Daily Show* for 12 weeks to direct the film *Rosewater*.

Chapter 1

THE (HAIRY) BACKSTORY

My grandfather had a talk show back in Russia: Getting Through the Pogrom with Nathan Laskin.

—Jon Stewart[1]

While his remark was tongue in cheek—the "Pogrom" is a reference to the relentless anti-Jewish riots and attacks upon Jews inflicted by the 19th-century Russian Empire—Jon Stewart correctly portrays his maternal grandfather, Nathan Laskin, as a funny guy—just not in the kinds of venues one might expect. Born in Russia in 1907,[2] Nathan Laskin worked as a young man in the family's fur business in Tientsin (now spelled Tianjin), one of China's most populous cities. At the time, Tientsin was under Western control in the form of foreign "concessions"; essentially, the city was divided up among eight countries each of which would control an area or district of the city. The eight countries—France, Britain, Japan, Italy, Germany, Austria-Hungary, Belgium, and Russia—each established a kind of miniature version of their culture in their assigned district. Roads that passed through more than one district had multiple street names; one such thoroughfare was named Victoria Street in the British zone and Rue de France in the French zone. U.S. president Herbert Hoover had lived, for a time, in Tientsin and called "a universal city, like a world in miniature."[3]

In the Russian concession of Tientsin, Nathan Laskin worked in the family fur business but also performed stand-up comedy for other merchants who did business in this city. Not much is known about the nature of these comedy performances, but one of the threads that connect Laskin to his grandson is his ability to recognize humor in everyday life and his desire to make people laugh.

But neither the fur business nor funny business succeeded in keeping Laskin in China; as many Jewish Europeans did, Laskin eventually made his way to the United States and then to New York City to make a new life and to earn enough money to start his own family. Laskin tried his hand at several small businesses, none of which resulted in great financial gain. He did, however, meet—and marry—Fannie, a New Yorker three years his junior, and in 1933, Nathan and Fannie Laskin welcomed their daughter Marian—Jon Stewart's mother—to the world. Ironically, in 1996 during a comedy showcase, Jon said about his grandfather, "Ninety years old. Huge bigot. I love the man to death. Huge bigot. Hates immigrants. [He came] from Russia . . . hates immigrants. I guess my grandfather's one of those lucky immigrants who got off the boat, signed in, and then turned to the people behind him and went, 'Now get off my land you foreign [Bleep],'"[4] But he also had what Jon recalls as a "dry sense of humor" and would, according to Jon, try to make his grandson laugh.[5]

On his father's side, Jon's great-grandfather owned a shoe store on Rivington Street on New York City's Lower East Side.[6] The street was named after James Rivington (1724–1803), who played a unique role in the American Revolution. Rivington was the editor (and generally the only writer) of the Loyalist "newspaper," *Rivington's Gazette*. In it, Rivington made public his support for British law and influence over the colonies, which, as you might imagine, earned him many enemies among the colonists who had come to America to escape those laws. Burned in effigy by the Sons of Liberty, Rivington eventually fled New York City, returning to his native England. In 1777, when the British armies had securely occupied New York City, Rivington returned and resumed publication of his Loyalist journal. However, soon after,

Rivington had a change of heart—and of loyalty—and began gathering and turning over secret information to General George Washington that aided Washington in the Revolutionary War–efforts. In effect, Rivington gradually drifted away from his earlier beliefs and became a spy for the Continental army.[7]

It was on the street named for this fascinating man that Stewart's great-grandfather sought to make a living in his shoe store. Surrounded by similarly small and busy shops, the Leibowitzs sold to, and mingled with, the growing community of Jewish immigrant shopkeepers and their families, many of whom kept up the traditions of Orthodox Judaism that had defined their communities in Europe. Jon's great-grandfather was a religious man and made certain that his grandson, Don (Jon's father) abided by Jewish customs and practices as well. According to Don Leibowitz, when he would visit his grandfather at the shoe store, grandfather Leibowitz "would pinch my cheek and make me recite prayers."[8] Although Don Leibowitz may have been raised in accordance with Jewish tradition, he, in his own way, drifted away from those traditions, especially after he started a family of his own. Indeed, many years later, when he was appointed adjunct professor of physics at the College of New Jersey, he took on the role of faculty advisor to the Secular Student Alliance.[9]

Jon's paternal grandfather—Don's father—worked as a New York City cab driver, picking up and dropping off passengers over the course of long work days, and earning the very modest living typical of city "cabbies." No one could say that these Leibowitz men lived in high style; like so many who lived in the Jewish immigrant sections of New York City, great-grandfather and grandfather Leibowitz were hardworking men who strove to make better lives for their children, one of whom was a boy named Don Leibowitz—Jon Stewart's father.

DON LEIBOWITZ

Don Leibowitz was born in Brooklyn, New York, in December 1931. He graduated from Stuyvesant High School in 1949. Located in the Tribeca area of Manhattan, overlooking the Hudson River, Stuyvesant High School, along with Brooklyn Technical High School and Bronx High School of Science, is one of the three original academic "specialized high schools" in New York City, and all three have always been known for their strong emphasis on advanced learning in math and science. Admission to any of these three schools is by competitive exam only, and Stuyvesant's exam is widely considered to be the most challenging.

After graduating from Stuyvesant, Don Leibowitz went on to earn a graduate degree in physics from the City University of New York, and an advanced degree in economics from Rutgers University.[10]

In 1960, Don married Marian Laskin, and that same year their first child, Larry, was born. Two years later, a few days after Thanksgiving, in 1962, on November 28, the Leibowitzs welcomed Jonathan Stuart Leibowitz to the world—the baby that would, as Jon commented many years later, grow up to be "a wiseass kid from New Jersey who has to comment on everything."[11] A father at 29 years old, and then again at 31, Don Leibowitz was surrounded by an impressive family—a brilliant wife and two healthy boys both of whom grew up to be remarkably successful. It should have been a comfortable and satisfying life for the Leibowitz family, and for a number of years it seemed to be exactly that.

But 11 years later, as Jon put it, Don Leibowitz "left my mother when he was about 40."[12] His father's departure may or may not have been one of the reasons Jon eventually discarded the name Leibowitz, but what is certain is Jon's disdain for the way in which his father had treated his family. During an interview with Oprah Winfrey in 2005, she asked Jon what kind of father he wanted to be. Stewart told her, "The kind who stays. The kind who doesn't say to a 9-year old kid, 'This doesn't mean your mother and I don't love you' as he's heading out the door."[13] Many years later, Jon described his father in this way: "He's a very scientific man, and we were the control group."[14]

In 1971, a couple of years before separating from Marian, Don became the energy coordinator for the New Jersey Department of Treasury. He remained at that position for more than 14 years, developing energy-saving techniques for the state buildings in Trenton. He also served as director of Distributed Generation of EnergySolve, LLC, and was president of his own company, the Leibowitz Energy Group, LLC. Don's scientific expertise in energy and conservation enabled him to play a key role in analyzing and solving a variety of energy-related issues in New Jersey. Don played an integral role in the early development of the "cogeneration district heating and cooling systems" in Trenton, providing more efficient heating and cooling with better pollution control than localized boilers.[15] Along the way, as he became a more and more highly recognized and respected energy expert, Don remarried in 1980. Don and Karen Beck Leibowitz had two sons, Matt and Dan.

In 1988, Don Leibowitz became president of the Trenton District Energy Company (TDEC) of the Trigen Energy Corporation, where he also worked while still with the Department of Treasury. Industrious and ingenious, Leibowitz currently holds more than a dozen patents (some have since expired) for different applications in engineering projects. One of his patented inventions, filed in 1998, was an ingenious device designed to minimize the hazards to roadside car and truck-inspectors as they peered beneath vehicles (the device was patented, appropriately enough, under the name "hazard device for a vehicle").[16]

After remaining with TDEC for 12 years, Don retired in 2000. Just one year later, he could not stand retirement any longer and applied for a teaching job at the College of New Jersey (TCNJ) in Ewing Township, a suburb of Trenton. TCNJ has long been regarded as a top-notch college that is both affordable and highly respected. (The 2014 edition of the Princeton Review ranked TCNJ in the top 15 of America's 2,500 four-year colleges.)[17] Somewhat ironically, this new career direction put Don Leibowitz into the profession in which his ex-wife, Marian, specialized: education. Given the zeal with which he had approached his previous professional ventures, it is no surprise that Don achieved a significant degree of success as a college instructor. Teaching several challenging interdisciplinary study courses, including one called "Human Survival—The Challenge of Science in the 21st Century," Don soon became a respected and popular instructor. One evaluator, on the website RateMyProfessor.com, wrote effusively that Professor Liebowitz was "without a doubt the greatest teacher I have ever had throughout the entire history of my education dating all the way back to day care. Ever. He is sweet, extremely funny, helpful, interesting and just a great all around teacher. He has a genuine enthusiasm for his subject. Unforgettable."[18] Don continued teaching at TCNJ until the end of fall 2008 semester. Enthusiastically keeping his hand—and mind—in both teaching and science, Leibowitz went on to teach an online course at Thomas Edison University.[19]

Yet, despite Don's general enthusiasm for his own careers, he was considerably less enthusiastic about the career trajectory that his son Jon took, as evidenced by one of the many remarks Stewart has made about his father over the years. During an interview with Oprah Winfrey, she told Stewart, "There are many people who realize you have a talent that they don't have." Stewart replied, "Do you mind if I put you on the phone with my father right now so you could repeat that last sentence to him?"[20] Although Jon eventually reconciled with his father enough to include him in the acknowledgments to one or more of his books, he also maintained a fairly sour view of his father's departure from Jon's childhood. "My dad had a kid when he was 50-something. I'm sure he's going to be like Anthony Quinn. He'll be 80 years old and he'll tell me, 'Guess what? You have another brother!' 'Oh, that's great, Dad.'"[21]

Don Leibowitz died on Saturday, June 8, 2013, at age 81, and was buried in Beth Israel Cemetery in Woodbridge, New Jersey.[22] In his father, Jon may not have had much of a fan. But Jon's mother, Marian, was a different story. She and Jon are among one another's greatest supporters.

MARIAN LASKIN/LEIBOWITZ

"My mother was a teacher for years, she worked in the education field, she's still in the education field. I couldn't be more impressed by what she did in her life."[23] To say that Marian Laskin was a "teacher" tells only a small part of the story. Respected both nationally and internationally not only for her career in teaching but also for her work as a creative education consultant, Marian Laskin's influence on her son Jon is evident even in small moments on *The Daily Show*. On one memorable occasion, Stewart was interviewing White House Domestic Affairs Chief, Melody Barnes, and Barnes had just told Stewart that "the work [the Obama Administration] has done around education has been a game-changer." Stewart's reply was, "The biggest complaint I hear from teachers, and by teachers I mean my *mom*: the teaching to the test. This idea, the Race to the Top, No Child Left Behind, these benchmarks that have been given from Washington have caused schools to focus entirely on whatever benchmark or requirement they need to get funding, and it has removed from education—I guess you'd call it: *the educating*."[24] Faced with Stewart's emphatic reply, Barnes could only agree with him. In another *Daily Show* exchange, this time with Education Secretary Arne Duncan, Stewart again spoke about his mother, emphasizing that Marian was a staunch opponent of the Obama administration's "Race to the Top" initiative. Stewart explained that his mother considered the initiative to be another version of former president George W. Bush's "No Child Left Behind" policy. Like Bush's initiative, Obama's would make it more difficult for teachers to be creative in their classrooms. Marian Leibowitz, obviously, disapproved of the "Race to the Top" policy and of Arne Duncan's support of it.[25]

Under the name Marian Leibowitz, Jon's mother was the primary contributor on a video titled "Coping with Stress: Teacher Proven Strategies."[26] The hour-long video provides a variety of strategies to combat the unique pressures that teachers experience. In her continued efforts to provide teachers with vital support and strategic resources, Marian was also a contributing author of a chapter in the book, *Supporting the Spirit of Learning*.[27] The list of efforts that Marian Leibowitz has contributed, and continues to contribute, to the culture of teaching and learning is a long one. She has served as president of the New Jersey Association of Learning Consultants and as president of the New Jersey Association for Supervision and Curriculum Development. In 1979, while she was special education coordinator at the Educational Improvement Center in Central New Jersey, Marian Leibowitz offered workshops for teachers of gifted students in 27 states.

Marian Leibowitz has devoted much of her career in education to the teaching of gifted children; one of her primary concerns has been the unique anxieties faced by children in such programs. In particular, she has said, "Once youngsters are identified as being gifted and talented, the pressure increases. Parents become very concerned about school and closely monitor everything that happens there." She also notes that children in these programs "quickly ascertain that they are doing twice as much work as everybody else. There is almost an underlying hostility on the part of regular classroom teachers who make comments like, 'Well now that you are in a gifted program, I would expect your papers to be neater.'" Ever the advocate for fine-tuning education for both students *and* teachers, Leibowitz adds that, "I would like to see people used in a dual capacity: working with students, doing things with them, for them, identifying their needs, but also helping regular classroom teachers provide the differentiated program students need in the regular classroom." She goes on to add, with a candor that also characterizes her son's approach to talking about issues, that one reason so many teachers have difficulty teaching gifted children is that they are "intimidated by youngsters who may know more than they do in a specific subject area."[28]

It is no wonder that Jon Stewart holds his mother, Marian, in such high regard. And he is hardly alone in his admiration and appreciation of his mother's generosity of intellect and spirit. In her summer 2010 blog, "A Life to Remember," Ellen Jin R. Kaufman, whose husband Bryn, had family members who were friends with Marian, wrote, "We even met one of the family friends, Marian, a very intelligent woman, the mother of Jon Stewart (of *The Daily Show of Jon Stewart*) and she gave a book as a present to [infant son] Zachary."[29]

LAWRENCE LEIBOWITZ—"JON STEWART'S UNFUNNY BROTHER"[30]

I have tried to fly under the radar.[31]

In many ways, Jon's older brother Larry Leibowitz is the polar opposite of his show-biz sibling. Whereas Jon ricocheted from job to job until launching himself into stand-up comedy, Larry Leibowitz pursued a much more direct and specific career path, as far from show business as one can get.

The divorce of Marian and Don Leibowitz was marked by another important moment in the life of the Leibowitz boys. Thirteen-year old Lawrence had his *Bar Mitzvah*, the symbolic rite of passage from childhood to adulthood in the Jewish religion and custom. Following the religious rites, Larry, his friends, and family celebrated at an expensive hotel and catering hall in Somerville, New Jersey. A few years later, at around age 18, Larry worked as an assistant manager at the local Woolworth's department store. Among the employees he supervised was a younger kid whose antics and lack of discipline forced Larry to fire him. The boy's name was Jon Leibowitz. The experience

represented an accurate view of the difference between the Leibowitz
boys; although both guys were undeniably smart and clever, Jon was a
cut-up and a jokester, Larry was, early on, the more serious and focused
of the brothers.

After high school, Larry Leibowitz attended Princeton University,
where he earned a degree in economics and graduated with highest
honors—summa cum laude.[32] It was a big step on his way to becoming
a powerful economic and intellectual force in the business world, particularly on Wall Street. His list of accomplishments is both extensive
and impressive, and yet it would take a diligent search to find big headlines about Lawrence Leibowitz. In fact, Internet searches for "Larry
Leibowitz" or "Lawrence Leibowitz" just as often yield links to Jon
Stewart as they do to Jon's older brother.

In 1996, Lawrence co-founded the hedge fund Bunker Capital.
A hedge fund is a type of investment partnership where, if they earn
profits for investors, the managers receive a percentage of those profits. Leibowitz served as Bunker Capital's managing director and Head
of Program and Proprietary Trading. He also became the director of
Global Equities Technology, at Credit Suisse First Boston. Leibowitz joined the business firm, Schwab Capital Markets in 2001, and in
2004, he became the managing director and chief operating officer of
Americas Equities at UBS Investment Bank. Before that, he was the
executive vice president of the Equities Division of UBS Capital Markets L.P. In 2007, Leibowitz was the head of U.S. Execution for the
New York Stock Exchange's Euronext, Inc., and in 2010, Lawrence
was named chief operating officer of the New York Stock Exchange
(NYSE). In that capacity, Leibowitz is responsible for the business and
product development for the U.S. cash markets. He has been described
as "a high-speed trading whiz" who has "changed the way in which
trading of stock happens."[33]

Currently, Larry Leibowitz, described as "a bit grayer and world wea-
rier" than brother Jon,[34] is also the chairman of the Nasdaq Quality of
Market Committee and serves on the Securities Industry and Financial
Markets Association's Market Structure Committee. This is the kind
of resume that can catapult someone into the brightest of limelights,
and Lawrence Leibowitz is a frequent honored speaker at industry
forums related to market structure issues. One place he does not speak,

however, is on "fake news shows." In 2010, when asked by a Reuters reporter whether there was a chance that he would appear on *The Daily Show* with Jon Stewart, Leibowitz replied, "I probably wouldn't make a very good guest . . . I have tried to fly under the radar."[35] To date, Lawrence has been successful in that effort, not having appeared even once with his brother on *The Daily Show*.

But in March 2010, Larry Leibowitz captured a moment of fame in a feature about him in the *Wall Street Journal*. In his capacity as CEO of NYSE, Leibowitz was responsible for speeding up the NYSE's electronic trading platform, making it more efficient—and more attractive to traders who sought faster and faster stock-trades.[36] Younger brother Jon may be on the cutting edge of comedy, but Lawrence Leibowitz has proven that he is at the forefront in the world of highest finance.

DAN AND MATT LEIBOWITZ—JON'S HALF-BROTHERS

Neither of Jon's half-brothers, Matt and Dan, has played a role in Jon's public career. Matt Leibowitz is a central New Jersey native with a passion for the arts and an interest in all things creative. After managing the 449 Room music club and booking acts at Conduit—A Music Club in Trenton, Matt went on to earn his Master of Arts degree in counseling from TCNJ in hopes of furthering his ability to help others. Currently, Matt is helping with the day-to-day proceedings of Urban Word, LLC, and hopes to have a positive impact on the Trenton arts and entrepreneurial community. In his off time, you might find Matt playing bass for the New York City–based band "The Constant," and developing new websites for local musicians and bands.[37] Recently, Matt wrote a review of Broadway smash hit, *The Book of Mormon*,[38] written by Trey Parker and Matt Stone—both of whom have been guests of Jon's on *The Daily Show with Jon Stewart*. Like half-brother Lawrence, however, neither Matt nor Dan has ever appeared on *The Daily Show*.

Dan Leibowitz graduated from Hightstown High School in Hightstown, New Jersey, in 1995 and is married to Sandy. Curiously, the year before Dan Leibowitz graduated from Hightstown High, Jon Stewart visited the school to receive an honorary T-shirt from the editors of

The Ram Page, the school's newspaper. The "ceremony" was aired on YouTube as part of the Ram Report. A youthful 32-year-old Stewart sits on a couch and says of the Ram Report that "if you give us twenty-two minutes, we'll give you some of the worst television you've ever seen in your life." He is soon joined by Eric, one of the student editors who hands him a signed white T-shirt that says "Ram Report: Always There." Stewart accepts the shirt saying, "I'm very moved. I'm very flattered. It still has a little stain on it, a little pizza stain, that's very nice."[39]

From grandparents to parents to siblings and half-siblings, the back story of Jon Stewart's life tells only a fraction of the tale. In fact, there is still one more Leibowitz to learn about, one whose contributions to Jon Stewart's life are immeasurable.

Chapter 2

BEFORE JON STEWART
WAS JON STEWART

The stories of my childhood lack any real magic. I was very much like a bad ABC Afterschool Special.[1]

Celebrities are always just "somebodies" before they become "*Somebodies*," and often the transformation is quite dramatic. In Jon Stewart's case, however, one could argue that his career as host of *The Daily Show*, along with his remarkable record of achievements since becoming one of America's funniest—and ironically, most trusted[2]—interpreters of politics and media, was inevitable. Having a personality punctuated by a self-deprecating sense of humor, and with the kind of sharp intelligence born as much from daily life as from formal education, Jon Stewart has already inscribed himself deeply into American popular culture. *The New York Times* has described Stewart and *The Daily Show* as a "genuine cultural and political force."[3] How did this compact comedian[4] become a power player in American culture? Why was a funny man taken so seriously? *The Daily Show* has become a nightly fixture for millions of viewers across the United States[5]—especially along the East and West Coasts—but it is really in the small town of Lawrenceville in the Garden State, New Jersey, that Jon Stewart's story begins. In fact, in those early days, there was no Jon Stewart—just a boy named Jon Stuart Leibowitz.

(A *BRIEF*) HISTORY OF A TOWN

Lawrenceville, New Jersey—most definitely not named after Jon's brother Lawrence—is roughly equidistant between New York City and Philadelphia, Pennsylvania. As part of Lawrence Township, the community of Lawrenceville boasts of a lively "Main Street" culture complete with historic churches and houses dating back to the colonial days, a wide variety of small "Ma & Pa" businesses, and even an annual "Scarecrow in the Village" event where, since 1999, Lawrenceville residents have crafted some of the most creatively rendered scarecrows ever seen. The scarecrows are then hung throughout the village and serve as a reminder of the ways through which so many small towns keep their history and common culture alive. As the *Lawrenceville Main Street* website puts it, "We're young at heart, but we're quaint."[6] Lawrence Township—originally called Maidenhead by the region's Quaker settlers—was founded in 1697, and there is a fascinating history that attaches to this "quaint" township. In fact, as it turns out, the area now known as Lawrence Township had a hand—pun intended, as we shall see—in the outcome of the American Revolution.

During the revolution, General George Washington anticipated aggressive counterattacks from the British army after the American victory at the Battle of Trenton (December 26, 1776). Washington ordered the Continental Army to establish a defensive position at Assunpink Creek, near Trenton, in order to meet this counterattack head-on. As Washington had anticipated, the British troops, under General Charles Cornwallis, advanced on Trenton, on January 2, 1777, with around 5,000 men for the Battle of Assunpink Creek, more commonly known as the Second Battle of Trenton. But under the leadership of the Continental Army's Colonel Edward Hand, the American rifleman were able to slow Cornwallis's advance toward Trenton. When Cornwallis decided to wait until the next day to try to finish the battle, Washington moved his army past Cornwallis's men in the middle of the night and attacked a large contingent of British troops at

Princeton, New Jersey. That defeat resulted in the British withdrawal of troops from New Jersey for the rest of the winter.[7]

Every year, to this day, residents of Lawrence celebrate Colonel Hand's contribution to the revolution by a march to Trenton from the Lawrence Township Municipal Building.[8] After the War of 1812, Maidenhead, New Jersey, was renamed Lawrence in honor of Captain James Lawrence, one of the naval heroes of the war. In the late 19th century, the establishment of Maidenhead Academy, which was later renamed The Lawrenceville School, helped to bring new money and resources to the region, which in turn resulted in the rapid development of the village of Lawrenceville. Today, this village is known as the Lawrenceville Main Street Historic District.

A (LESS BRIEF) HISTORY OF A COMEDIAN

He once claimed that his first words were "I think I'm coming down with something."[9] It's easy to be fooled by his self-deprecating point of view, but in reality, Jon Leibowitz was born into a strikingly intelligent family, and while he did not become a teacher, college professor, or finance expert, Jon's sharp eyes and ears were picking up a vast collection of material through which he honed his own razor sharp intellect.

Jon and his brother Larry were born in New York City but grew up in Lawrenceville, New Jersey. Their house was just a few of miles from the Princeton University, down Route 206. Lawrenceville was a "little fishing village," in New Jersey, as Jon described it 32 years later in an interview for *People* magazine.[10] About his childhood, Stewart recalls it as "typical." As he put it, "I played a little Little-League baseball. I never wanted for food. I always had shoes." Life for the Leibowitz family was, in Jon's view, normal. "I had a room. There were no great tragedies . . . We were Jewish and living in the suburbs so there was a slightly neurotic bent to it, but I can't point to anything where a boy overcame a tragedy to become a comedian. As my grandmother used to say, 'I can't complain.'"[11]

In fact, Jon rarely complains about his New Jersey childhood, but a few of his remarks suggest that his early years presented some unique challenges. "I grew up more as an outsider. I was the only Jew in the neighborhood . . . Latchkey kid, basically unsupervised, most of the time thinking up ways to entertain my friends." What type of stuff was entertaining to Jon and his childhood friends? "My fart humor back then was very sophisticated. I did top-notch stuff."[12]

Although they were just a few miles from the multicultural Princeton University, the people of Lawrenceville had little experience with Jewish families. While the Leibowitzs enrolled Jon in a Yeshiva kindergarten in nearby Trenton, thereafter, Jon—along with brother Larry—attended Lawrenceville's public schools, where he was frequently teased by schoolmates who called him less-than-flattering names that rhymed with Leibowitz.[13] It didn't take Jon long to feel that "it was an odd thing to be Jewish" in Lawrenceville.[14] A sense of humor, developed at a very early age, became one of the young Jon's most valuable assets. "Some people make a joke of everything. I've done that since I was 4 or 5 years old. I don't remember a time when people didn't think I was a wiseass."[15] That sense of humor returns when he recalls his grade-school days at Ben Franklin Elementary School. "I remember having a grade-school teacher I thought was a hard-ass. When you're that age, you think the guy is Himmler. Then you visit him eight years later and he's wearing polyester pants, he's four foot eight, you think he's gay, and you're like, 'Are you the guy I was afraid of?' "[16] Jon's old school mate, Eric Fundin, recalls the young Jon Leibowitz having something of a crush on the school librarian, Mrs. Fundin (Eric's mom).[17]

When Jon was nine years old, and until he was 11, he played trumpet in the Lawrence Stage Band. At the time, a Philadelphia-based television program, *Captain Noah and His Magical Ark* regularly featured performances by local talent, including children, and sure enough, Jon Leibowitz and the Lawrence Stage Band played on the show. Captain Noah (played by W. Carter Merbreier), the show's host, was a former Lutheran minister; his wife, Patricia Merbreier ("Mrs. Noah"), was a singer and puppeteer. In later years, a number of celebrity guest-hosts appeared on the program, including master puppeteer, Jim Henson, basketball great Charles Barkley, superstar Elvis Presley, tennis great Martina Navratilova, chicken czar Frank Perdue, and none other than Jon Stewart after he changed his name![18] About his Lawrence Stage Band appearance with Captain Noah, Stewart recalls that "Captain Noah didn't know anything about kids. He was a guy who wasn't happy about things . . . he would say hi to the kids, but there was more to it than that. He would go off after that and have a smoke."[19]

During those early years, Jon and his family would vacation, each year, on the Jersey Shore in Asbury Park. Later, when he was in high school, he would head to Seaside Heights Long Beach Island, or with his friends, "If we thought we could get into a bar illegally, we would go to Wildwood."[20] To this day, the Jersey Shore remains a favorite vacation spot for Jon, who despite any stereotypes about his home state has always been a champion of all that New Jersey offers.

Although the Leibowitzs were not, according to Jon, particularly traditional in their observances of Jewish tradition, the Leibowitz family did attend religious services at Princeton Jewish Center. While older brother Larry celebrated his Bar Mitzvah at a posh hotel, Jon's rite of passage had to be scaled down. His parents had separated in 1973, when Jon was 11 years old, and with money having become more of an issue, his more modest and cost-efficient Bar Mitzvah was held at Princeton Jewish Center on Nassau Street.[21] (Egalitarian in its approach to Jewish worship and culture, The Jewish Center distinguished itself from traditional orthodox synagogues by encouraging both men and women to participate in reading from the Torah and leading services.)[22] Not surprisingly, 13-year old Jon made the transition from Jewish boy to "man" a bit more interesting. When he took this symbolic step into adulthood, Jon had to use crutches. He had discovered the hard way that "playing basketball on a skateboard" wasn't the best way to prepare for his big day.[23] References to his Bar Mitzvah, and to the idea of Bar Mitzvahs in general, have peppered Stewart's comedy throughout his career. One evening, Jon joked with *Daily Show* guest Gene Simmons—also Jewish—that he'd met his wife, Tracy, at a Bar Mitzvah.[24] In a typical Jon Stewart fashion, this bit of personal "history" was not intended to be accurate; it was just another amusing riff on the momentousness of Bar Mitzvahs, a bit of youthful humor. As he put it in 2010 at age 48, "In some ways I think you're always the kid you were when puberty first destroyed your life."[25]

After their parents separated, Jon and his brother, Larry, remained in Lawrenceville with their mother. Marian was a teacher of gifted children, a fact that Jon would remain proud of throughout his life. Jon's father, Donald, more or less estranged from his ex-wife and children, was a physicist working for Recording Company of America (RCA).[26] What kind of kid was Jon Leibowitz? By his own (tongue-in-cheek) account, "I was a smallish young man. Very pleasant. You know, those were the days when kids played outdoors. And used their arms and legs, and ran."[27] Like many kids of his generation, Jon also grew up watching a lot of television, and had a crush on Eve Plumb, who played Jan Brady on *The Brady Bunch* (1969–74).[28] Nearly 20 years later, in 1994, Plumb appeared on MTV's *The Jon Stewart Show* (1994–95) to promote the Saturday morning show *Fudge* (1995–97). When she walked out to join Jon on stage, Jon was obviously delighted to have a chance to chat with his childhood heartthrob. As if thrown back to those days of his youth, he even called her "Jan" and she had to correct him, gently, that her name is actually Eve.

Along with the rest of the country, Jon was deeply affected by the dramatic events occurring during his childhood: the assassinations of Robert Kennedy and Martin Luther King, Jr., and the 1969 NASA mission to the moon. Of course, as his memory of these events incubated over the decades, they grew into comedic bits and pieces for Stewart. On his show of July 20, 2009—the 40th anniversary of the lunar landing—Stewart would celebrate the 1969 moon-landing as the day of America's "officially claiming the moon as America's Space-Puerto Rico." While these powerful moments made a vivid impression on the young Jon Leibowitz, he wouldn't be the comic wise-guy we've come to know if he didn't also recall his own momentous childhood experiences, like "throwing up in kindergarten from a bad ham sandwich."[29] In another moment of candor—tongue firmly in cheek—he reminisces about the mischief he and his buddies would get into, especially at places like the Santa Fe Café on Nassau Street near Princeton. Stewart "confesses" that "we were the ones who kept burning down that restaurant." Stewart and friends ran around "like idiots" on the grounds of Mercer County Community College on 20-degree winter days, suffered the "humiliation of being fitted for hush-puppies" every year for school, and on at least one occasion, Stewart spent an evening hanging out at a local "eating club" getting drunk on one of his favorite beers—Genesee Cream Ale—and shooting pool.[30]

The breakup of Jon's parents' marriage was also processed, in part, through Jon's comedy filter. He said, in a 1995 interview, that the breakup was almost a cliché. "My dad left my mother when he was about 40, and he married his secretary. I thought, wow, that is so hackneyed. Dad, couldn't you come up with something a little more original, like marrying maybe a cheerleader?"[31] Characteristically, Jon rarely remarks in public about the breakup of Don and Marian Leibowitz. On those occasions when he does address the issue, he finds a way to deflect the seriousness of it with a joke. Once, when asked about one of his father's worst traits, Stewart recalled that it was his father's body hair. "You know, when you're swimming as a kid and you want to crawl on your dad? None of us went anywhere near him. 'My god, a beaver! Everyone out of the pool!'"[32]

But Jon's sense of humor about his father also has an edge to it. In 1999, Jon responded to another reporter who asked him what the young Jon had learned from his father. "If you don't get it right with your first family, you can always do it again with another."[33] He characterized his father's affair with his secretary and subsequent departure as "the way my family got divorced."[34] Although by some accounts, Jon and his father were estranged for most of the time since the divorce, as recently as 2009, Don Leibowitz told reporter Randolph Portugal that he still kept in touch with Jon despite his son's busy schedule. As the elder Leibowitz put it, "All my sons had their own experiences and I am absolutely proud of all of them."[35] Still, it's hard not to wonder about how sure Jon himself is of his father's pride. When he was asked what was the one question he'd like to ask his father in a *Daily Show* interview, Jon replied, "Ain't I doin' good, Pa? Ain't I?" Although he was, at least in part, joking, when he was asked whether he thought his father had really doubted his accomplishments, Jon answered, "No, I think he thinks it's fine—probably."[36] In typically sly humor, Stewart responded to an interviewer's question about whether he was "scarred by your experience with the breakdown of the American family": "I am still bitter and hurt, and when I get big enough to criticize [my parents] on the cover of *People* magazine, the bitterness will come out. I'm sure at some point I'll be able to use it to my advantage, as the seed for my alcohol addiction or some sort of rehabilitation that I'll have to go through."[37]

But before whatever rift took hold between Don Leibowitz and his younger son, Jon's home life was, by his own account, fairly ordinary.

"I come from a straight-up middle-class existence . . . I don't think what I went through is any more remarkable than what anybody else goes through. My way of handling it was with humor."[38] On another occasion, when asked whether his comedy grew out of pain, he responded, "I have a very suburban background. My comedy doesn't come from pain. At times I wanted a pair of Keds and didn't get them, but it's hard to make a 20-minute stage routine out of that."[39]

Part of Jon's suburban background included the kinds of after-school jobs that kids in the neighborhood took for their pocket money. When he was around 15 years old, Jon got a job at the popular department store, Woolworths in the Quaker Bridge Mall. No doubt, he had a little help; his brother, Lawrence, was an assistant manager, and according to Jon, "the head cheese there,"[40] and "a bit of a taskmaster, but good people."[41] Jon's job was downstairs "in the catacombs," restocking shelves, retrieving items to bring to the main floor, returning items from the main floor to the stock shelves, and so on. Jon and his fellow shelf-stockers tried one thing after another to combat the boredom. At one point, the guys had invented a "game" where they took turns making acrobatic jumps from some of the empty shelves onto piles of beanbag chairs. "Unfortunately, I hit a bag wrong and it shot across the room and wiped out thousands of dollars' worth of aquariums."[42] There was a scramble to get the place cleaned up in a hurry. Although Jon was able to dump the debris into the incinerator, the noise of all that glass breaking reached the ears of the management team. "I paid with my job and the humiliation of having my brother actually have to fire me."[43] It wasn't Jon's only experience with being hired and fired, however. Within a span of less than two years following his Woolworth's experience, Jon was summarily fired from five more retail stores, all within the Quaker Bridge Mall.

Sometimes Jon and his friends would make mischief of a more historical kind. Speaking in 2000 with a reporter from *The Daily Princetonian*, Princeton's student newspaper, Jon fondly recalled three things from his childhood: "Hoagie Haven, Genessee Cream Ale and whizzing on the Mercer Oak."[44] It was the latter that, in a weird way, connected Jon and his friends with a bit of local history. The Mercer Oak was an enormous white oak tree, approximately 250 years old, and grew in Princeton Battlefield Park. The tree was named for American brigadier general Hugh Mercer who, as some stories have it, was near—or per-haps even beneath—the great oak when he was fatally wounded by the British during the American Revolution. In more modern times, the tree was the site of marriages, picnics, and teenagers' parties. It was also regarded as the symbol of Princeton Township and of Mercer County.[45]

In March 2000, the Mercer Oak was blown down by strong winds. Tragically, the majestic tree collapsed just a few days after the death of a man named Richard Baker who had spent a quarter of a century car-ing for, among other Princeton Battlefield landmarks, the iconic tree. The Mercer Oak, in addition to being the target of Jon and his friends' "whizzing," was also a movie extra of sorts, appearing in the movie *I.Q.* with the stars Meg Ryan, Tim Robbins, and Walter Matthau. In the last few scenes of the movie, the Mercer Oak can be seen on screen for several minutes.[46]

LAWRENCE HIGH SCHOOL

Growing up in what he jokingly refers to as the "rough and tumble of Jewish life in New Jersey,"[47] Jon Leibowitz was known at Lawrence High School as a funny guy. Located on Princeton Pike in Lawrence Township, Mercer County, New Jersey, Lawrence High School is a fairly typical suburban school. A boxy concrete and brick building built in 1967, just five years after Jon Leibowitz was born, Lawrence High School educates approximately 1,100 students, in grades 9 through 12. Among the numerous athletic programs, Lawrence High School boasts an outstanding soccer team—Jon's chosen sport—that has, to date, won nine New Jersey State Championships, including five in a row from 1967 through 1971. A number of celebrities and sports figures claim Lawrence High School as their own: magician and comedian Teller (of Penn & Teller), former New York Giants quarterback Scott Brunner, and Glenn Meyernick, former captain of United States Soc-cer. (Meyernick died in 2006.)

Jon's experience of high school was, as he has said on more than one occasion, unremarkable. He played soccer, he played a little French horn in the school band, he occasionally did homework, and he hung out with friends. He was also a member of the Lawrence High School German Club. "There was me, Klaus, Gunther—and that was about

it. Just the three of us. Small school. No one liked German Club."[48]
(While it may have been true that German Club wasn't as popular as
others at Lawrence High, there were around 20 students in the club.)[49]
Of course, Jon Leibowitz wouldn't be, well, Jon Leibowitz if he didn't
also goof around—a lot—in high school. Teachers don't always appreciate a class clown, and while Jon's sense of humor may have worn thin
for most of his teachers, there was one, Selma Litowitz, who, according
to her daughter, Debra Frank, may have been "the first who recognized
that [Jon's] humor was something he could make a living at."[50]

Mrs. Litowitz left a deep impression on Jon. When she was diag-
nosed with Parkinson's disease in 1991, she refused to let it rule her
life. Parkinson's disease is considered a terminal disease that attacks the
nervous system and erodes the sufferer's motor skills. The disease could
easily have made Selma give up, but she was made of tougher stuff than
that. Selma kept up her determination as well as her sense of humor.[51]
In the decade following their mother's diagnosis, Selma's children,
Rob, Debra, and Carol, were inspired by her strength and composure.
In 2001, they visited Lawrence High School, where Selma had taught
for over 20 years, and pitched the idea of a benefit concert to raise
money for Parkinson's research. The school administration got right on
board, and the resulting event, called *ParkinSong*, featured uplifting and
inspiring music performed by acts including master singer-songwriters
Ana Egge and Terri Hendrix, David Crosby and Graham Nash, Bonnie
Raitt, and adult alternative buzz band Grey Eye Glances. Hosting the
incredibly successful event was none other than one of Selma Litowitz's favorite students Jon Stewart. It was an easy commitment for Jon
to make; Mrs. Litowitz had always seen something special in him, and
the feeling had been mutual. "She was one of my favorites. It's not
easy to teach teenagers. And she did it with great joy and aplomb, and
that's a rare thing."[52] She and her family lived on the same street as the
Leibowitzes, Glenn Avenue, and in his opening remarks at *ParkinSong*,
Stewart joked that for years as a kid, he thought that Jews had to live
alphabetically.[53] Selma Litowitz died on December 26, 2005.

Jon graduated from Lawrence High School in 1980 and found a
one-of-a-kind job: collecting and sorting mosquitoes for the New
Jersey State Project on encephalitis for the underwhelming salary of
$119 per week. "We had these huge bell traps that had car batteries

attached to them, and we would go there at night . . . and what we did is we put women's pantyhose around large coffee cups, and the battery would power a light in the fan. All the bugs would fly towards it; then they'd get sucked in through the fan and get trapped. So we would have giant cups, you know, I believe at Starbucks they'd be called Vente Lattes, filled with bugs . . . and you would knock them out with chloroform."[54] He could, he said more than 20 years later, "spot a male or a female [mosquito] from across the room . . . the males are a lot cockier, arrogant."[55] As summer drew to a close, he did what most of his fellow graduates of Lawrence High School did; he headed off to college. He'd been accepted to the freshman class at the University of Virginia (UVA), in Charlotte, which was no small accomplishment. UVA accepts less than a third of the students who apply and only around 10 percent of the school's undergraduates are Jewish.[56] Jon really didn't know what he wanted to study, but with his UVA acceptance, that was his next destination.

Chapter 3

"LEIBO"

Little and hairy.[1]

                    —(Jon Stewart on how he would describe himself)

As a freshman I was quite a catch. Less than five feet tall, yet my head is the same size it is now.[2]

Get a sense of humor. If you don't, it'll be incredibly frustrating.[3]

                    —(Jon Stewart on the new millennium)

In a book devoted to the College of William and Mary's soccer team, one photograph shows a young man dribbling the ball with strong, muscular legs, obvious skills, and his face a picture of intense concentration. He appears to have outrun his opponents, obviously confident and at home on the field. He plays for The Tribe—the College of William and Mary's varsity soccer team. Who is this compact, skilled, and focused soccer player? It's *Leibo*, as Jon Leibowitz's teammates called him, the diminutive, funny, hardworking midfielder who garnered his fellow Tribesmen's respect as much for his sharp-tongued humor as for his considerable talent on the field. "My years with Tribe soccer were the best of my college experience."[4] Not surprisingly, Jon later joked about his soccer skills, saying that he'd begun playing soccer at Law-rence High School "as a way out of the suburbs." After the games, he fibbed, "other kids would say to me 'Way to try!'"[5] In truth, Jon was so committed to excelling at his chosen sport that he would often practice his soccer skills until late at night with a friend at a local field.

"Leibo" was, it turned out, an enigma—a notorious jokester, an impressively skilled athlete, a serious competitor, and, at the same time, a young man deeply uncertain about what he should be preparing himself to do in life. He had started out in the sciences as a chemis-try major, contemplating a possible career as a veterinarian. Indeed, that might have proved incredibly ironic years later when he would marry a veterinary technician named Tracey McShane. Grinding his way through an essentially pre-med program, and going on to become an animal doctor, however, was not in the cards for Jon. After a few semesters, and for no particular reason he could put his finger on, Jon shifted his attention from the sciences to the social sciences, chang-ing his major to psychology. Far less difficult than four years of hard science, a bachelor's degree in psychology was at least a respectable one. It was also a degree, Jon said later, that would have made him "unemployable."[6]

Although the College of William and Mary's website claims that "There's no such thing as a typical W&M student," and that the col-lege boasts "over 400 student clubs and organizations,"[7] including a German club, what was becoming clear for Jon was that while his fresh-man classmates were variously sorting themselves into the kinds of aca-demic programs that would become majors and yield solid employment later on, he was still casting about for an idea of what he was supposed to be doing in college. How about a fraternity? Nearly a third of all William and Mary students were members of fraternities and sororities; why not Jon? He joined Pi Kappa Alpha, one of the largest fraternal organizations in the world, a frat with a long and interesting history, and with more than a quarter million lifetime initiates in the United States and Canada.[8] Ironically, Pi Kappa Alpha's birth was at Jon's for-mer college, the University of Virginia, in 1868. Now, Jon Leibow-itz was a part of the fraternity that boasted such distinguished alumni as television journalist Ted Koppel, Chicago Bears quarterback Kyle Orton, senior vice president of Universal Studios Robert L. Ward, and award-winning actor Jeremy Pivin. The members of Pi Kappa Alpha, according to their website, "strive to be *Scholars*, *Leaders*, *Athletes*, and *Gentlemen*, and they seek excellence in everything they do."[9] Maybe not all of those were goals for Jon, but it couldn't hurt to be part of such a prestigious and respected fraternity. And yet, despite Pi Kappa Alpha's dedication to "developing men of integrity, intellect, success and high moral character, and . . . fostering a truly lifelong fraternal experience,"[10] Jon remained a Pike—as the frat brothers of Pi Kappa Alpha were known—for a grand total of six months. He'd been completely turned off by the whole fraternity "hazing" process and decided, finally, that fraternity life—even as a revered Pike—was pointless.[11] The Pi Kappa Alpha motto, "Once a Pike, always a Pike," did not, in Jon's case, apply, although the Pike website continues to list "Jon Stewart" as one of the famous Pikes of William and Mary.

College life seemed to have generated more puzzles than solutions for the young Jon; the young Leibowitz had not yet found the direction that would, once he discovered it, propel him to the Big Apple—New York City, comedy, television, movies, and national renown. He may not have known what he wanted to do with his education, but what he and others around him knew was that Jon could make people laugh. His William and Mary soccer coach, Al Albert, remarked "He was always the locker-room cut-up, but we've had other locker room cut-ups who haven't gone on to be comedians."[12]

College, for many, means freedom, discovery, new friendships, romantic relationships, profound intellectual growth, and the pleasure of entering into adulthood. For Jon, it also meant being a funny guy without a plan. About his time at William and Mary, Jon says, "I was miserable there."[13] How did he come to be at a prestigious and historically significant college without a clue about why he was there?

BECOMING LEIBO

In 1980, after graduating third in his high school senior class, not quite 18-year-old Jon Leibowitz did what around three-quarters of U.S. high school seniors do; he headed off to college. First stop: the University of Virginia (UVA) where, according to Stewart, he "got lost on campus." UVA is well-known for being a tough nut to crack. Applicants need high grade point averages, evidence of participation in extracurricular activities, and, if they are from outside Virginia, they have to have plenty of money to be able to afford UVA's sizable tuition. With some combination of these and other factors, Jon entered UVA as a member of the class of 1984. Notably, June 2013, Jon's friend and colleague, Stephen Colbert, delivered UVA's valedictory keynote address at the university's commencement ceremony. He told the graduates, "This is an impressive institution because it rejected my application."[14]

As impressive a university as UVA was, and is, after one semester there, Jon did what nearly a third of all U.S. college students do before they earn their bachelor's degree; he transferred to another college,[15] the College of William and Mary. William and Mary, also in Virginia, and occasionally described as the University of Virginia's academic rival is a nationally and internationally acclaimed college located in historic Williamsburg, Virginia. It was America's first college to become a university in 1779, and its name reflects its royal origin, the result of a charter granted by King William III and Queen Mary II to establish the college in Virginia in February 1693.[16]

With around 260 fellow students, Jon lived in Yates Hall, a long rectangular red-brick building named for Reverend William Yates (1720–1764), the college's fifth president. According to Stewart, the basement (or *Yatesment*, as some students referred to it) section of Yates Hall, where he lived—located within the open square formed by Ukrop Way, Yates Drive, and Gooch Drive—combined "the cheerfulness of a bomb shelter with the prison-like comfort of the group shower."[17]

By his own reckoning, Stewart was a "mediocre" student.[18] He was also one of the few Jewish students at the college and one of only a tiny number of Jewish people in that region of the country.[19] Although hardly observant of most Jewish traditions, Jon was nevertheless conscious of how few Jewish students were at the college. The Jewish population at William and Mary was, and is, around 285 out of 8,200 students, less than 4 percent, and much less than the Jewish population of UVA.[20] In typical comic fashion, Stewart remarked, "I came to William and Mary because as a Jewish person, I wanted to explore the rich tapestry of Judaica that is Southern Virginia."[21]

The College of William and Mary has a rich history; it's the second oldest college in the United States[22] (Harvard is generally recognized as the oldest), and is typically regarded as the top "Public Ivy League" college in the country.[23] The so-called Public Ivy League colleges share the characteristics of having a rich history, a tradition of excellence, renowned graduates, classically beautiful campuses, and an exemplary academic reputation. Equally important, these respected colleges are all much more affordable than any of the traditional, private, Ivy League colleges. Jon Leibowitz's choice of the College of William and Mary— and their choice of him—placed him at the heart of these nationally and internationally respected institutions of higher learning. For a young man with virtually no idea about what to study—or why to study it—Jon had now been accepted to a pair of the nation's most esteemed universities.

Four U.S. presidents—George Washington, Thomas Jefferson, James Monroe, and John Tyler—are among the college's prestigious alumni. Washington went on to serve as the college's chancellor, as did Tyler in his day. Jefferson eventually founded none other than the University of Virginia, a fact that adds a touch of irony to Jon Leibowitz's early life. On its website, the students at the College of William and Mary are described as being "not only some of the smartest in the world, but passionate about serving others and serious about having fun."[24] An historic college for smart, passionate, and fun-loving students sounds like the ideal place for a young Jon Leibowitz to thrive. Graduates of William and Mary include a number of other notable individuals, including the fourth chief justice of the United States, John Marshall (1780), former director of the Central Intelligence Agency and current U.S. secretary of defense, Robert M. Gates (1965), fashion designer Perry Ellis (1961), actress Glenn Close (1974), comedian Patton Oswalt (1991), and General Winfield Scott (1805), the longest serving general in the history of the U.S. Military.[25] The fact that Jon Stewart's name appears among these and hundreds of other renowned alumni is impressive.

But Jon thought so little of his undergraduate experience that he once said, "I earned a degree in making bricks out of straw and water at Colonial Williamsburg."[26] Although he would one day become one of the "most trusted names in news,"[27] his college career, as he described it in a 1994 interview with *New York* magazine, consisted mainly of "waking up late, memorizing someone else's notes, doing bong hits, and going to soccer practice."[28] Despite his self-described detachment during his undergraduate years, Jon managed to make humor the connecting thread between the various aspects of his college life. He would sum up his collegiate experiences in dismissive comments like, "I drank beer, met some nice people, made some good friends, stared at the desk where James Madison once sat, played soccer."[29] Madison (who did not play soccer) was the cousin of James Madison, the fourth president of the United States. The James Madison of William and Mary notoriety graduated from the college in 1771. In 1777, he was appointed as the college's eighth president, and the first following the college's formal separation from England.

But while this may, in fact, be what Stewart recalls of his college years, his old roommate and soccer teammate, John Rasnic, remembers that Jon was "very popular with girls" and that he "dated some very attractive women."[30] The truth was that Jon had little time for more than his academic responsibilities, soccer practice, and travel to games. Of course, he enjoyed the typical college student's distractions—a few beers, an energetic social life, some television, video games, and concerts—but for the most part, there wasn't much that was remarkable about his college years. With friends and teammates, he hung out, partied, and talked politics. One of his soccer teammates, Mike Flood, recalls that Ronald Reagan's election during their freshman year was a source of consternation for them as well as for a number of people in their social circle. Ironically, back in high school, Jon was assigned to play Ronald Reagan in a school debate in which he had to pretend to *defend* political positions with which he disagreed profoundly.[31] As so many of his peers did in those days, Jon turned to familiar sources of humor for perspective on politics and popular culture. He read *Mad Magazine* and *National Lampoon*, soaked up the comedy of Lenny Bruce, Woody Allen, George Carlin, and Steve Martin. He made interesting friends, including, for example, a young man named Anthony Weiner, who had arrived at William and Mary as an exchange student in 1983.

Weiner joked 27 years later, that back in the William and Mary days, Stewart seemed to have spent much of his time without pants.[32] But in this case, Weiner's teasing of Stewart was, in retrospect, profoundly ironic. Stewart's 2010 *Daily Show* interview with Weiner would prove to be an uncanny foreshadowing of Weiner's public downfall a year later when he was caught having sent lewd images of himself, wearing only his underwear, to as many as a dozen young women, none of whom were his wife.[33] By mid-June 2011, Weiner was compelled to resign from government, but not before his old friend, Jon Stewart, expressed both sympathy for, and criticism of, the disgraced congressman's actions. He told viewers, "This is my friend Anthony!" Stewart then put to rest a rumor that he and Weiner had been roommates at William and Mary, saying that he and Weiner had, with other friends, only rented a summer house together in Delaware. He joked, "Think *Jersey Shore* meets *Yentl*."[34] Weiner spent the next two years regrouping with his politically savvy wife, Huma Abedin, whom he'd married just one year before the scandal. In early 2013, he announced not only a return to public life, but his candidacy for mayor of New York City, his second try at the coveted office.[35]

NUMBER 11

As comically critical as he sounds about his college life—he once said of his time at William and Mary that "I stayed four years but never learned anything I would use later in life"[36]—there's little doubt that he absorbed much more than whatever may have been etched into the surface of "Madison's desk." The general curriculum at William and Mary is a challenging one, as are the requirements within the major fields of study. As lost as he may have felt, Jon managed to find enough of interest to keep him there through his graduation with a bachelor's degree in psychology. Jon's education also extended well beyond the classroom. He learned to handle encounters with anti-Semitism, relying, as usual, on both his sense of humor and his ability to turn such experiences into the raw material of his future work as a comedian. Recalling an incident where Jon had to face anti-Semitism directly, soccer teammate Resnic describes a time when the soccer team played a game against Randolph-Macon College, another college in Virginia. One of the opposing players called Jon a "kike," one of the most derogatory terms for a Jew. Originally, the word was a put-down invented by American German-Jewish immigrants for those Jews who had come from Russia and other East European countries. According to Jewish historian Stephen Birmingham, the put-down arose because "so many

Russian [Jewish] names ended in 'ki', they were called 'kikes.'" The word then drifted into usage by non-Jews and became an insult to all Jewish people in general.[37] As John Resnic recalls, although Jon was surprised and "a little upset," he shrugged it off and kept a cool head. Jon's version of the experience was that "In 1982, I was playing soccer at William and Mary, and a kid from Randolph-Macon called me a kike. I ran after him. 'I'm not a . . . well, yes I am.'"[38] While Jon Leibowitz may have been short in stature and reluctant to get into physical fights with bigots, coach Albert remembers that "everybody was always a little afraid of messing with Jon because he was so quick witted."[39] In this case, he had used his quick wittedness to allow a vicious insult to slide right off his back.

Always a funny guy, Jon's teammates liked him for his sharp tongue, lightning fast talent for clever comebacks, and his ability to keep them laughing. He said, many years later, "Some of the best people I've ever met in my life I met on my college soccer team."[40] Jon was, additionally, no slouch on the field. A varsity player from his sophomore year on, he was moved from the wing position he played as a freshman on junior varsity to midfielder on the varsity squad with the number "11" on his jersey. As his coach put it, "Jon was very feisty as a player, very high-energy sort of guy." In 1983, before his final season at William and Mary, Jon's coach, Al Albert, recruited him to play for the U.S. squad in the first Pan-American Maccabi Games in São Paulo, Brazil. These games were the stepping stones to the World Maccabiah Games, the Jewish version of the Olympics. Stewart actually *started* for the U.S. team, a remarkable accomplishment and honor in itself. And just as he had done throughout his high school and collegiate soccer careers, he became the locker room cut-up. "He created a little bit of levity," says David Coonin, one of Stewart's Maccabi teammates. For the American team, the Pan-American Maccabi Games entailed a 10-day trip to Brazil, with plenty of socializing among members of the various squads. The players danced—both Israeli and Brazilian style—and partied as much as their rigorous practice and game schedules allowed. The Latin American Jews evidently did not quite know what to make of their American counterparts. "When we walked out on the soccer field, they called us 'gringos,'" says Fred Schoenfeld, co-chair of the Pan-American Maccabi Games that year. Few thought the American "gringos" could play. But the U.S. team most definitely could play, winning four games, going all the way to the finals, where, in the end, they lost to Brazil. The "gringo" squad from the United States ended up winning the silver medal.[41]

With the Pan-American Maccabi Games under his belt, Jon returned to college, not quite ready to hang up his soccer cleats. William and Mary was scheduled to play the team from the University of Connecticut at Storrs that boasted a more powerful soccer program. There was a good chance that the UConn Huskies would thrash the weaker Tribe of William and Mary. But the game was closer than anyone expected. Both teams played well, with The Tribe more than holding its own against the significantly stronger Huskies. Jon had a couple of chances to score, but for a while, it looked like neither team was going to get the ball past their opponent's goalie. UConn was decidedly not whipping William and Mary. Instead, and in dramatic fashion, The Tribe beat their rivals by a score of 1-0. And the guy who scored the winning— and only—goal? None other than Jon "Leibo" Leibowitz.[42]

"Leibo" might have become an outstanding professional soccer player; the thought had crossed Jon's mind more than once. But as fate would have it, injuries helped to change his mind about playing soccer beyond his college years. After he graduated, Jon had to undergo orthopedic surgery on his frequently injured knee as well as hernia-repair surgery, both sustained during his years of playing soccer.[43] In a fitting tribute to their very own player-comedian, Jon's Tribe teammates created an award in his name, still being given, for the player who demonstrated most outstanding effort, work ethic, and, of course, a good sense of humor. The award is called the *Leibo*. Years later, in 2006, the National Soccer Coaches Association of America (NSCAA) gave Jon an Honorary All-America Award in recognition of his earlier days as a talented player.

AN EDUCATION, GRADUATION, A DIPLOMA, AND A CAREER . . . NOT.

Although he has said of his college years that he was a "lost person," people who knew him were impressed by his intellect and his obvious gift for outwitting others. Still, by his own accounts, Jon's years at

William and Mary were somewhat baffling to him. He told the 2004 graduating class that "If you had been to William and Mary while I was here and found out that I would be the commencement speaker 20 years later, you would be somewhat surprised, and probably somewhat angry." Of his scholarly life, he told the graduates, "You could say that my one saving grace was academics where I excelled, but I did not."[44] With a mind that was far from "mediocre," Jon's restless intellect just needed more satisfying material on which to feed.

Upon graduating in 1984, Jon found himself "shell-shocked" when he realized that, unlike the college experience, the real world is an "elective" where the "paths are infinite and the results uncertain."[45] Armed with his bachelor's degree in psychology, and feeling completely ill-equipped for any kind of career, Jon entered the working world, taking a variety of jobs without any particular aim. The jobs may have had little or nothing to do with what he'd studied at the university, but Jon's diligence about finding work and his willingness to do what he had to do for an income were completely in character with the guy who was admired by his college soccer coach for his energy.

So, with his diploma in hand and with a degree that he had no intention of using, Jon entered the working world, taking a string of jobs from which he would quickly quit or be fired. He worked in a cancer research lab. He tended bar, bussed tables, and stocked shelves in a store. He was fired from a bakery job for forgetting to rinse the soap out of a bread barrel, producing sudsy but inedible loaves. Perhaps more in character with Jon's desire to be an entertainer, he even worked as a puppeteer, performing in skits as "a cerebral-palsy puppet, a blind puppet, a deaf puppet, a hyperactive puppet," to educate children about physical disabilities.[46] As Stewart told television interviewer Ted Koppel in 2002, "At 23 you sort of find yourself wondering what the hell you're going to do. You could join the softball team, and bartend at the bar, and work for the state, and pretty much stay in that equilibrium for the next 50 years. Or you could figure out something else that you're going to have a passion for, and make an attempt."[47]

What was Jon Stuart Leibowitz passionate about? In 1986, he sold his car—an old Gremlin—left New Jersey, and moved to New York City, hoping to find a place for himself in the comedy scene. It was, as he once put it, "an exercise in 'Outward Bound' for neurotics."[48] For money, he worked for a catering company, driving a van. At night, he put himself in front of open mikes in what Ben Karlin, Stewart's *Daily Show* production partner, calls "the wretched comedy clubs of New York," hoping to attract sufficient attention to his material. Trying to make live audiences laugh at your jokes is difficult work, and newcomers to the New York City comedy scene often find their few minutes at the microphone to be discouraging. Not Jon Leibowitz. He had come to New York City to make a new beginning and had no intention of being run out of the Big Apple. As he now understood it, college "is not necessarily predictive of your future success." At William and Mary, he may have felt disillusioned, "mediocre," and thought of himself as having a "repugnant personality." But with his decision to make it as a professional comedian in New York City, Jon "Leibo" Leibowitz was determined to take his own advice to the graduates of his alma mater: "Things change rapidly, and life gets better in an instant."[49] What Jon didn't yet realize was that some "instants" take a little longer than others.

Chapter 4

THE BITTER END
AND A NEW BEGINNING

[T]he one thing I did that was great was I moved from Trenton, New Jersey to New York to try and become a comedian.[1]

Trenton is a lovely area filled with—OK, I'm trying to think of what it's filled with—nothing. That's why I left.[2]

With comedy role models like Woody Allen, Steve Martin, and Lenny Bruce, how did rock and roll giant Bruce Springsteen fit into the equation? After all, Jon once said that insomnia was his greatest inspiration! But more than 20 years after leaving New Jersey, Jon thanked his favorite musician, and one of his idols, Bruce "The Boss" Springsteen on *The Daily Show*, saying, "You introduced me to the concept of the other side. You introduced me to the concept of: you go through the tunnel and you take a chance . . . the joy of it is chasing that dream, and that has been my inspiration for leaving New Jersey and going to New York."[3] In 1986, Jon had already sold his old car, packed his things into a rented truck, and with a cassette tape of Springsteen's songs cranked up loud, he drove "through the tunnel"—the Holland Tunnel to be precise—and arrived in The Big Apple, ready to vault into his career as a comedian. But it didn't quite start out as he might have hoped. Estranged, by then, from his father, Jon did not know what his father's reaction was to his moving to New York City. Jon's mother was supportive, but like so many parents feel when their children leave home to seek fame and fortune, Marian was a bit nervous, too. "I didn't say it, but I figured, New York City is an hour and a half away." If need be, Jon could always come home.[4] As Jon himself recalled it, "When I told my family what I was doing, there was this sense of, 'For *what?*'"[5] But the 24-year-old Jon Leibowitz had no intention of returning home or of failing to achieve his goal. As Jon saw it, "The one thing I did that was great was I moved from Trenton, New Jersey to New York, to try and become a comedian. . . . Because I gave myself the opportunity to express whatever it was that I thought I needed to express."[6]

Whatever it was that he had wanted to express would have to wait, though. In fact, months went by before Jon worked up the nerve to try out his jokes on a New York City stage. It was one thing to make it through the tunnel, but quite another thing to face being, at least at first, a really tiny fish in an incalculably enormous pond. As 1986 came to an end, and as the first few months of 1987 began to roll by, Jon had a big decision to make, and the decision was to start the comedy ball rolling.

One night, in April 1987, Jon appeared at the oldest rock and roll club in New York City: The Bitter End. On stage, he stood in front of the famous red-brick wall and fought off the nervousness of a 25-year-old performing comedy in the Big Apple's most venerable venue. While he did not become a sensation instantly—in fact, he was by most accounts terrible—he gained enough confidence to believe that he just might be able to make a living being funny. Gigs at Stand-Up NY and other well-known clubs led to performances at Las Vegas's renowned Caesar's Palace, and for a couple of years, Jon made progress toward the goal of "making it" in show-biz. But "it" didn't happen quickly or easily. Hundreds of performances, dozens of attempts at making it big on television and in the movies, and countless moments that were a mixture of determination and doubt all stood between Jon Leibowitz and a career whose success would lead, one day, to his being listed among The Bitter End's "Legends" featured on the powerhouse club's website.[7]

THE BITTER END

I wanted to write. I wanted to do anything comedic.[8]

Being small and Jewish is a good recipe for developing a wit.[9]

At 147 Bleeker Street in the downtown Manhattan neighborhood known as Greenwich Village, a couple of blocks southwest of Washington Square Park, and around 3,500 feet from the Hudson River, The Bitter End opened its doors in 1962. Originally owned and managed by Fred Wintraub and later by Paul Colby, The Bitter End was a unique-looking establishment wedged beneath and between apartments and other small Greenwich Village businesses. With its unusual wood-slatted front, a long blue doorway awning, and bulletin boards featuring fliers and posters for everything from musical performances to listings for apartment rentals, The Bitter End was, by the mid-1970s, a fixture in the neighborhood. In its colorful history, The Bitter End's crowds have been entertained by comedians such as Lenny Bruce, George Carlin, Joan Rivers, Bill Cosby, Ray Romano, Billy Crystal, Chris Rush, and Lily Tomlin. Dozens of world famous musicians have brought their sounds to the club as well. From Chuck Berry to Janis Joplin, Marvin Gaye to Stevie Wonder, Bob Dylan to Norah Jones, Taylor Swift, Gavin DeGraw, and Lady Gaga, The Bitter End has long been a giant stepping stone for performers in New York City, and, as pointed out on its website, "At The Bitter End, you never know who or what you'll hear next."[10] Like so many before him, Jon Stuart Leibowitz's time onstage at The Bitter End was the start of something much bigger. Sort of. But first, as the diminutive comedian pushed his way into the New York City comedy scene, the young Jon Leibowitz would be made to feel much, much smaller.

While The Bitter End looked like it was going to provide a springboard for Jon's career, it was, as it turned out, a painful start that could have easily wound up, perhaps appropriately, as a very bitter end. Jon had carefully prepared about four minutes of material for his first time at the microphone. At one o'clock in the morning, right after a rock band finished performing, it was Jon's turn. He got through less than half of his jokes. The audience did not find him particularly funny; to

The exterior of The Bitter End coffeehouse, a venue specializing in live music and comedy in Greenwich Village, New York City, circa 1960. (Hulton Archive/Getty Images)

them he was just another boring wannabe like so many who had tried and failed on The Bitter End stage. Jon had, in his inaugural moment, "bombed." It was, by his own account, "brutal . . . a terrible night."[11] It took him another four *months* before he worked up the courage to get back in front of a comedy club audience. But despite his initial experience, his commitment to becoming a professional comedian was as strong as ever.

At that time, in the mid-1980s, the most well-known up-and-coming comedians were people like Sam Kinison, Whoopi Goldberg, Eddie Murphy, Andrew "Dice" Clay, Sandra Bernhard, Denis Leary, Rosie O'Donnell, Paul Reiser, Bob "Bobcat" Goldthwaite, and Roseanne Barr. A number of these folks went on to have their own television shows. Others moved on and up to bigger and bigger performance arenas, sometimes filling whole sports stadiums with devoted fans. Some changed their names, too. Andrew "Dice" Clay was born Andrew Silverstein. Whoopi Goldberg's birth name was Caryn Johnson. Woody

Allen had changed his name from Allen Stewart Konisberg. Whether for simplicity or, to some degree, to mask their Jewish heritage, these performers believed they had a greater chance of success if their names sounded simpler, less ethnic.

According to various sources, it was after his act at The Bitter End that Jon Leibowitz changed his name to Jon Stewart. Depending on who you talk to, he chose this new name because: (a) He wanted to distance himself from his father, Don Leibowitz; (b) Emcees kept mispronouncing his name; (c) "Leibowitz" sounded too "ethnic" (i.e., Jewish); or (d) "Jon Stewart" was just a better show-biz name than Jon Leibowitz. Whatever his true reasons for the name change, The Bitter End in effect was the platform on which Jon *Leibowitz* morphed into Jon *Stewart*. As many of his comedy idols had found, a name change could open doors. Once the doors were open, however, it was up to the comedian to figure out the best way to walk through. Jon Leibowitz, newly minted as Jon Stewart, would have to turn an experience at The Bitter End into a sweeter beginning.

The life of a stand-up comedian is a strange one; telling jokes is a kind of science that sets out to discover what will make people laugh. Every good comedian learns how to deliver those jokes, but comedians also know that even the best jokes can, for any number of reasons, fall flat on an audience. Woody Allen once said that "Being funny is not anyone's first choice." The great satirist, Calvin Trillin, considered being funny is "like a mild disability." Comedian Fred Allen thought of a comedian as being "on a treadmill to oblivion." It would not have been much of a surprise if, after reflecting on his horrendous first experience on a Manhattan stage, the newly arrived Jon Stuart Leibowitz had repacked his things and headed right back through the Holland Tunnel to the safe haven of New Jersey. Then again, Jon hadn't left everything behind just to return to his former life. He just needed to re-tool, to do some more writing, and to get his next comedy gig. And he had to get over a temporary loss of nerve. That would take nearly four months, and in the meantime, as Jon realized, living in New York City was expensive. He needed an income and was able to find a job as a "contract administrator" for the City University of New York. It was, at least, an impressive-sounding title for a 25-year-old with an unused degree in psychology and a disappointing inaugural joke-telling performance on the comedy stage. So, what does a City University of New York "contract administrator" actually do? Jon organized files, made phone calls to individuals and agencies at the University, and got bored. It provided him with a modest salary, but little else. At least he had his nights free, and that meant he could still grab a microphone at a nightclub. He could still pursue his dream. He just had to find a place to do just that.

THE COMEDY CELLAR

People say "Where do the jokes come from?" They come from a place of pulling your hair out.[12]

Months after the letdown at The Bitter End, Jon got another gig—a small one, but an important one. It was a job that further convinced him that what he wanted to do with his life was to be a professional comedian, to make an ongoing study of life's absurdities, and to make people laugh. Jon secured a regular "show" Sundays through Thursdays at The Comedy Cellar. Located on historic MacDougal Street in the heart of Greenwich Village, The Comedy Cellar was just a half-dozen blocks west of a street with a familiar name: Mercer, named for the very same General Hugh Mercer of Princeton Battlefield Parks's Mercer Oak fame. It was also around a dozen blocks from Jon's first passageway into his New York City life: the Holland Tunnel. MacDougal Street had, in the early 20th century, felt the footsteps of people like Jack London and Emma Goldman who hung out at the Liberal Club. There's also the Minetta Tavern, which gets its name from the Minetta Brook, which is actually a stream running beneath the building. Among other famed literary figures, Ernest Hemingway used to spend long hours with friends here. The Provincetown Playhouse was relocated to MacDougal just a few doors down from The Comedy Cellar.[13] In this neighborhood rich with tradition, Bill Grundfest—himself a former stand-up comedian and now a television writer and producer—opened The Comedy Cellar in 1982. It is a venue familiar to all comedians, big and small. Typically, The Comedy Cellar featured "showcases" of comedians, five or more in one show, with each getting around 15- or 20-minute sets in which to perform. The list of comedians who have taken the stage at the Cellar is impressive; over the years, some of the regular performers have been Louis C.K., Dave Chappelle, Amy Schumer, Nick DiPaolo, Jim Norton, Opie and Anthony, Jimmy Fallon, and Jerry Seinfeld. Just landing a regular time slot at The Comedy Cellar had put Jon Stewart in some pretty great company. Then again, there are time slots, and there are *awful* time slots.

Jon's slot—the last of the "night"—started at around 1:45 a.m., when most (if not all) paying customers had already headed home. The two or three who might have hung around could be counted on to heckle, insult, or just ignore the guy at the microphone. But stand-up comedians who get discouraged by bored or even hostile audiences don't last long. Jon Stewart did not let any of the usual trials and tribulations of young comedian-hood divert him from his determination to succeed. As he told one reporter, "The thing is, there are no training programs for comedians. There are no schools where you go and learn everything you have to know. You just get drunk enough one night and go onstage and try to stay there as long as possible."[14] Performing comedy sets at The Comedy Cellar had the potential at least to keep Jon in front of live audiences. Unfortunately, his audience of closing-time stragglers, Comedy Cellar waiters, busboys, and management—all of whom just wanted to clean up and get home—provided very little useful feedback for a comedian looking to fine-tune his routines. At the same time, while he may have, as he has said, almost quit every night he performed there, he also knew that he was learning an invaluable lesson about the life of a stand-up comedian: how to try and fail and then try again. "It was a mental challenge . . . Until I got on stage, it didn't actually make sense."[15] Stewart made "sense" of things at the Comedy Cellar for a little over two years. As he put it, "When you start out, you're bad, and getting good isn't easy. You just don't start out knowing exactly what your approach to comedy is going to be. It's a matter of trial and error."[16] And Stewart was trying, making mistakes, filing away ideas to use again and those to discard, and collecting stories, observations, and experiences. He was performing. He was refining his craft while also earning a few bucks. Very few. Jon's typical take-home from a night at the Cellar was less than $20 a night. But he was doing something much more important; he was putting the name Jon Stewart on the comedy map, and for nearly two years, Jon's time at The Comedy Cellar mike kept him hungry for a wider audience.

CAROLINE'S COMEDY HOUR

Performing stand-up comedy was not the only thing Jon was doing; he was also *writing* comedy material, and in 1989, he joined a hip group of writers for *Caroline's Comedy Hour* (A&E), a team that included, at various points in the show's life span, Louis C.K., Dave Attell, and Richard Jeni. The show featured comics such as Richard Belzer (now of *Law & Order SVU* fame), Gilbert Gottfried, Joy Behar, Dennis Leary, and David Cross—all of whom were filmed performing stand-up at Caroline's, one of New York City's most famous comedy clubs, and all of whom have gone on to successful careers in stand-up comedy, television, and movies.

In a way, Jon's move to Caroline's was, in effect, a move "upward" in that the club is located considerably farther "uptown" than either The Bitter End or The Comedy Cellar. It's also a much more commercially recognized venue that Caroline's on Broadway, as it is known, is now located in Times Square on Broadway between West 49th and West 50th Streets. Originally Caroline's was just a small cabaret club in the Chelsea area of downtown Manhattan that opened in the same year as The Comedy Cellar—1982. Its owner Caroline Hirsch was so successful in bringing in comedy acts that she moved the club to the South Street Seaport where it became the site of the A & E Network's series *Caroline's Comedy Hour*. Soon, even those expanded quarters weren't enough to hold the standing-room-only crowds, and Caroline's was again relocated, this time to Time Square. So many of the most famous comedians have performed there over the years, including Jay Leno, Tim Allen, Rosie O'Donnell, Tracy Morgan, Joel McHale, Kathy Griffin, and Billy Crystal, to name a few.[17]

A & E's *Caroline's Comedy Hour* had a relatively small but loyal audience. The comedians were developing their own fan bases, and the 28-year-old Jon Stewart was pushing hard to acquire the "chops" that would enable him make the next moves toward success. He was writing, occasionally performing on Caroline's stage, and, equally important, spending time with some of New York's most talented comedians.

Jon's persistence paid off. His comedy act was noticed by a number of agents who booked talent at some of the big Las Vegas hotels. He was hired to do gigs like opening for singer Sheena Easton at Caesar's Palace. Caesar's was, in many ways, a Mecca not just for comedians but for singers, dancers, and the high-rolling crowds they attracted. An enormous and lavish casino hotel, Caesar's offered its guests and gamblers the kinds of shows that they would keep talking about when they returned to their home cities and towns. Such exposure, along with continued stints in front of New York comedy club crowds, served to transform Jon from a local comic to an increasingly recognizable figure in the crowded world of stand-up comedy. The exposure may have been a good thing, but Jon didn't always "kill" in Vegas. He told one interviewer, "I think [Sheena Easton] spoke to me only once because I bombed so badly at one gig. She opened the door to my dressing room and said . . . 'Don't worry, Jon. Tomorrow's another day.'"[18]

Still, Jon Stewart's name and his ability to think quickly on stage had been noticed by sharp eyes from the cable channel Comedy Central. In 1991, Jon was offered a job hosting a comedy sketch show called *Short Attention Span Theater*, which aired from late 1989 until 1994. Although he stayed on as the host for only about a year, Stewart's brief tenure at Comedy Central foreshadowed a much more rewarding future. *Short Attention Span Theater* provided Jon with the kind of stepping-stone that comedians, far more often than not, can only dream of.

Short Attention Span Theater

Merely *writing* jokes, nevertheless, was not Jon's primary goal at all. *Telling* jokes, performing in front of audiences—live and on camera that would bring him into people's homes—that was where Jon wanted and needed to be. He would get that opportunity in 1991, with *Short Attention Span Theater*.[19]

Short Attention Span Theater was a collage of comedy sketches, commentary by an assortment of comedians, and clips from movies shown on HBO and Cinemax. Stewart was invited to join the show as co-host with Patty Rosborough. Rosborough was a fellow actor and comedian; she'd appeared in the film *Jacob's Ladder* (1990) and had been a featured comedian in the documentary *New Wave Comedy* (1986). In addition, among the many celebrity hosts, *Short Attention Span Theater* featured names like Dennis Leary, Laura Kightlinger, and Brian Regan, all of whom have become well-known comedians and television personalities.

The show was not particularly successful, nor particularly good. Most of the sketches were more silly than funny, and nearly all of them ran far longer than anyone with a truly short attention span could have tolerated. But the show provided Stewart with ample opportunity to further refine not only his comedy, but also his skills at hosting a multi-featured program. His delivery was confident, he was a good-looking guy typically clad in his leather jacket, and he had a voice and a television stage presence that, in 1992, caught the attention of another channel, one recognized as among the "coolest" on the tube: Music Television (MTV).

You Wrote It, You Watch It

In the late 1980s, New York University student Todd Holoubek created a performance group called "The New Group" (which later evolved into The State) as an alternative to the local comedy ensembles in the New York City area. One of the unique aspects of "The New Group" was its emphasis on improvisation and collaboration—there was no "leader" and every member would have opportunities to write and perform material. This was an attractive format for local performers. New members came and went as the group refined its vision for comedy performance, and before too long, The State had earned a solid reputation for performances on and off the NYU campus. The group even had a brief Off-Broadway run of a show called "Molt,"[20] which attracted the attention of MTV. MTV, taking a serious interest in the 30-year-old comedian's gift for comedy, offered The State an opportunity to collaborate with Jon Stewart, who was to host a new show called *You Wrote It, You Watch It*.

The premise for *You Wrote It, You Watch It* was quite clever; it combined a traditional comedy improvisation motif with some of the hip and edgy characteristics of the very popular MTV program line-up that included such shows as *The Grind* (1992–1997), *Headbangers Ball* (1987–1995), and *Yo! MTV Raps* (1988–1995, 2008). For *You Wrote It, You Watch It*, viewers would send in stories or scenarios they'd written, and the show's resident comedy troupe, The State, would perform them, often producing wild scenes drawn from the daily lives of their viewers. Stewart opened each show, and introduced each scene, usually with at least one or two wry comments. Typically, he wore a flannel shirt over a t-shirt, sported untamed hair, and an expression suggestive of just a little too much partying the night before. The rolling "disclaimer" at the beginning of the show added to its manufactured carelessness. It read: "THE STORIES YOU ARE ABOUT TO SEE ARE TRUE. THE NAMES HAVE NOT BEEN CHANGED SO THAT YOUR FRIENDS CAN MAKE FUN OF YOU TOMORROW. ANY SIMI-LARITY BETWEEN THE CHARACTERS DEPICTED HERE AND ANY ACTUAL PERSONS IS COMPLETELY INTENTIONAL." The show was funny—at least some of the time, but *You Wrote It, You Watch It* was, ironically, *not* actually watched by many people, and it was quickly canceled. While the show made it through only one season, The State went on to have their own MTV show, which ran for two years. Of the short life of *You Wrote It, You Watch It*, Stewart joked, "You wrote it, you just didn't watch it."[21]

When *You Wrote It, You Watch It* was cancelled, MTV gave the group a show by the same title: *The State*. It was another sketch-comedy show, 30 minutes long, that catered to a largely teenage audience. The sketches were dominated by outrageous characters and situations, all written, acted, and directed by the cast of 11 actors. Stewart's very limited role was as the "fan-mail guy" who reads letters written to the cast of The State. This time, the show lasted a little longer, most of a second season. Then, another cancellation. That didn't mean Stewart would be out of work. He just needed to work on his next step. He wasn't getting rich—"I haven't told my family yet what I actually do. But I'm sure if I did, they'd be delighted to know that I'm not a urologist. Anyway, I have an older brother who works on Wall Street—who will provide for them in their time of need."[22] Stewart was being disingenuous. At this point, there was no way that his family members remained ignorant of Jon's career trajectory. Others were well aware of the talent Jon Stewart possessed. He was starting to show up on the radar of bigger and bigger show business power brokers, though it would still be just a little while longer before that notice would turn into something truly substantial. First, Jon had to be turned away again, and it was a rejection that ultimately "saved" Jon from the constraints of network television.

Chapter 5

A SHOW OF HIS OWN—PART I

I have complete faith in the absurdity of whatever's going on.[1]

LETTERMAN'S REPLACEMENT . . . NOT

Jon Stewart's presence on television was about to become much more interesting. In fact, the world of TV talk shows was, from the perspective of the major networks, becoming perhaps a little *too* interesting. Whereas today audiences young and old prefer to rent from Netflix or order movies and programs from the various digital providers, audiences in the 1970s, 1980s, and well into the 1990s regarded late-night TV as the place to watch cutting-edge comedy, interesting interviews with movie stars, and all kinds of "reality" gossip that now would seem antiquated. In the early 1990s, Jon Stewart was very much part of that "old" television world, and, in fact, he was about to be swept up—or nearly so—into a tense network skirmish.

At around the same time as the cancellation of *You Wrote It, You Watch It*, in 1993, David Letterman was making plans to leave NBC. A hugely popular comedian and talk show host, Letterman had, by the late 1970s, become the permanent guest-host on *The Tonight Show with Johnny Carson. The Tonight Show*'s roots go all the way back to 1954 when it was hosted by comedian-writer-musician-actor Steve Allen. Allen stepped down in 1957, and Jack Paar became the new host. In 1962, a young, sharp-witted comedian named Johnny Carson took over and, in effect, made history by remaining with the show for 30 seasons. His version of the comedy and guest-interview show enjoyed off-the-chart ratings every year. In a medium where anyone can be replaced in a heartbeat, Carson himself was considered to be irreplaceable by the network. But Dave Letterman performed so well in his role as *Tonight Show* guest-host that in 1980 that NBC offered him his own daytime talk show, to be called *The David Letterman Show*. After just a few months, however, the show's dismal ratings prompted NBC to cancel it.

A few months later, another late-night talk show host, Tom Snyder, was himself facing a rough patch. Snyder was on air with NBC since 1973 with *"Tomorrow Coast to Coast,"* with his show coming right after Carson's. But by 1981, Snyder had fallen out of favor with NBC, and his show was canceled. Fortunately for NBC, the ideal replacement was at their fingertips: Dave Letterman. Letterman took over the post–*Tonight Show* time slot and began to build up an impressive audience share of his own. By then, because he had his own late night talk show, Letterman could no longer serve as Johnny Carson's guest-host. That role was filled by a popular stand-up comedian named Jay Leno. Still, *The Tonight Show* was very much Carson's turf, and many thought that if and when he retired—and most hoped that he never would—Letterman would be his most likely replacement.

Meanwhile, as Jon Stewart was wrapping up his own job with *The State* on MTV, Johnny Carson was about to make the shocking announcement that, after 30 years of being American's talk show king, he was going to retire. NBC was pushed to replace one of the most popular television personalities in history. But the next shock came when NBC decided not to go with Letterman; instead, they picked Leno to take over the coveted show. Disappointed and angry, Letterman let his irritation be known at the network, and NBC executives were not happy about the negative publicity. For his part, Leno expressed resentment over the idea that Letterman didn't think much of him as the replacement for Carson. Letterman still continued hosting *Late Night with David Letterman*, and just a few months later, he too announced that he was leaving NBC. Johnny Carson was gone. Tom Snyder was—at least for now—gone. Jay Leno was in, and David Letterman was, by choice, out. But not for long. CBS offered him a lot of money to come over to that network. His show *Late Show with David Letterman* on CBS was aired directly opposite Leno's *Tonight Show* on NBC. There were other late night talk show hosts; Arsenio Hall and Ted Koppel, for example. But the two 11:30 p.m. talk show giants were Leno and Letterman, and in the early-going, Letterman was the ratings winner. In the midst of the late-night talk show chaos, Jon Stewart was invited to appear on Letterman's show, got to sit down with the late-night giant and be funny. It was a wonderful opportunity for Jon to be seen with one of the comedians he most respected. Ten years later, during an interview with ABC's Ted Koppel, Jon explained what that appearance on Letterman had meant. "I had a great time and felt really good, and went home to my illegal sublet and was still as short as I was the night before, still had roaches."[2] In other words, Jon knew that he was not going to become an overnight sensation simply because he knew the right people.

But now NBC faced a new problem. Who would replace Letterman? To Jon Stewart's amazement, he was considered a finalist to become the new host of *The Late Show*. It was a job that would have vaulted him into the show biz stratosphere. In the early 1990s, and ever since, David Letterman had been one of the main players in sparking the night time talk show competition. Hosting different guests every night from Hollywood and beyond, Letterman—like his main rival, Jay Leno—represented the kind of maximum television exposure for which nearly any performer would give his or her right arm. For Jon Stewart to take over Dave Letterman's spot would mean nightly network stardom. But NBC had someone else in mind. As it turned out, the veteran comic and comedy writer Conan O'Brien landed the treasured time slot, and Jon Stewart was, effectively, unemployed and, it may have seemed, without any immediate prospects.

After his short stints at *Short Attention Span Theater* and *The State*, and after being passed over as Letterman's replacement, Stewart might have headed back to downtown Manhattan to continue his stand-up training at the microphones of the local comedy clubs. But while MTV may have dropped *You Wrote It, You Watch It* and *The State* from its program schedule, the forward-thinking MTV station executives were not planning on dropping Jon Stewart. Instead, MTV launched a new show featuring interviews, sketches, and some time for stand-up comedy, to be hosted by Jon Stewart and, even more remarkably, to be called . . .

THE JON STEWART SHOW . . . FOR NOW

A 30-minute talk show on MTV, *The Jon Stewart Show* first aired on October 25, 1993, and was targeted at the young, savvy audiences who wanted to see their favorite celebrities, particularly from the music world, sitting and talking with a cool and funny host who could keep the show lively and provocative. The first few episodes proved Jon's hipness, as he delivered jokes, danced with musicians, traded barbs with celebrities, and seemed genuinely to know the cast of characters of a large number of musical groups. Jon's sidekick, comedian Howard Feller, would make oddball introductory comments like "And now here's your host; he makes his own gravy . . ." Among Jon's early guests were radio "shock-jock" Howard Stern, actor Daniel Baldwin, actress Alicia Silverstone, comedian Dennis Leary (who said to Jon, "I can't believe you have your own show"), *Star Trek* icon William Shatner (who held Stewart on his lap, about which Stewart told him that he'd just "boldly gone where no man has gone before"), supermodel Cindy Crawford, comedian Chris Rock, rock bands Gin Blossom, Heart, The Cranberries, and rappers Run DMC. Those first-season episodes were hilarious but also a little rough around the edges. It's not that Jon was anything less than professional about his preparation for each show. Despite the appearance of his complete casualness, Jon was almost never at a loss for words, for clever insights, or for a good joke. The roughness came from Jon's efforts to make his talk show something qualitatively different than those iconic network shows. Stewart was slowly and deliberately finding his comfort zone as host of his own show. By late 1994, viewers could count on seeing and hearing wildly popular guests on *The Jon Stewart Show*, and more and more viewers were tuning in. Unfortunately, although the show was regarded by critics as a solid addition to MTV's repertoire, not enough of those young hipsters were watching; the ratings were poor. Jon had fallen into the danger zone again. With all the sameness of the nighttime network programs, the one show that tried to be different was about to go under.

Less than a year after its launch, *The Jon Stewart Show* was bought by Paramount in September 1994 and went into syndication. This meant that Paramount could air *The Jon Stewart Show* on any or all of its affiliated television stations, which would increase its audiences substantially. The show would be twice as long and would have a much better chance of surviving for the longer haul. With a new, 60-minute format, Stewart's show enjoyed a modest success for an equally modest length of time—around nine months. Although the show was cancelled in June 1995, those two years as the host of his own show, with

Jon Stewart at Radio City Music Hall for the 1994 MTV Music Awards. (Jeff Kravitz/FilmMagic/Getty Images)

his own name as the name of the show, represented a giant step forward in Stewart's career. Refining his talents for having entertaining conversations with guests, writing sketches on topical themes, introducing and often interacting with musicians all gave him excellent tools for a career as a comic writer, host, and performer. He had also gained a tremendously valuable resource—access to a wider variety of interesting people. Guys like Conan O'Brien might be bigger than Jon and better at keeping their jobs but, as Jon put it, "I'm harder to knock over."[3] Still, the again-unemployed host of *The Jon Stewart Show* had to come up with another plan.

Just prior to the complete demise of *The Jon Stewart Show*, Jon was cast in a TriStar Pictures movie, appropriately titled *Mixed Nuts* (1994). Directed by award-winning writer-producer-director Nora Ephron, *Mixed Nuts* boasted a very strong cast, including Juliette Lewis, Anthony LaPaglia, Rob Reiner, Parker Posey, and one of Jon's idols, Steve Martin.[4] As the opening credits appear, sure enough, there's Jon Stewart's name—evidently one of the stars. Well, not really. The story begins with a pregnant Gracie (Lewis) chasing after her ex-con boyfriend Felix (LaPaglia) down the road. Felix collides with two rollerbladers carrying a large Christmas tree between them. The skaters are played by Parker Posey and, yes, Jon Stewart. The two actors are actually skating for much of this scene, and it's worth noting that Stewart is evidently a decent roller-blader. The three of them argue and as push comes to shove, a good Samaritan, Philip (Martin), comes along and tries to talk everyone down. His efforts to restore calm and sanity don't work, which is particularly comical since Philip is the manager of a suicide prevention hotline called "Lifesavers."

At this point, the story earns the movie title. We soon learn that Philip and "Lifesavers" face eviction by their landlord, Stanley (Garry Shandling). Philip hides the eviction notice from his staff, Catherine (Rita Wilson) and Mrs. Munchnik (Madeline Kahn). Instead, he approaches his bank loan-officer girlfriend Susan (Joely Fisher) to give him a loan. She not only refuses, but also informs him that she has been cheating on Philip and now wants to break up.

From this moment on, there are elevator rescues, fruitcake tosses, an overdose of animal tranquilizers, slapstick head-bonks from carelessly opened doors, a hilarious dance between Philip and the transvestite,

Chris (Liev Schreiber), and then, a few minutes later, Felix shoots Chris in the foot. When Gracie takes the gun away from him, she accidentally shoots and kills Stanley, the landlord. Philip and the others dress the dead Stanley up as a Christmas tree and plan to leave the newly decorated tree on the boardwalk. As (bad) luck would have it, they run into the same roller-bladers who, with vengeance in their eyes, skate like missiles into the group. When Felix drops the tree, the dead Stanley is revealed.

After that, the plot becomes an even madder rush toward absurdity; the police arrive, Felix falsely confesses to the murder, and Gracie counterconfesses to the police that she killed Stanley and shows them the gun. Felix snatches the gun and sprints to the roof a building, threatening to jump. Using his skills as a hotline counselor, Philip talks Felix down and is now a hero, and when Catherine gives Stanley's bag to the police for evidence, they find the materials Stanley used in his double-life as the "Seaside Strangler." Gracie's killing of Stanley results in her receiving a reward of a quarter million dollars, some of which she offers to Philip to cover the expenses of moving "Lifesavers" to new quarters. But at that moment, she also goes into labor in a farcical scene reminiscent of the *Nativity!*. Dr. Kinsky, played by Rob Reiner, has Grace (whose name is suddenly more meaningful) brought beneath a large Christmas tree where he can assist in the delivery of her baby. At the end, Philip proposes to Catherine, and, with the possible exception of those roller-bladers, they all live happily after.

Somehow, despite having fewer than five minutes on screen in *Mixed Nuts*, Jon Stewart had already garnered enough of his own audience to merit having his name appear with the other main players of the movie. True, a review of *Mixed Nuts* said that it was "Truly alarming . . . watching some fine performers . . . at their very worst."[5] But for Jon Stewart, *Mixed Nuts* proved to be an important turning point. In 1996, Miramax Films offered him a three-year contract for which he would be required to be co-writer, coproducer, and costar in two movies per year. The films might or might not ever seen the light of distribution, but for three years, Jon had an assured income and, more importantly, the attention of one of the largest movie production companies. This was big. Jon was learning, and earning, but not quite doing what he'd set out to do: making people laugh. It was time for another breakthrough, another step into the main arena. Jon Stewart had already proven himself to be a funny and intelligent comedian, a better-than-average talk-show host, a competent actor, and a sought-after comedy writer and producer. He now needed to draw upon all of the strengths as well as strengthen any of the weaknesses. That breakthrough came soon enough—after a couple more "almosts" that, as it turned out, were just the ticket Jon needed. But first, a blind date!

MEXICAN RESTAURANT MIRACLE

The date wasn't blind for me.

—Tracey McShane

I thought she hated me.

—Jon Stewart[6]

Fired from the show that bore his name, Jon fully expected to feel as disappointed as he'd been when he was turned down to replace Dave Letterman. Instead, as he said in an interview with Oprah Winfrey, "I thought, 'Okay, my apartment is now worse, and I can still write jokes.' In that moment, I realized I had suddenly become competent."[7]

In fact, Jon's "competence" proved to be a kind of magic in its special appeal to one member of his audience. Tracey McShane had been feeling depressed after her long-term relationship ended. As friends do, her set of friends kept trying to fix her up with dates, and when none of them seemed to work out, her friends wanted to know what, or who, she was looking for. She'd recently been watching *The Jon Stewart Show* and she told her friends that she wanted to meet "someone funny and sweet, like Jon Stewart."[8] As luck—or magic—would have it, Tracey's roommate happened to have a job on a filmset and one of her co-workers was a friend of Jon Stewart's. One day, Jon showed up on the set to hang out with his friend and some of his colleagues—including Tracey's roommate, who told Jon that Tracey had seen him on TV and liked what she saw. But what Tracey did not like was being set up by her roommate with actors, and her roommate actually told Jon that his being on TV was really a potential strike against him. Then she told him much more about Tracey and whatever she said must have been just the right things; Jon decided to ask her out for dinner at a Mexican restaurant.

While Tracey felt a little shy about the setup, Jon wasn't exactly Mr. Cool, either. "The date was literally me talking and eating. I cleaned my plate and part of hers." But soon, Tracey started to talk a little and then, by her own account, kept talking and talking. Jon's show was canceled in June 1995, and he'd just met—a month later—the woman who, less than five years later, he was going to marry.

For the next few years, Jon did what hundreds of actors and comedians do to support themselves: he took whatever jobs he could get that would keep his name and his face in the eyes of producers, directors, and casting agents. He appeared in small but interesting roles on television shows such as *The Nanny* (1993–2000), *Newsradio* (1995–1999),[9] and *Spin City* (1996–2002), and in a couple of respectable movies. While in no way delivering award-winning performances, Jon was able to keep putting money in his pocket and got invaluable exposure to other writers, directors, and producers in the world of situation-comedy television. With a beautiful girlfriend and a growing list of accomplishments, it seemed the sky was the limit for Jon Stewart.

Chapter 6

A SHOW OF HIS OWN—PART II

I can be in twenty movies. But I'll never be an actor.[1]

In 1996 Jon took at least three more giant steps. First, he was co–executive producer—as well as writer and star—of a TV special, *Jon Stewart: Unleavened*. Next, he now had his own production company, called Busboy Productions, named for the time when he worked as a busboy in a Mexican restaurant. And as a further sign of his versatility and audience appeal, he was cast as a romantic lead actor in *Wishful Thinking* (1996). The momentum was building, and from that point on, Jon Stewart was steadily becoming an unstoppable force.

Jon Loses His Shirt

Wishful Thinking, directed by Adam Park, was a more complex movie than most reviewers acknowledged. The story follows the waxing and waning passions among and between a network of characters: Max (James LeGros), Elizabeth (Jennifer Biels), Lena (Drew Barrymore), Henry (Jon Stewart), and Jack (Eric Thal). Max fancies himself a writer who will make it big, even as he works as a projectionist in an out-of-the-way theater that shows only black and white films. When Max rescues an abused dog and brings it to a veterinary clinic, he meets Elizabeth, whose heart is warmed by this dog rescuer. Romance ensues, and before long, the two are living together. Elizabeth wants marriage, but Max shows no desire to tie the knot, and it becomes apparent that the two are not likely to make it. Meanwhile, Lena, who sells tickets at the same theater where Max works, is attracted to Max and willing to do whatever it takes to win his affection. Max sees Lena merely as a friend and is somehow oblivious to her obvious desire for him.

Jon Stewart as Henry is a genuinely nice guy who is also chronically insecure and believes he stands little chance of ending up in a healthy relationship with a woman. When, for example, he is first introduced to Lena and she says, "Nice to meet you," Henry does a double-take and replies, "It is?"

In a classically "Stewart-esque" bit of dialogue, Henry and Lena have the following exchange:

Henry: I'm really surprised you called me.
Lena: Well, I had a really nice time with you at the party.
Henry: I did too with you, it's just, I was really sorry about spilling that wine on your dress. I could have sworn that bottle was empty.
Lena: It was okay. I actually had a harder time getting the brie out.
Henry: Yeah, I mean you gotta admit after a couple of drinks those things look a lot like a sponge.

As they eat what, for Henry, is an appalling meal of sea urchin and other raw delights, Lena tells him that she and Max like to add a phrase to the end of cookie fortunes, like "in bed." Henry replies that he likes to do that too, and that one of his favorites is to add, "and then you die" to the end of fortunes. It's a line that could have come from the real Jon Stewart during any interview he's done or in any conversation he's had with reporters. Lena finds Henry clever and amiable company, but her heart yearns for Max. Henry finds Lena attractive, especially because she seems to like being with him, but it doesn't take long for him to figure out that her interest in him is limited.

But then a kind of magic happens—Henry meets Elizabeth (Biels) in a late-night diner and the two feel a spark of attraction. Elizabeth had been alone, contemplating her shaky and unsatisfying relationship with Max. Henry had stopped in for a cup of coffee before heading home. Both Henry and Elizabeth are shyly pleased to find one another there, and at one in the morning, Henry proposes that they go to Coney Island to go on the rides and walk the boardwalk. To his evident surprise, Elizabeth agrees to go. From this point on, Henry becomes Elizabeth's "forbidden" man; she can't seem to tell her boyfriend, Max, the truth about wanting to leave and about having met someone to whom she feels so drawn. It isn't long before Henry and Elizabeth are headed to her bedroom. On the way, in what may be perhaps the only time he does so in a movie, Jon Stewart peels off his shirt, revealing a toned, muscular torso.

Stewart as Henry is attentive, caring, observant, and intelligent. The sharp wit and wry smile that have made Jon Stewart such an icon on *The Daily Show* are also very much a part of what made him the right casting choice to play the leading man to Biels as Elizabeth. Equally significant is that director Adam Park recognized that Stewart's handsome face would, in fact, make for a credible pairing with Jennifer Biels's beauty.

The following year, Stewart got to be part of a production starring a number of Hollywood heavy hitters: Goldie Hawn, Bette Midler, Diane Keaton, Sarah Jessica Parker, Dan Hedaya, Stockard Channing, Maggie Smith, and Rob Reiner, to name a few. Also in the film were noted personalities such as former New York City mayor Ed Koch, socialite Ivanna Trump, and feminist author Gloria Steinem. So where did Jon Stewart fit into the Hugh Wilson hit *The First Wives Club* (1997, Paramount Pictures)? Precisely on the cutting room floor! According to the Internet Movie Database (IMDb), the scenes in which Stewart appeared were deleted from the final version.[2] But 1997 was a busy year for the 35-year-old Jon Stewart. He had reached the point where guest appearances on regular network television shows could boost ratings while also expanding Jon's own media reach. And what could be more up Jon's alley than to play a Jewish doctor on the "Kissing Cousins" episode of the popular 1990s CBS situation comedy *The Nanny*, starring Fran Drescher?[3]

"I'm a doctor. I can park anywhere."

Three attractive women are sitting at a bar, chatting. A handsome, well-dressed man enters and, approaching the women, says, "Excuse me, ladies. Which one of you ordered the short Jew?" All three women quickly turn around and call out, "Me!" The "short Jew" is Jon Stewart, playing the part of "Bobby." When he tells the women that the one with whom he spoke to on the phone had a "very distinct voice," he can mean only one of them, the star of the show, Fran (also known as "Nanny Fine" on the show). Famous for her very nasal voice, Fran Drescher's character, just as nasal, has been hoping for a long time to marry a "nice Jewish man." She smiles demurely at Bobby and says in her nasally "distinct" voice, "Hiiii!" Hearing her voice in person, Bobby tells her, "You must have really deformed adenoids." Not impressed with this "come-on," Fran turns away, at which point Bobby tells her, "I'm sorry. I'm a doctor." With an even bigger smile, Fran turns back to him, drapes one arm over his shoulder, and says, "Come onnnn!"

It's a funny start to a show that, despite a relatively weak premise, often features well-known guest stars and moments of true comedy. Fran is the live-in nanny for the somewhat aristocratic Mr. Maxwell Sheffield (Charles Shaughnessy) who secretly loves his employee. The audience understands that Fran just as secretly cares for her boss, but neither can find a way to let the secret out. In the meantime, one episode after another, Fran manages to attract a variety of characters to date, which only adds to Mr. Sheffield's frustration.

Arriving next evening for a date with Fran, Bobby drives up in his $80,000 car, fueling Mr. Sheffield's growing jealousy. When Fran cautions Bobby that he has parked his car in an illegal spot, he tells her, "Fran, I'm a doctor. I can park anywhere"—a remark that is particularly ironic in that Stewart has frequently made jokes about his parents wishing he had gone to medical school. When he goes on to say that he would be allowed to park at a fire hydrant in front of the department store Loehmann's, Fran swoons.

Back at Bob's house after their date, Bob is checking the glands in Fran's throat and pronounces them healthy. Fran just can't get over her good fortune: "Oh wow. Lobster, dancing, and a free check-up!" It just gets better when she learns that Bob wants children and that his mother is no longer alive. The show takes a further comic turn when Fran, in a passionate embrace with Bob, fantasizes that they have married and now live the privileged life of the characters in the soap opera *Dynasty*. When Mr. Sheffield arrives with his own wife, she and Fran confront one another and the two start brawling. They both topple over the couch, choking each other and each trying to pull the other's hair. As the fantasy ends, Fran is still in Dr. Bob's embrace, thinking that she has found the perfect mate. But not for long. Jon's role as the passionately romantic suitor is about to undergo a comedic transformation.

At the "Hillcrest Jewish Center," Fran attends the wedding of her cousin, and as she walks up the aisle in her role as bridesmaid, she bumps into her boyfriend, Bob, who is obviously one of the ushers. Surprised, they kiss, and Fran asks what he's doing there. Before Bob can answer, Fran's overbearing mother sees them and says beaming, "Isn't it adorable! Let me get a picture of you and your cousin, Bob." The classic "spit-take" ensues, with Bob and Fran spitting out their kiss. The scene dissolves into the photo that Fran's mother had taken.

"I have green eyes, you have blue . . ."

At around the same time, Jon was asked to guest-star in an episode of the popular CBS comedy *Newsradio*. Directed by Tom Cherones, the show centered around "New York's #2" news radio station, WNYX. The cast members formed a talented ensemble, many of whom, such as Andy Dick, Joe Rogan, Moira Tierney, Dave Foley, and Phil Hartman went on to become much bigger stars. (Sadly, Phil Hartman was killed in 1998.) Jon was tapped to play a strange role in the1997 episode entitled "Twins." Andy Dick's character, Matthew, one day introduces his colleagues to his "identical twin brother" Andrew, played by Jon Stewart.[4] In a moment reminiscent of a scene in Arnold Schwarzenegger's movie *Twins* (1988) where Schwarzenegger and Danny DeVito play completely un-identical twins, Matthew's colleagues stare in disbelief from one "identical twin" to the other, waiting for the joke. But Matthew is completely serious and genuinely happy to have his brother there with him. Both are wearing sweater-vests, both know the same fist bump, and both seem to believe that they look and sound exactly alike.

At one point, while hanging out in the break-room with some of Matthew's co-workers, Andrew "confesses" to the obvious truth that he is not Matthew's twin and is not, in fact, really even Matthew's biological brother. Andrew's parents had adopted Matthew and had always told him that he was Andrew's twin brother. The rest of the WYXN staff promise to keep the secret, but naturally the secret gets out just a few moments later. When Matthew confronts Andrew, Andrew tries to soothe him telling him, "Dude, we're still brothers. It's just that we're not twins. And biologically speaking, we're not actually brothers, either." Matthew is stunned, replying, "But we look so much alike!"

In tones that make it impossible not to see Jon Stewart the real person in the character, Andrew explains, "I'm three inches shorter . . . you have blond hair, I have brown hair, I have green eyes, you have blue . . ." But the real punch line comes when Andrew adds, "I'm Jewish!" Once again, the theme of his Jewishness crosses over from Stewart's real life to screen in typical good humor.

"I'm a Jewish guy"

Jon did not have to play a fictional character to explore the range and depth of Jewish humor. In his self-titled TV performance, *Jon Stewart: Unleavened*, Jon served as writer and sole cast member, and his Busboy Productions company was behind the project. Directed by Beth McCarthy-Miller, *Unleavened* was literally a million-dollar—that was its budget—stand-up comedy production.[5] More importantly, it was a true showcase of the Jon Stewart who had set out, 10 years earlier, to become a professional comedian in the Big Apple. The title Jon chose for the show was obviously significant. "Unleavened" is the term closely associated with the traditional Jewish flatbread, called *matzoh*, eaten during the Passover holiday. In their haste to escape their enslavement in Egypt, Jews did not stop long enough to allow their bread to rise, to leaven. Stewart's use of the term for his stand-up showcase evokes the double sense of something being imperfectly nourishing.

With a black and white montage of film footage showing images of "the magic city of Florida's Gold Coast," *Jon Stewart: Unleavened* begins on a nostalgic note, a nod toward the heyday of the allure of Miami Beach, Florida. Beautiful beaches, resorts, and show business night-spots all served to make Miami a true hot spot for both celebrities and their fans. Stewart's one-man show was taped live at the Coconut Grove Playhouse, and upon being announced to the sellout crowd, a dapper Jon Stewart strolled across the stage, waving to his delighted fans. His first words into the microphone: "Gracias! Gracias! Muchos Gracias! Hola Miami!"—in deference to the fact that, by 1996, a large percentage of Miami's population was Latino. He actually continued for a few more sentences in rough Spanish that gradually deteriorated in "quesadilla" and then, finally, into the start of the traditional Hebrew prayer, "Baruch Atah Ado . . . that's all I know!"

But it most certainly was not all he knew. He was just getting warmed up. In the typical self-deprecating humor so characteristic of the great Jewish comedians, and peppered with a ton of profanity so characteristic of Jon's speech, Stewart told the audience how much he loved coming to their city, and that it reminded him of his "carousing" years when he would come to Miami because "I loved getting rejected by women I couldn't even understand." Then after a few funny bits about the summer Olympics games, including references to the evident civility between Iraqi and Iranian athletes, he seemed to get serious for a moment, telling the crowd that he didn't think America had any business getting into a war in the Middle East. The audience loved it and cheered loudly; Jon was clearly going to be mixing comedy with politics, and his audience was right on board. But *Unleavened* was a comedy special, and true to form, Jon undercut the seriousness by "informing" everyone there that Jesus, Mohammed, and Moses all went to the same high school. He spoke about America having the world's best military but only the 15th best education system. "Smart bombs, and really stupid children." More laughter.

Over the course of the hour, Jon frequently reminded his audience, "I'm a Jewish guy" as the preface to bits of humorous social commentary on topics that included the legalization of marijuana—he's not in favor; wars in the Middle East—they're inevitable; American politicians—they're mostly hypocritical bigots who form the militias throughout middle America—their blame of Jews and blacks for virtually all social problems is idiotic, and so on. Jon's riffs on popular American culture were a compelling blend of intellectual insight and brilliant humor that kept the audience laughing. In one instance, he praised the commitment and dignity of the Million Man March in Washington, and then said that he had gone to the Capitol a week later for "30 Jews pulling a falafel wagon." Even more laughter.

In and among the jokes and social commentary, Jon also managed to acknowledge his relationship with Tracey, saying, "I have a girlfriend. She's lovely, and I'm so in love with her. She inspires me." Then, back to the edgy material, Jon talked about Louis Farakhan and his combination of charisma and virulent anti-Semitism. Stewart wondered, "Jews and Blacks fighting each other. That has to be the dumbest [bleep]-ing thing I have ever heard of . . . what are we fightin' about? Who's got more people in show business?"

Around 40 minutes into it, Jon's jokes became increasingly graphic, full of sexual innuendo and a few vulgar bits that, not surprisingly, had the audience laughing even more. Maybe it was because he told these stories in the same kind of earnest, intellectual tones as his more G-rated material. At one point, in the midst of some R-rated material, he asked the audience, "Am I sharing too much?" Then he shifted more specifically to religion. After a brief joke about the Pope's head-dress, the audience's laughter quieted just a little bit. "Oh, it's not so funny when it's about your guy, is it?" Stewart asked them. A few people even booed.

But then Jon did what he does best, he shifted gears ever-so-slightly and won everyone back over. In musing about the lack of connection between Easter and the tradition of painting and hiding eggs, he wondered aloud, "How many disciples did Jesus have?" The audience and Jon said, simultaneously, "Twelve." Then Jon asked, "How many eggs are in a carton?" The audience roared. Then he talked about some of the quirks of Judaism and Jewish "rules": "Thou shalt not kill. Thall shalt not commit adultery. Thou shalt not eat pork." Stewart speculated that maybe that particular commandment had been authored by some nervous pigs. Comfortable again, the audience was with him all the way. At the end of *Unleavened*, nearly everyone in the audience stood in appreciation of the remarkable performance from the "Jewish guy." Jon Stewart had put on quite a show of his own, but *Unleavened* was just the appetizer, and Jon was hungry for more.

Chapter 7

A SHOW OF HIS OWN—PART III

TOM SNYDER'S REPLACEMENT . . . NOT

On October 21, 1996, Stewart was the first guest-host on *The Late, Late Show with Tom Snyder* (CBS) and was scheduled to fill in for the next four days.

Snyder, a brash, chain-smoking, sharp-tongued radio and television news anchor and commentator since the 1950s, began hosting *The Late Late Show* when David Letterman moved from NBC to CBS in 1994. Letterman, who had always been a big fan of Snyder's, had insisted on having control of the show that would come on at 12:30 a.m., after his own *Late Night* show. In 1995, he brought Snyder over to host that show. *The Late, Late Show with Tom Snyder* was unique in that it was aired live, with viewers allowed to call in and talk with Tom and his guests. When Snyder took ill with the flu, in October 1996, Jon Stewart became the first substitute host for the show. (Later, comedian Martin Mull also took on some of the guest-host duties.)

Some of Snyder's loyal fans worried that Tom Snyder was being dropped and that Jon Stewart would be taking over the show. While Jon had fans, Snyder was considered an icon in the 12:30 a.m. time slot; his supporters were not happy about Stewart's increasingly frequent stints as host. David Letterman, owner of Worldwide Pants, the producer of Snyder's show, assured audiences, through a spokesperson, that Snyder would be welcome to continue doing *The Late, Late Show* for as long as he cared to, and that he was definitely not leaving the program. But Snyder's absences were becoming more frequent, and Stewart, who, along with Mull, was filling in more often, looked like an excellent candidate to take over the show when the irascible Snyder retired. Where Snyder liked to come across as a mostly serious and occasionally aggressive TV journalist, Stewart was much more laid back. Jon's approach to his stints on Snyder's show was to foreground his sense of humor while interviewing his guests and taking phone calls from viewers. That sense of humor was evident on an occasion when Stewart appeared as Snyder's guest, and the two exchanged comic banter for much of the show.

Unfortunately, as skilled a substitute as he was, Stewart did *not* get the call to replace Snyder. Instead, when Snyder left *The Late, Late Show* in 1999, the job was given to Craig Kilborn, who remained the host until 2004. Kilborn, a handsome writer and occasional actor, was the physical opposite to Jon Stewart. At six-feet five-inches tall, blond, a former collegiate star basketball player, and supremely confident, Kilborn had spent three years as an ESPN sportscaster, where he had also anchored a regular feature segment. There was one other significant qualification on Kilborn's resume: for the three years prior, from 1996 through 1998, Kilborn had been the host of a trailblazing Comedy Central talk show called *The Daily Show!*

Jon was, however, already at work with Letterman's production company, Worldwide Pants, to develop new shows. One of the possibilities was a show—a very, *very* late (or very, very *early*) show that would air right after Snyder's. But signing a deal and getting a new show into the network schedule are two different things. It was looking like it would be a long time before a Jon Stewart–hosted talk show would see the light of day. Fortunately, another opportunity arose for Jon. He had signed on with *The Larry Sanders Show* (CBS, 1992–1998) starring well-known comedian Gary Shandling. *The Larry Sanders Show* was a clever parody of late-night talk shows. It was so clever, in fact, that there was little difference between Shandling's show and any of the iconic late-night shows hosted by Leno, Letterman, O'Brian, and for that matter, Kilborn. In fact, Shandling himself had been a frequent, and favorite, substitute host on *The Tonight Show with Johnny Carson* from 1986. Although Sanders had been offered a variety of standard-format talk shows over the years, it was *The Larry Sanders Show* that provided him with the golden comic opportunity to host a show about hosting a show. Beginning in November 1996, Jon's role was to play a character named "Jon Stewart," the fictional guest-host for the often-absent fictional "Larry Sanders." Anyone tuning into Shandling's show would have a hard time knowing that it was intended as a spoof; it didn't seem any spoofier than the talk shows it parodied. If on that particular night, "Jon Stewart" was sitting in the host's chair, audiences would know that he was playing the part of a fictional substitute for a fictional host. In a way, although *The Larry Sanders Show* was a wonderful opportunity for Jon to be out front and center on a talk show, it still wasn't his show, and it wasn't even really him.

When word got out that Shandling would be leaving *The Larry Sanders Show*, there were rumors that Stewart would become the full-time fictional host. Larry's fans were worried, *sort of*. They half expected that Larry's departure would just be part of the show's storyline. Even on the show itself, the fictional producer, Artie (played by veteran actor Rip Torn), believed he has inside information that Stewart would be taking over the show, which might put Artie and Larry's sidekick, Hank (Jeffrey Tambor), out of work. Stewart's going from "permanent guest-host" to full-time host of *The Larry Sanders Show* might have made for an ingenious and hilarious double-parody, but, as Stewart told *Entertainment Weekly*, that rumor was just "a little something called fiction."[1] Equally fictional was the rumor, two years later, on the set of *The Larry Sanders Show* that the network was incensed at a parody that Jon Stewart had written. In that skit, Hank had starred as Adolph Hitler. In fact, CBS did little to dispel the rumor, though neither Sanders nor Stewart ever confirmed it, either.

Then, in 1998, there was yet another little earthquake in the world of talk show hosts. Craig Kilborn was leaving *The Daily Show* to take over Tom Snyder's job duties on CBS's *The Late, Late Show*, where he went on to appear in over 1,000 episodes (1998–2005).

During Kilborn's tenure, *The Daily Show* featured, almost exclu-
sively, television and movie stars along with the occasional musical
act. In most cases, the guests had come on to hawk their latest projects, not to provide any particular insights into any particular topic. As
an interviewer, Kilborn was intelligent but often abrasive—some said
nasty—and he did not seem to have a lot of respect for many of his
guests. Still, he rarely got any of them to deviate from their mission of
self-promotion. In September 1996, his first year as host, Kilborn interviewed a young guest who'd come on to promote his upcoming HBO
special titled *Unleavened*, a 52-minute solo stand-up comedy showcase.
The guest's name was Jon Stewart. Two years later, when Kilborn was
on his way to CBS, Stewart's name came up as a solid choice to replace
Kilborn on Comedy Central's *The Daily Show*. It was as though Stewart
was caught in a spiral of parodies. Once a potential candidate to replace
Tom Snyder, and then a fictionally potential candidate to replace Larry
Sanders, Jon was now in the running to replace the guy who was replacing the guy who Stewart might have replaced. But was this going to be
another "almost" for Jon?

You would think that Jon Stewart would be chomping at the bit,
just waiting to sink his teeth, at last, into a television venture that he
could mold and shape as his own—really his own. And he *was* excited.
But he was also committed to a few projects he had to complete. Now
in his mid-thirties, Jon may not have found stardom, previously, in his
few moments of film exposure, but not long after his minimal work in
Mixed Nuts, his respectable showing in *Wishful Thinking*, as his nonap-
pearance in *First Wives Club*, Jon had a role in a new film that would
make him a somewhat more credible leading man.

In *Playing by Heart* (1998),[2] Stewart again plays a nice but insecure
guy who ends up in an unexpected romance. As Trent, Stewart's initially reluctant love interest is Meredith (Gillian Anderson). Trent is
frustrated by love because, ironically, he is a guy that women can actually trust and who would be genuinely worthy of their love. With one
of the central roles in this film, Stewart had more opportunity to flex
his acting muscles. One reviewer wrote that "high points come with
Jon Stewart's sweet courtship of Gillian Anderson."[3] Another wrote
that despite generally sub-par performances from many of the very talented actors and actresses, "The couple that comes off best is Stewart

and Anderson. He's a pleasing film presence and very funny."[4] In *Playing by Heart*, Stewart found himself among a truly A-list, or in some cases future A-list cast, including Angelina Jolie, Amanda Peet, Sean Connery, Gena Rowlands, Dennis Quaid, and Ellen Burstyn. Although his performance isn't quite Oscar-worthy, Stewart acquits himself more than competently as the sensitive and charming young architect who finds himself attracted to an emotionally vulnerable theater director, Meredith. Unfortunately, Meredith is more or less fed up with men and their lack of honesty. She shows little interest in Trent's attentions and resists Trent's efforts to get to know her. But Trent—with so much of Stewart's real charm and charisma built into the character—uses a wry sense of humor and a sensitive intelligence to win her over. There are a half-dozen other co-plots involving other couples, a mother and her dying son, a pair of adulterers, and more, and eventually, all the plot lines converge at the scene of the renewal of wedding vows of Paul and Hannah (Connery and Rowlands).

What makes this movie, and Stewart's acting in it, so significant is the ways in which Stewart gets to play a character who borrows liberally from the actor himself. Like Jon, Trent is attentive, insightful, a good listener, and above all genuinely funny. And it works. At one point, Meredith tells him, "I have a hard time trusting men." Trent replies, "I'm not men. I'm not a group. I'm just me." In another moment where Jon Stewart's self-deprecating humor becomes inseparable from his characters, Meredith tells him, "I don't deal with passion well." Trent suggests that she may be afraid of losing control that she may "prefer to be the director, telling everyone what to do." Sighing, she replies, "It's pretty painfully obvious, isn't it?" But then Trent turns the tables and says, "You know, there's something to find out about *me*. I take direction pretty well." Trent has cleverly turned Meredith's admission of a "flaw" into evidence that the two belong together.

But shortly after Christmas in that same year, 1998, audiences were treated to another movie in which an entirely different Jon Stewart showed up. Playing Professor Edward Furlong (no relation to the actor by that name), a character way off the charts of normalcy, Stewart showed audiences that he could also be very, very strange. Robert Rodriguez's *The Faculty* (Dimension Films, 1998)[5] starred Piper Laurie, Bebe Neuwirth, Salma Hayek, Elijah Wood, and a number of other

highly respected actors and actresses. The story is that something weird
is happening to the teachers, staff, and even some of the students at
Herrington High School. They look normal enough, but their behavior
gets increasingly stranger, and a handful of students begin to suspect
that their teachers are really aliens determined to destroy them. It turns
out that they're right. The teachers are, one after the other, quickly
being possessed by alien parasites.

The suspicious students form a loosely connected group—somewhat
like the one in the movie *The Breakfast Club* where one of each "type"
of student is represented. At Herrington High, the group is comprised
of a jock named Stan (Shawn Hatosy), a moody loner; Zeke (Josh Har-
nett); Stan's popular and worldly girlfriend Delilah (Jordana Brewster)
who edits the school newspaper; the quiet, unpopular kid, Casey (Elijah
Wood) who secretly pines for Delilah; the outcast brainy girl, Stokely
(Clea DuVall) who secretly pines for Stan; and the "new girl," Marybeth, orphaned and living with relatives, and is a friend of Stokely, and
who secretly pines for Zeke.

The sharp-eyed students notice that although their teachers look
more or less the same as they always do, there is something fundamentally wrong. In fact, for some strange reason, the teachers keep
sending students to the blatantly attractive nurse (Selma Hayek) for
hearing checks, providing the aliens with the perfect opportunity to
inject themselves into human bodies by way of the ear canal. Casey
figures this out and warns his friends, and when they find themselves in
Mr. Furlong's (Jon Stewart) class, they realize that their trusted teacher
has been completely taken over by an alien and is now attempting to
infect Zeke. Armed with a pen filled with a drug that causes liquid to
dry up, Zeke stabs Mr. Furlong in the eye. Because the aliens need lots
of liquid to survive, this particular alien is destroyed. So is, it *seems*,
Mr. Furlong, himself.

Eventually it looks like nearly everyone at the school has become
infected with the alien parasite, and the uninfected gang-of-six escape
from the building and end up at Zeke's house. There, they inoculate
themselves with the drug that would, if they were infected, kill them.
What follows is a chaotic stream of events whereby the remaining teens
are infected, but not before they manage to kill the "queen" parasite. As
a result, all the other alien parasites die off, leaving the students, most

of the faculty, and staff restored to health. In fact, Zeke, Stan, Delilah, Casey, Stokely, and Marybeth are all now much better adjusted to life in general, and Herrington High School is miraculously saved.

But the movie is not really over; during the credits, Mr. Furlong reappears, alive, though missing an eye and a few fingers. (While Stewart appears for less than a minute during this sequence, he has joked that "When you do a role like that, Hollywood doesn't stop knocking on your door," and "I get calls all the time: "Jon, we were thinking you should diversify—what about a Magic Marker in your eye?"[6]) Despite its somewhat predictable plot and over-the-top acting in some cases, critics actually kind of liked the movie, even the ones that kind of did not. One wrote that *The Faculty* was "a crappy teen horror movie, but in director Robert Rodriguez's hands, it's at least agreeably crappy."[7]

He'd played a roller-blader, a couple of nice marriageable guys, and an alien-infested high school teacher. Incredibly, Jon had more movie work to do in 1998, this time to appear in film directed by Tamara Davis who had already directed features starring Chris Rock (*CB4*, 1993) and Adam Sandler (*Billy Madison*, 1998) among others. Now she was putting together a movie called *Half Baked* (1998, Robert Simonds Productions)[8] starring Dave Chappelle, who plays two roles: a janitor named Thurgood Jenkins and a rap star named Sir Smoke-A-Lot. The story is, of course, ridiculous. Kenny (Harland Williams) kills a cop's horse. But not just any horse; this one happens to be diabetic, and Kenny has—with all good intentions—fed the horse some of the junk food he'd just purchased while stoned on pot. Kenny is arrested, thrown in jail, and, absurdly, the judge sets his bail at $1 million, which, as you might expect, Kenny cannot pay. Kenny's pals now take it upon themselves to come up with a way to bail their friend out of jail, and to do it fast. Otherwise, they fear, Kenny will become a victim of Nasty Nate (Rick Demas) who is, well, nasty.

The group of stoner friends decides that selling marijuana is the best and fastest way to raise the million dollars needed for the bail, and it just so happens that Thurgood, who works for a pharmaceutical company, can get his hands on plenty of pot. Along the way, Thurgood and the "gang" make friends with Sir Smoke-A-Lot and some of *his* friends who also happen to deal in "weed." Meanwhile, a rival drug dealer, Samson Simpson (Clarence Williams III), finds out about Thurgood and his friends' little operation and does his (comic) best to eliminate the competition.

So, just where does Jon Stewart fit in to this goofy plot? He plays what the credits call an "enhancement smoker"—a guy who believes that everything is made more fascinating when experienced "on weed, man!" In a classic stoner scene, Stewart, one of Thurgood's new customers, tells his dealer how cool it is to see the back of a $20 bill "on weed, man"—"there's a dude, sittin' in the bushes, man. Does he have a gun? I don't know, man! I don't know!" Then, as he does so often on *The Daily Show* when he pretends that his nonexistent earpiece has informed him of something, Stewart suddenly "hears" something in his ear: "Wha? What? Red Team go!" In a way, Stewart's "enhancement smoker" character was probably not that different from the youthful Jon Stewart himself when, by his own characterizations, he spent many hours and days at college getting high. But to play this role in a feature film meant that Stewart was learning to channel things he knew how to do naturally into professional experiences for which he was rapidly gaining the respect of directors, producers, and fellow actors.

It was an exhausting year, and no one could have blamed Jon for taking a break. But as if to put an exclamation point in his own resume, and while Craig Kilborn was starting to pack up his *Daily Show* luggage to move to CBS, Jon managed to squeeze one last acting project into his 1998 yearbook.

Children's Television Workshop (CTW), under the direction of Tom Trbovich, was putting together a made-for-television celebration of *Sesame Street*'s 30 years on the tube. Trbovich had the daunting task of directing a whole gaggle of muppets and needed a star who could host the show. For that role, who better than a guy whose career was picking up a huge head of steam, a guy who had once worked as a puppeteer, a guy who really wasn't that much bigger than some of the Muppets themselves? Trbovich put in the call to Jon Stewart and Stewart accepted the job hosting *Elmopalooza!*.[9] As it turned out, Jon's puppeteering skills were not needed. Jon just had to play himself—or, once again, a version of himself that might actually interact with Muppets as though they were as "real" as he was.

For the event, the Muppets and all their celebrity friends come together at Radio City Music Hall, in New York City, to perform in

"Elmopalooza," a tribute to *Sesame Street*. Jon Stewart arrives backstage to begin preparations for the show, and as he enters his dressing room, he is set upon by a large make-up crew comprised mainly of Muppets. "Prairie" the Muppet is the "producer" of the extravaganza, and she fires off tips for Jon's performance as host. She tells him, "Jon, try not to peak too early!"

A few minutes later, Elmo arrives to thank Prairie for her efforts and Jon for agreeing to host the show. In character, Stewart interacts with Prairie and Elmo as though they are human participants in the event. Unfortunately, when Elmo exits to take his place in the theater, he makes the mistake of closing the defective dressing room door. The result? Jon and Prairie and an assortment of others are now locked in the room. The show must go on, and various Muppets and celebrities scramble to compensate for Jon's absence and to get the various acts on—and then off—the stage. There are performances by En Vogue, Gloria Estafan, Shawn Colvin, The Mighty Mighty Bosstones, Kenny Loggins, Jimmy Buffet, and the Fugees. Comedians Chris Rock, Richard Belzer, David Alan Grier, and Rosie O'Donnell make appearances, as do supermodels Cindy Crawford and Tyra Banks.

Meanwhile, Jon tries everything he can to get the door opened, but he and the others fail in their attempts at lock-picking, tunnel-digging, and door-knob yanking. Finally, after most of the show is over, Oscar the Grouch announces that he can get the door open. He just needs some pepper, which Bert (of Bert and Ernie) just happens to carry in his pocket. One quick sprinkle of pepper onto the face of Oscar's friend Slimy-the-worm, and the worm's sneeze breaks the door down—right on top of Jon Stewart. He's okay, though, and in true show biz spirit, he rushes to the stage, to join the other characters for the last few minutes of the program. Jon and Elmo sing a duet ("Songs are around when you need them") that is picked up by Big Bird and a few dozen others in the grand finale.

Critics weren't particularly kind in their reviews of *Elmopalooza!* One wrote that the comedy was "inferior to what you'd find on an average episode" of *Sesame Street* itself.[10] Variety critic, Tony Scott, called *Elmopalooza!* "a woeful collection of musicvideos" that are connected only by virtue of the "charming presence" of the Muppets themselves.[11] Interestingly, despite the campiness of his role and the "inferior" comedy, Stewart caught none of the reviewers' flak, and could chalk up his *Elmopalooza!* performance to experience.

Less than a year later, Craig Kilborn would be fully installed on CBS's *The Late, Late Show*. Jon was poised for his launch as host of *The Daily Show*. But first, he still had another movie contract to follow through on. For this one, Jon had another opportunity to flex his trim Hollywood muscles again, appearing in the movie *Big Daddy* (1999), directed by multitalented actor-director Dennis Dugan.[12] Dugan had, three years earlier in 1996, made a movie called *Happy Gilmore*, starring Adam Sandler, a good friend of Stewart's. The Dugan–Sandler collaboration was renewed with *Big Daddy*, this time with Sandler playing Sonny Koufax, an unambitious, unemployed, immature, 32-year old law-school graduate who never bothered to take the Bar exam. Stewart plays Sonny's best friend from law school and roommate Kevin Gerrity, who is now a successful attorney. Sonny lives off of a cash award won in a lawsuit after a cab driver ran over his foot. He works part time in a toll booth mainly to give him something to do other than watch TV, eat snacks, and vegetate. Meanwhile, Kevin travels the world on legal business and is gearing up for a trip to China for his law firm. Unfortunately, Sonny's girlfriend Vanessa (Kristy Swanson) has no intention of staying with such a slacker, and she leaves him for a rich, much older man, Sid (Geoffrey Home). Kevin (Stewart) plans to propose to his girlfriend, Corinne (Leslie Mann), which just adds another source of irritation to Sonny's life as he and Corinne can't stand each other.

That same day before leaving for China, Kevin reveals to Sonny that, years before, he fathered a child, but that he doesn't really know anything about the boy. As luck—and a comic plot—would have it, the next morning, Sonny opens his front door to find a young boy named Julian (played alternately by twins Cole and Dylan Sprouse). Julian hands him a note that explains that his mother will no longer care for her son. Sonny has no intention of baby-sitting and calls Kevin who is at the airport about to board a plane. What can Sonny do? He decides to "use" the boy as a way to win Vanessa back. If he can be a responsible adult pseudo-dad, maybe Vanessa will see him in a new light. That's not going to happen. When Vanessa again rejects Sonny, he takes Julian with him to the Department of Social Services where he tries to give Julian back. Sadly, Sonny learns that Julian's mother has in fact died of cancer and that, for the time being, Julian will have to be placed in a foster/group home setting. Feeling a spark of paternal instinct, Sonny decides to keep Julian with him and develops a real bond with the boy. But, to keep things complicated, a Social Services agent (played by Josh Mostel) finds out that Sonny is not actually Julian's father and has Sonny arrested for kidnapping.

At this point, the events all start to stream toward a finale . . . and a twist. In court, Sonny is represented by Kevin and, wouldn't you know it, Corinne's sister, Layla (Joey Lauren Adams), who is now Sonny's girlfriend. Sonny's friends all testify on his behalf, but the judge intends to convict and sentence Sonny for kidnapping and fraud. At that moment, however, Kevin has a kind of flashback. He'd been drunk and had a one-night stand with a waitress from Hooters during the '93 World Series. Julian had just testified that he'd come from Toronto and that he'd been born in July—nine months after that Series. Kevin connects the dots and realizes that he is, in fact, Julian's father, and he explains all of this to the judge. Because he is the true father, Kevin argues, successfully, that all charges against Sonny should be dropped. Unfortunately for Julian, who has come to love Sonny as his dad, the judge awards full custody to Kevin. (Happily, the boy is assured that he and Sonny will remain close friends for life.)

And now for the twist. A little over a year later, Sonny, who is now a lawyer, and Layla are married and have a child of their own; Kevin and Corinne are married and raising Julian. For Sonny's birthday, his buddies have surprised him with a party at Hooters. Their waitress? None other than Sonny's old girlfriend Vanessa. The cook? Vanessa's "rich" older husband Sid. Critics found *Big Daddy* to be an unpleasant mix of "crude humor and mawkish sentimentality"[13] and the movie was nominated for five Razzie Awards, which are "awarded" each year by the Golden Raspberry Award Foundation for the worst in that year's motion pictures: Worst Picture, Worst Supporting Actor (Rob Schneider), Worst Screenplay, Worst Director, and to top them off, the Razzie for Worst Actor went to Adam Sandler,[14] who later went on to become one of only three people to win this "distinction" twice in a row—in 2012 and 2013.[15]

Although some have poked fun at Stewart's movie career, one writer saying that it "is so unremarkable that Stewart himself lampoons it,"[16] his involvement with film and television projects was creating an increasingly impressive track record. Mostly self-deprecating about his acting prowess, Stewart nevertheless was showing his willingness to be cast in productions ranging from drama to farce.

Interestingly, when Stewart plays "himself" in movies and on television, he becomes very much the guy audiences are now accustomed to seeing on *The Daily Show*. In a particularly odd moment where TV character and real-life guy seem to merge, Jon appeared on one of the celebrity episodes of Regis Philbin's TV show, *Who Wants to Be a Millionaire*. Stewart told Philbin that he was playing for Alzheimer's research because his grandmother had died of complications from the disease. Philbin expressed sympathy, and Stewart then joked, "I told you this already before the show!" It took a moment for Philbin to realize that Stewart was only joking, and another moment for it to dawn on him that he'd been subtly accused of being forgetful. Philbin laughed, Stewart laughed, and the studio audience laughed. Philbin was outmatched, but Stewart just let the joke—and the point—pass.

Taped Shows and Real Animated Life

Few people could, as Jon Stewart was doing, pack more projects into the "moment" before taking his seat behind *The Daily Show* desk. Jon was in demand more than ever before, both as a real-life actor and as an animated version of himself.

Michael J. Fox was starring in a hit prime time television show, *Spin City* (ABC, 1996–2002), and he invited Jon to appear in the Wall Street episode as an unscrupulous stock broker. Anyone who knows Jon Stewart knows of his love for dogs (he has rescued a number of them, including several that he adopted). When he took over *The Daily Show*, one of the things visitors discovered was that there would frequently be lots of dogs around the set and in the offices, and photographs taken of Jon taking walks along downtown Manhattan streets often showed one or more of Jon's dogs accompanying him. When he agreed to appear on *Spin City*, he convinced the writers to call the episode's hot stock "Barky.com." The story itself had even more interesting connections to Jon's life. Briefly, Mike Flaherty (Michael J. Fox) has offered to invest co-worker Alex's (James Hobert) money in a conservative portfolio of mutual funds. But Alex wants Mike to make a high-risk investment in a new technology stock, Barky.com. Although Mike takes the check for $8,700, he does not invest in the tech stock because he knows it's too new to be a good risk. Two days later, when the stock's value soars from $2 to $68 per share, Alex believes he is now rich, and Mike believes he is now in big trouble. It's time to call his stockbroker to help fix the mess. Enter Jon Stewart as Parker the slick broker: "Hey, Flaherty, you big bag of dirt! What can I do you for?"

What Mike needs Parker to "do him for" is to buy shares of Barky.com "two days ago." He tells Parker that he *meant* to buy it two days before. With the exact same kind of sarcastic voice and expression that Stewart himself has all-but-trademarked, Parker replies, "Well, you know we can use the New York Stock Exchange's 'Oh-I-meant-to-buy-it clause,' I'm amazed more people don't take advantage of it." Mike persists, and Parker finally asks, "How much have you got?" Mike tells him "Eighty-seven hundred," and he now needs 300,000 by next day. With a low whistle and a grin, Parker tells him, "I can totally do that!"

But come next day, after Mike has tried to win the money by buying hundreds of "scratch-off" lottery tickets, Parker shows up and tells him that Barky.com's value has once again gone "through the roof." Mike *would* have been a very rich man, Parker tells him. Unfortunately, Parker confesses, he has a slight gambling problem, and after cashing in the enormous stock gains, he lost it all on bets at the track. Of course, Mike finds a way to at least get Alex's original money back again, and, of course, Barky.com crashes in value so that, had Alex actually invested in it, he would have lost everything—a happy ending.[17] But what viewers would not have seen, or likely know anything about, is the irony of Jon Stewart's role as Parker and his joke about the New York Stock Exchange. In real life, not only is Jon quite knowledgeable about economics and finance, Stewart's older brother, Larry Leibowitz, is a brilliant financial expert and investment analyst who became the chief operating officer of the New York Stock Exchange in 2010.

At around the same time, Jon had also agreed to appear as the animated "Jon Stewart," on the grown-up cartoon series, *Dr. Katz, Professional Therapist* (Comedy Central, 1995–2002). Dr. Katz was the creation of Jonathan Katz, a stand-up comedian who also knew a ton of other comics on whom he could draw to voice Dr. Katz's "patients."

Among them were Louis C.K., Wanda Sykes, Kathy Griffin, Jim Gaffigan, and Patton Oswalt. Like those folks, the animated Jon Stewart played/voiced himself in the role of one of Dr. Katz's neurotic patients. The show was a unique way of integrating these comedians' stand-up routines into the various responses they would give to their "therapist's" questions. It was also unique in its use of producer Tom Snyder's innovative animation technique called Squigglevision, where the only things that moved, for the most part, were eyebrows and mouths. But to give the impression of near-constant movement, the lines around everything—people, furniture, houses—would be in constant "squiggling" motion.

In the "Guess Who" episode,[18] Jon Stewart takes the couch, and in many ways, the animated Jon Stewart, voicing the lines he delivered, primarily, on his special *Jon Stewart: Unleavened*, provides us a lens directly into the daily concerns of the man himself. For instance, he tells Dr. Katz, "So, um, yeah. I'm Jewish. Not serious, not a serious Jew, obviously. I don't wear protective religious headgear." Dr. Katz listens, nods, says "Mmm hmm" and Stewart continues that he's traveled to Israel: "They're cocky there. God was born there, so there's no talking to those people."

The theme of Stewart's Jewishness and his quasi-outsider perspective on it is often coupled with his self-identification as just a regular guy from New Jersey. He tells Dr. Katz, "I mean, I'm from Jersey. We've got Springsteen, so it's a different thing, but you get off the plane in Israel and immediately they're like, 'Welcome to Israel, the *Holy Land*,' and I'm like, 'Great, I'm from America, home of the Whopper.'" The therapy session with Stewart takes up over a third of the episode and while all of Stewart's lines are from stand-up routines, somehow hearing them cut and pasted into the mock therapy session lends greater emphasis on the personal and social issues that persist in his comedy. In fact, the whole context of the show makes you forget, temporarily, that the things "Jon" says are just parts of jokes and not expressions of emotional turmoil. At one point, Jon tells Dr. Katz that "the reason that Jews are bitter is we have to sit through all those TV shows around Christmas—they're always the same . . ." When Dr. Katz prompts Jon to talk about his childhood, he tells him: "I went to an elementary school that was all Italian and Irish, you know? And I'd show up on

Passover with matzoh and a boiled egg on 'Spaghetti Day,' you know? The Fitzpatrick twins would be sitting across from me, like, 'Whaddya gotta eat them crackers for?' and all I could think of was 'Years ago, my people were slaves in the land of Egypt, and Moses came forth unto Pharaoh and set *Let my people go*. And we fled through the desert to the Promised Land.' [And the other twin would say] 'Yeah, whaddya gotta eat them crackers for?' So finally I just told them I had stomach cancer and couldn't have anything spicy."

During the rest of Jon Stewart's session with Dr. Katz, he tells him about his feelings toward Canada, the Emergency Broadcast System, and his concern about the poor education that today's kids are getting. As he puts it, "That's our legacy . . . Smart bombs, stupid children." He also complains about his tiny apartment and that he can "sit on my toilet, turn on the TV, and shut the front door without moving," hearkening back to the real Jon Stewart's days as a fledgling comedian, newly arrived in New York City, and living in a tiny sublet.

A couple of years later, "Jon" again appears on Dr. Katz[19] and tells the therapist that he and his girlfriend/fiancé have adopted a dog together. Because the dog is depressed, he was put on Prozac. (This was true. Jon and Tracey had adopted a pit bull that had been abandoned.) Once again revealing something about his real life, Stewart and Dr. Katz discuss Jon's relationship with his non-Jewish fiancée/wife. Dr. Katz tells him that such marriages involve a "leap of inter-faith." Stewart replies that it's confusing. "Guy comes down to Earth, and takes your sins, and dies and comes back three days later, you believe in him, you get to go to heaven forever. So how do you go from that to 'Hide the eggs!'?" When Stewart asks Dr. Katz, "Is there anything I can do at home, for free, that would help me?" the doctor reminds Jon that he'd advised him to try to "enjoy the day before the day takes over." Stewart replies that yes, the doctor told him that, but that he hasn't yet had time to "embroider it on a pillow." Finally, after the two bicker for a moment about whether therapy can boil down to a single phrase, Dr. Katz says it cannot, but Stewart "recalls" that Dr. Katz had once told him precisely that—Dr. Katz tells him, "You hear what you want to hear" and then realizes that that may be the phrase they were looking for.

At his next appointment, Jon enters the waiting room and encounters Ben, Dr. Katz's son who has a long-standing crush on Laura, the receptionist. As Stewart and Ben stumble over introducing them-selves, Stewart, who doesn't know who Ben is and assumes he is another patient, tells him that there's no need for discomfort and that everyone has problems. Finally, Ben tells Jon that he is Dr. Katz's son. Surprised, Stewart tells him that he doesn't look like Dr. Katz; Ben tells him that he looks more like his mother, but that Jon Stewart, in fact, looks a little like Dr. Katz. Jon replies, "Okay, then, if you want, I'll go with you; I'm his son, too!"

The Daily Show

This whole life [of comedy] is a journey. There is no "made-it." [20]

But, in fact, Jon was just about to "make it" in big way. He was, at long last, hired by Comedy Central and given a four-year contract to host *The Daily Show*. On January 4, 1999, Jon was given one week to write and co–executive produce his first episode of *The Daily Show*. With a dream job, a team of excellent writers, a regular and sturdy paycheck, and a built-in audience, Stewart should have been ecstatic. He would have the opportunity to talk with celebrities, engage in juicy gossip, and tell the occasional joke to both studio and home audiences. It was the kind of show he was already good at. It was a hosting-gig that would be the culmination of years and years of hard work. But, incredibly, Jon had lost his taste for hosting a television show devoted to syrupy conversations with show-biz celebrities, celebrity gossip, and celebrity public-relations appearances. After setting himself up in his new office on January 4, 1999, within a couple of months, Jon realized that he could not continue hosting *The Daily Show*, *not* if it was going to be just another nighttime talk show where movie stars came on to be human advertisements for their movies and television shows. He had grown weary of serving as a prompter for celebrities to tell less-than-fascinating stories about their glamorous lives. Jon knew that to survive and make the most of this opportunity, he would have to smarten up the show. Comedy Central was now taking a big risk. Their new host was about to change the course of Comedy Central's sec-ond highest rated show (*South Park* was number one). The outgoing host, Craig Kilborn, had a sizable following, striking looks, imposing size, and aggressive personality. The incoming host was much smaller, perhaps a bit less striking, and had not been on the air with his own show for a long enough period of time as to garner as large a fanbase as Kilborn's. But whereas Kilborn's humor tended to be caustic to the point of meanness, Stewart's humor was often directed as much toward himself as toward others. He was a sharp observer and critic of popular culture without becoming nasty about it. As one journalist put it, Jon Stewart's delivery comes "with more of a conspiratorial wink than a condescending smirk."[21]

His interest in political and social issues and the ways in which media represented those issues drove him to make an effort to reshape the show. Not surprisingly, the writers, who had enjoyed a predictable format that afforded good pay, found Stewart's efforts to reconfigure *The Daily Show* obnoxious. If Stewart himself had not been such a strong writer, he might have gone down with the ship, as more than half of his *Daily Show* writing staff left the program. But *The Daily Show* did not dissolve with the loss of a bunch of its writers. Instead, Jon now found himself with an opportunity to introduce his audience to a radically different kind of comedy show, one that would, as *The Larry Sanders Show* had, *resemble* existing talk show formats while satirizing many of those very shows. But Stewart's *Daily Show* would be much more than a parody of talk shows. It would be a forum in which television media itself was under the comedian's microscope.

Thirteen years after leaving New Jersey to make a career in comedy in New York City, Jon Stewart now had a stage on which to produce a television show into which he could throw his full range of talents. It would be intelligent, topical, entertaining, and of course, funny. Had he packed up and quit after being booed off the stage at The Bitter End or after making no impression at all on the exhausted 2:00 a.m. staff at the Comedy Cellar, Jon Stewart would have been giving up on the one career he'd truly wanted. But what could have been the "bitter end" of a comic career was, instead, the bright beginning to one of the most respected comedy shows, and comedy show hosts, on television. For the next 14 years, right into the present, from his Comedy Central desk, Jon Stewart's unique perspectives on politics, culture, economics, history, news media, and, yes, Hollywood would throw a gigantic wrench into the machinery of mainstream media.

Chapter 8

THE DAILY SHOW
WITH JON STEWART

You know how some musicians can play by ear? I felt like I had that—like there was a certain "comedy by ear" that I knew how to do. And producing our show is somewhat of a musical process.[1]

We're not on a traditional network: We're on the goofy, juvenile delinquent network . . .[2]

MY SHOW, MY WAY

You are the glue, my friend, you are the caulk.[3]

Jon was no Craig Kilborn. He was, from the start, much more interesting. More relevant. And more exacting—especially when it came to his own contributions to the new *Daily Show*. That meant he was going to ruffle a few feathers. In a way, it started two years before Jon took over the show. In 1996, around six weeks after Kilborn had been hired as host, he interviewed a very relaxed, goatee-sporting Jon Stewart. (Jon had grown the goatee for his role in the movie, *The Faculty*.) At one point, Kilborn told Jon that he was enjoying his transition from sportscaster to talk show host and that he still played a little basketball. Kilborn asked Jon if he played any basketball. The audience was then treated to a funny moment as Stewart told Kilborn to "stand up." (As he started to stand, Kilborn joked that doing so was going to make him look like Robert Wadlow, the eight-foot ten-inch man featured in nearly every edition of the *Guinness Book of World Records*.) When the two men stood side by side with Kilborn nearly a foot taller, Jon turned to Kilborn and said, "Now ask me again if I play hoop."

The interview itself was somewhat flat, with Stewart seeming to be in much greater control of the show than Kilborn, whose ability to generate conversation and humor was obviously not nearly as good as his guest's. When Kilborn asked why his upcoming HBO comedy special was being filmed in Miami and not New York, Stewart replied, "Miami's like a second home to me, being Cuban."[4]

One of *The Daily Show*'s regular features was Kilborn suddenly putting his guest on the spot to answer five random questions. When the energy was about to drop out of the conversation, Kilborn announced dramatically to Jon that it was now time for those questions. Kilborn asked, "What's the capitol of Kentucky?" to start off. Stewart guessed wrong. It was the same for the next three questions, none of which got many laughs—either in the asking or the answering. The last question, evidently something Kilborn thought Jon would appreciate, was to translate from the Yiddish, "Nisht Gedaiget." (It means "not to worry.") Stewart smirked and deliberately mistranslated the phrase to mean something about how Germans had put the Jewish people into concentration camps. The audience chuckled. Kilborn told Jon, "I can't accept that answer," and Jon interrupted, telling Kilborn that "of course you can't accept the answer. You're cut from the same Aryan cloth!" It was a joke. The audience laughed. Kilborn looked a little confused and turned to the audience saying "That was fun." Jon, who had just taken a sip of coffee, spit it back into the cup to laugh.[5]

Two years later, on December 16, 1998, Craig Kilborn hosted his second-to-last show. His guest was Jon Stewart, and the purpose of the interview was for Kilborn to introduce Jon as the next host of *The Daily Show*. As usual, the show began with the voice-over: "The most important television program . . . ever!" Then Kilborn got right down to things, telling his audience that Jon had already checked out his "new digs." As the two chatted about the early days of the show, Craig told the audience that during the preliminary days of rehearsal for the first broadcast of *The Daily Show*, Kilborn had received a "good luck" phone call from none other than Jon Stewart. Kilborn then presented Stewart with a gift—a thick edition of the *Yellow Pages* on which Jon could sit, to make himself look taller. Jon took it in stride, sat on the phone book, and joked about how great it felt to be "way up here." He actually looked comfortable, as usual, in his role as the incoming host, while Kilborn seemed ill-at-ease and in a bit of a rush.

While Jon was joking about his new height, Kilborn interrupted to ask about the movie, *The Faculty*, in which Stewart plays a high school teacher infested by aliens. First, of course, they rolled the publicity clip that showed a surprisingly menacing Mr. Furlong (Stewart) turning to confront a student. When the clip ended, Kilborn commented briefly, and then—again somewhat awkwardly—asked Jon, "Did you die?" Careful not to be a spoiler for his own movie, Stewart joked, "I turn out to be a beautiful Jewish woman."[6]

Once again, Jon Stewart was in "command," while Craig Kilborn was clearly a man with one foot out the door. But in a moment of surprising candor, he asked Jon about changes he would be making to the show. Stewart, gracefully, pretended to be taken aback, telling Kilborn that changing the show would be like "drawing a moustache on the Mona Lisa."[7] Suddenly, as though rallying for his last sprint to the finish line, Kilborn announced that it was time for the five questions. This time, everything he asked Jon was tailor-made for a correct answer. One question was, other than Sandy Koufax or Rod Carew, "name your favorite Jewish athlete." With only a moment's hesitation, Jon answered, "Art Shamsky," one of the heroes during the New York Mets 1969 "miracle" season. The last question of the night was to name the song that Randy Newman put on the charts in 1977. The answer was "Short People,"[8] and Stewart—having guessed correctly—added that he wasn't as tiny as people seemed to think. He then pointed to his coffee mug and said, "Why don't I just go for a swim right here." Jon also joked—sort of— that one change he would make was to get rid of Kilborn's staff of "correspondents." Kilborn's "glue" and "caulk" were giving way. He had one last show to do on Thursday, December 17, 1998. Then, despite the fact that Jon had never set out specifically to become a talk show host, just a couple of weeks later starting on January 4, 1999, Jon Stewart would begin a 14-plus year stint as the new host of *The Daily Show*. Something else Jon had never set out to do, or even thought possible was that in that same year, *People* magazine chose Jon Stewart as one of the fifty "most beautiful people in the world."[9] He ranked 16th in the voting, ahead of Cate Blanchett, Jessica Biel, Matthew Perry, and Taye Diggs. Jon told one interviewer, "I made sure some of the people above me got eczema, blotchiness—until there was nowhere left to go; they had to turn to me. And it was a dream come true."[10] But it wasn't necessarily a dreamy experience for the staff at *The Daily Show* who had "grown up" with Craig Kilborn. When Jon Stewart took over, he immediately shifted the focus of the show more to politics than show biz, and gave a much bigger and more creative role to many of the correspondents— most notably Stephen Colbert, Steve Carell, and Ed Helms. Stewart himself found that taking a show over made for ruffled feathers. "I can't tell you my first year here was particularly pleasant." Jon found himself, on more than one occasion, engaged in what he called "knock-down, drag-em-out yelling" squabbles with members of the staff who initially didn't understand the increasing focus on current events and politics.[11] In fact, Jon nearly quit before he even started. "I walk in the door, into a room with the writers and producers, and the first thing they say is 'this isn't some MTV bull . . . ' And then I was told not to change the jokes or improvise." Jon walked out, called his agent, and told him that he wanted out. It took over two years before Jon had the kind of staff with whom he felt completely comfortable.[12]

FAKE REAL (REAL FAKE?) NEWS

I'm actually too valuable to live my own life and spend most of my days in a vegetable crisper to remain fake news anchor fresh.[13]

The Daily Show *has achieved an undeniable, potentially disturbing, cultural significance . . .*[14]

By now it's an introduction millions have heard: "January 2nd, Two-Thousand, from Comedy Central's World News Headquarters in New York, this is *The Daily Show with Jon Stewart*!" Cue the theme song, "Dog On Fire," go to camera one, then two, and maybe a quick shot of the studio audience, and then the lens settles squarely on the man behind the semicircular desk. He is, typically, scribbling with his left hand furiously on the top sheet of a small, pale blue, and totally irrelevant pile of "notes." As the music ends, he looks up, as though mildly surprised to find "us" there, and tells us, "Welcome to The Daily Show! My name is Jon Stewart, and *man* what a show we have for you tonight. My guest tonight is [movie star, politician, author, pundit, scientist, fellow comedian . . . you can fill in the blank] who'll be talking to us about [a book, a movie, a discovery, a political campaign, a war, a foreign country, a television show . . .]. But first, our top story . . ."

Of course, the top story, and the several that follow, are pulled from current events—political campaigns, speeches, scandals, wars, peace talks, elections, revolutions, movies, marriages, divorces, and more. Or, more accurately, the stories are more often about the ways in which other networks, journalists, and "talking heads" have covered one or more of these stories. *The Daily Show with Jon Stewart* is less about news than about the *packaging* of the "news." And it is even more about the remarkably sharp wit of Jon Stewart and his team of writers, contributors, and "correspondents."[15] Whether he launches into "coverage" of national or international stories, a local event, or, often, the way in which one or more news broadcasters has done something stupid, Jon Stewart pries open every person, place, event, or media outlet to find both the humorous and the outrageous. He is also fully aware of his role as a kind of antidote to the mainstream approaches to these absurdities. Stewart once remarked, "If you watch the news and don't like it, then this is your counter program to the news."[16]

Interestingly, at this point in Jon's life, he was working toward a completely *different* kind of role—that of husband. In June 1999, Stewart proposed to his girlfriend, Tracey McShane, five months after beginning his tenure on *The Daily Show*. An avid crossword puzzle fan, Jon had recruited puzzle-master Will Shortz to create a special puzzle in which the marriage proposal would be embedded. Then, as he and Tracey lounged together to work on the puzzle, Tracey made the happy discovery. The two were married in May 2000.[17]

What better moment, then, for Jon to be cast in a small movie role in a film entitled *Committed*.[18] Actually, the role was very, very small—in

Jon Stewart on the set of The Daily Show, *Comedy Central's award-winning, satiric look at politics. (Norman Jean Roy/Comedy Central)*

fact, it was "uncredited" in the cast listing. But Jon was there, on set, playing the part of a "birthday party guest" where for a few brief frames audiences were treated to a truly funny moment.

Following from the movie's title, the story is about the extent of the commitment in the marriage between Joline (Heather Graham) and Carl (Luke Wilson). Carl wants to hit the road to find himself, and Joline wants the commitment that their marriage should reflect. When Carl heads off, Joline follows him—surreptitiously, from New York to El Paso. Whereas the rest of American society seems to shrug its collective shoulder at the growing number of dissolved marriages, Joline refuses to accept any abdication of commitment that, for her, marriage embodies.

Stewart's role is limited to a visual scene; he is one of four partygoers squashed onto a couch, smoking and "chilling," and visibly "uncommitted" to anything at all. With a cigarette dangling from his lips and his head thrown back as he watches Heather Graham, Stewart perfectly embodies the "birthday party guest" that no one needs to know much about, but who somehow ends up showing up at people's parties.

Whereas Jon's acting in *Committed* was, for most audiences, forgettable, his part in a short film entitled *Office Party* (2000) was harder to ignore. On screen, once again for just a few moments, Jon plays a "pizza guy" in director Chiara Edmands's expertly crafted little film that packed a lot of story into just 12 minutes. Every character is a scene stealer. A typical corporate office staff has had an over-the-top holiday party, complete with hard drinking, dancing, weed smoking, and a guy, Don (Dave Attell), who gets so drunk that his co-workers think he's dead. Before they dispose of his body, they make a series of photocopies of his face. The film alternates between party scenes and the morning after, where the employees and the boss all seem to be hungover, bruised, and curious about where Don is. In one flashback scene, the "pizza guy" (Jon Stewart) arrives on the elevator and finds Linda (Carol Kane) slobbering over the office's "special boy" Rodney (Rob Munk). Stewart gives them a long, withering look before saying, "Large pepperoni for Don?" He then steps past Linda and Rodney to find the guy who ordered the pie. In another flashback scene, the pizza guy finds Don, who has passed out, and Bill (Tate Donovan) and Sean (Ralph Macchio) who are photocopying Don. The three conscious guys have a cigarette together, and Don slumps off the photocopy machine. Stewart looks from Don, to Sean, to Bill, and tells them, offhandedly, with flawless comic timing and without a shred of real concern, "I think that guy's dead."

The rest of the story follows the employees and their boss, Mr. Fingerberger (Bill Tatum), as they try to figure out what happened the night before. Bill and Sean have actually buried Don, and we presume he really did die, but during the film credits, Don shows back up without a clue as to what happened to him. When he asks Bill if he's missed anything, Bill assures him that he hasn't.

When Jon Stewart had originally come to New York to become a comedian, he may have envisioned himself in front of microphones, telling jokes. He may have imagined that one day he would be a recognizable face on television, maybe even the movies. The connecting thread was always to be deliberately funny, to make people laugh. However, in a 2001 movie in which Stewart plays a news anchorman, the laughs he produces are the direct result of his characters' efforts *not* to be funny at all.

In Kevin Smith's film, *Jay and Silent Bob Strike Back*,[19] Jon plays Reg Hartner, a news anchorman. The movie itself could be described as an adventure story, a kind of "hit the open road to discover life's purpose" kind of tale. But the road, here, is one that is both outrageously intricate and completely over-the-top in its silliness. Once again, Stewart found himself surrounded by an intriguing array of stars, including Carrie Fisher who plays a nun, Ben Affleck and Matt Damon (who play themselves as well as two other characters), Judd Nelson, George Carlin, and even singer Alanis Morissette who plays God.

The story in a nutshell is that Dante (Brian O'Halloran) and Randal (Jeff Anderson) get a restraining order to stop Jay (Jason Mewes) and his pal, Silent Bob (Kevin Smith), from dealing drugs from the front of the local Quick Stop store. When they are successful in their campaign, they discover that their lives are now without much purpose. But when their friend, Brodie (Jason Lee), tells them that he's learned about a movie, entitled *Bluntman and Chronic*, being made featuring two notorious characters based on Jay and Silent Bob, Dante and Randal decide to go and grab a piece of the credit—and money. They pay a visit to one of the movie's producers, Holden McNeil (Ben Affleck), who doesn't seem to appreciate their position. But Randal and Dante persist, motivated, in part, by the desire to refute the slanderous assumptions people have been making about them on the Internet.

George Carlin, in a satisfying cameo role, picks up the hitch-hiking Dante and Randal and schools them about life on the road. Armed with this new knowledge, the two catch a ride with a "gang" of sexy female jewel thieves who will figure in the story later on. But not before they "free" Suzanne, an orangutan in captivity, provoking the fury of federal wildlife marshal Willenholly (Will Ferrell). Everything comes together—sort of—when Dante and Randal end up in Hollywood and have to face a barrage of consequences for their road trip, including squaring off with the police on the hunt for jewel thieves, the producers of *Bluntman and Chronic*, Suzanne the orangutan, and Jay and Silent Bob.

Reg Hartner (Stewart) is a resolute and serious TV "journalist" who must deliver dramatic stories, such as the one about the stolen orangutan as well as a feature story on a "terroristic primate rescue syndicate," the Coalition for Liberation of Itinerant Tree-dwellers (C.L.I.T.—with all conceivable groan-worthy jokes), and he must do so with poise and without a trace of mirth. When he interviews Marshal Willen-holly (Ferrell), it's hard not to envision a blooper-reel in which the two burst out laughing at the utterly silly exchanges that their char-acters must dead pan their way through. One reviewer wrote that the movie is "irreverent, self-referential, twisted, cheap and tasteless. And, of course, I mean that as the highest compliment."[20]

The Thrill of Creating Comedy

Comedy and hosting a talk show is about the closest thing to sports that I have found.[21]

As Reg Hartner, Jon was required to report on current events, no mat-ter how ridiculous the stories might be, with unquestioned seriousness. But as himself on his own talk show, Jon had the freedom to "report" on anything he chose and in any style he liked. In referring to his work on *The Daily Show with Jon Stewart* as akin to sports, he chose an interesting metaphor. As a collegiate soccer player, Jon Stewart had been both a dedicated and talented athlete and a team jokester. But if that were really the bottom line for *The Daily Show*, Jon Stewart would be just another late-night talk show host, in the tradition of Johnny Carson, David Letterman, Jay Leno, Jimmy Kimmel, Conan O'Brien, and more recently, Jimmy Fallon. Indeed, the formats for the "big" late night shows are similar, almost as though there is an unwritten law for how to run a late-night comedy talk show. The formula goes something like this:

- Voice-over announcing the show, with [Host's name].
- Host emerges and tells the studio audience and the rest of us "at home" that the night's show will be *particularly* good, with *espe-cially* great guests.
- Opening monologue—dealing with topical events, celebrities, and "news" stories as they have been packaged into jokes writ-ten by staff members and occasionally the hosts themselves. If a

member of Congress has been caught in a scandal, the host may simply say something like, "A Congressman caught in a scandal? Now there's a surprise!" If there's a band, they'll play a note or two, signaling to the audience that they just heard something funny, in case they missed that point. In some theaters, a lit-up sign will blink on, calling for "APPLAUSE!"—to which studio audiences respond with the kind of audible laughter, hooting, and whooping, which reassures viewers from home that the joke— and the host—are very funny.

- Hosts then introduce and/or ask the audience to "say hello to" the band leader and the band. The hosts then interact for a moment or two with these band leaders, trading the occasional inside joke or innuendo, that is, Letterman with Paul Schaefer, Leno with Ricky Minor (or, for many years prior, Kevin Eubank), and Conan with Max Weinberg of E Street Band fame. The banter between host and bandleader often gives the impression that the two guys (and late-night talk shows have long been the nearly exclusive domain of men) have been up to who-knows-what-kind-of-craziness in the time between the previous show and this one.

- Recurring segment—i.e., Leno and *Headlines*, Letterman and the *Top-Ten List*. The studio audience is ready for this segment, applauds wildly and happily when the host tells them it's time for "tonight's Top-Ten List" or for "Headlines!" In most cases, the hosts present their lists or "headlines"—which may actually include mainly quirky print ads or back-page newspaper articles—in a manner suggesting that these items reflect the silliness, carelessness, or just plain stupidity of everyone *other* than the host and his audience.

- First Guest(s)—Leno's first guest typically stays after his or her interview segment is finished. He or she simply moves over to the other couch. Letterman's first guest almost always leaves after the interview, and Conan's first guest sometimes stays, as do Kimmel's guests.

- On occasion, the guest(s) on all five shows will perform—music, comedy, magic, animal-taming, and so on.

- "My Next Guest"—Leno's guests sit near each other, with the most recent at Leno's right side. The guest has to look back a bit over his or her left shoulder to see Leno. Letterman's guest also sits to the host's right. Letterman's chair swivels so he and the guest—both facing mainly forward—can to some extent make less neck-straining eye contact. On Conan O'Brien's show, Conan's guests also sit to the host's right. Conan is able to look directly at his guests, who must turn their heads to the left to see their host. Like his fellow hosts, Kimmel sits to the guests' left. Although the guests are able to look left to see Kimmel, they, too, are seated to face the audience.

- In all of these shows, at least one guest is almost always a television or movie star who has come to promote a new film, television show, or occasionally a book he or she has "written"—most often with a ghostwriter who has managed to create the illusion that Hollywood stars also sit at their computers composing works of literature. There are the inevitable film clips with the guests frequently acting as though they had no idea which promotional clip would be shown. Without much difficulty, audiences could predict who will appear on these shows; it will be those with a new "project," those who are, at the moment, "hot." In any given one- or two-week period, audiences can, in fact, accurately anticipate that the *same* guests will appear on *all* of the mainstream late-night talk shows. For instance, when the movie, *The Girl with the Dragon Tattoo,* hit the theaters, the star, Rooney Mara, appeared on *Late Night* with Jimmy Fallon (NBC), *The Tonight Show* with Jay Leno (NBC), and *The Late Show* with David Letterman (CBS), all within a single week in December 2011. She also appeared on *The Today Show* (NBC) and several others during that same week. 2012 Summer Olympic female gymnasts appeared together and individually on most of the network (and a few non-network) talk shows within a week in August of that year. Few guests on any of these shows are of the more serious variety; Letterman is more likely to have a guest whose pet does a "stupid pet trick" than one who has written a key piece of Federal legislation. Leno's guests might perform a stand-up comedy routine or be representatives from the U.S. Olympic Gymnastics team, but are not likely to know much about the nation's economy. Guests appearing on Conan and Kimmel seem mainly to be there to give the hosts fodder for jokes about show business, or, on occasion, sports.

- After taking a commercial break, each of the shows comes back with their bands peppering the audiences with covers of contemporary music. Sometimes the host will act as a "conductor" and wave the band back to silence before resuming the conversations.
- The shows end with some kind of announcement by the hosts about the next night's guests. Theme music rises, and the credits roll.

The Daily Show with Jon Stewart is, decidedly, a significantly different animal. The show's structure may, at times, vaguely and humorously, mimic the formats of the others, but Jon's agenda is always, in part, to highlight the peculiarities of those programs. For one thing, although Stewart often warms up his studio audience with funny banter, with a few significant exceptions, he offers no traditional on-camera monologue. He is a comedian, but he doesn't tell the kind of punch-lined jokes on his show that the other hosts do for the classic "rim-shot" from the studio band. (During commercial breaks, he does, on occasion, tell a joke or two to keep the audience happy.) He mines comedy from the issues and people who populate current events and particularly from the approaches that network newscasters take in reporting them. As guests do on Letterman, Leno, Kimmel, Fallon, and Conan, the guests on *The Daily Show with Jon Stewart* sit to the host's right—at least at first. They may occasionally sip from the official guest cup of coffee, water, or tea. But that's where the similarities to the aforementioned talk shows end. As Jon and his guest sit, they both swivel around so that they are face to face, talking across the narrow desktop, in *profile* to the audience. They talk *to each other*, not *at* the studio audience.

Jon and his guests talk about books,[22] current events, politics, the economy, and, of course, movies and television shows (complete with promotional clips). One essential difference between Stewart and the Letterman-Leno-Kimmel-Conan-Fallon quintet is that, with the possible exception of his show biz guests, Jon Stewart and his guests have genuinely thoughtful conversations, real dialogue, and authentic give and take. Whereas Letterman, Leno, Kimmel, Fallon, and Conan mainly provide platforms to assist in the showcasing of their guests' newest movie or television shows, Stewart's agenda for his guests is more complex. Whether they are political figures, leaders of cities or states or even nations, scientists, journalists, scholars, or even other talk show hosts, like Bill O'Reilly, Rachel Maddow, or—notably—Bassem Youssef (who has been called the Jon Stewart of Egypt and who has been, on more than one occasion, arrested by Egyptian police for, among other things, joking affectionately about Islam), Jon's guests can anticipate a lively discussion—full of intelligence, thoughtful remarks, and, of course, humor. And just as often, whoever occupies that chair across from Jon can expect to be asked one or more challenging questions that they did not expect at all, the kinds of questions that prove, once again, that Stewart is a formidable interviewer who knows how to set his guests at ease one minute and then on edge the next.

For a "fake" news show, *The Daily Show with Jon Stewart* may be one of the most successful television programs with regard to hosting very real and powerful guests and discussing real and often critical events. Equally remarkable is the fact that, increasingly, the people who appear on Jon's show quite obviously welcome the opportunity to appear on *The Daily Show with Jon Stewart* because, along with the American public, they regard *The Daily Show* as a respected forum and Jon Stewart, himself, as a deft and insightful host who will, at the very least, provide opportunities for his guests to speak intelligently. Occasionally, his conversations with pop stars are a bit superficial, sometimes even awkward. He has called these kinds of interviews the "weakest part of the show, through no fault of anyone's but mine."[23] But Jon's interviews with scholars are usually eye opening, and his discussions with political figures are famously candid and startlingly well-informed. He refers to these kinds of interviews as "the most erratic portion" of the show because "those are the most spontaneous and the least structured" minutes of the night—all of which, he said, make them the most fun.[24]

Stewart relies on staff members to help keep him up to speed about the content of the hundreds of books he seems to have read in their entirety in impossibly short amounts of time, but he reads enough of each one to have found points of interest, and his knowledge of national and international politics and governance, economics, and history is extensive, thorough, and obviously respected by his interviewees. Remarkably, Jon has little difficulty switching gears—one night chatting with a television actor who may or may not be able to sustain much of a dialogue about anything substantial, and the next evening asking probing questions and demanding honest answers from a U.S. senator, a political leader from Pakistan, or a candidate for the U.S. presidency.

Another characteristic that distinguishes Jon Stewart and *The Daily Show* from the other late-night shows and their hosts is a skill set that includes lightning-fast comedic wit, a deep intellect, relentless attention to network media's approach to current events, and an ability to have at least a basic familiarity with a new and complex publication virtually every single night. The other hosts are often funny, and sometimes clever in their own remarks, but few viewers would argue that they are as quick, well-informed, and as erudite as Stewart. Toward the end of 2000, Stewart was asked, "So how did a short Jewish stand-up comedian come to be the political spokesperson for this generation?" The question was one Jon was starting to hear more and more often, and his reply was typical: "I don't think there's a spokesman for anything in this country anymore. There are 200 million people and 120 freaking channels to choose from. I'm not even a spokesman for my own viewers."[25]

The Daily Show is self-consciously satirical, with Stewart frequently drawing attention to the fact that his show is *not real journalism.* Just as frequently, of course, he draws attention to the ways in which the so-called real journalists and newscasters aren't real either. In one notable episode on October 28, 2002, while *The Daily Show* was taping in Washington, D.C., Senator John Edwards (D-VA) sat down with Stewart and when Jon asked the senator if he would consider a run for the presidency, Edwards replied that he was not considering it at that "point in time." Stewart jokingly asked whether Edwards would tell him first if he should change his mind, and Edwards joked right back that he would.[26] Or maybe it wasn't a joke. Less than a year later on September 15, 2003, Jon reminded his studio audience of Edwards's promise as he replayed the tape of that interview. Then, via live satellite, Senator Edwards appeared on screen. Stewart prompted him: "Senator, I believe you have something to tell us." Edwards responded, "Jon, I'm here to keep my promise. I am announcing my candidacy for the Presidency of the United States on *your* show." The audience went wild, cheering, laughing, clapping, and as their noise died down a bit, Stewart said, "Thank you very much, Senator. I appreciate that. That's very nice of you. That's excellent. Thank you so much." Stewart then asked Edwards if he would just make his announcement one more time because Stewart wanted to "add something." When Edwards reminded Jon that he'd promised not to make fun of him, Stewart assured him that he just wanted to make the announcement more "special." Senator Edwards complied and with a smile he again announced his candidacy. That was when Stewart turned the moment on its head. "Now Senator, I didn't tell you this before when we were in Washington, D.C.—and by the way thank you again for that interview as well—uh, and I guess I should probably tell you now, uh (long pause), we're a fake show. So, I want you to know that this may not count."[27] In the somewhat awkward moment that followed, it was not clear that Senator Edwards knew whether Jon was telling the truth about his show being "fake." Of course, *The Daily Show* is "fake" only in the sense that its stated agenda is comedy. It may be a fake news show, but its unique perspective on what is generally understood as "the news" is quite real. Senator Edwards's confusion was, no doubt, a result of that ambiguity: *The Daily Show* may not take itself very seriously, but *Daily Show* audiences surely do.

Unlike other talk show hosts such as Glen Beck and Bill O'Reilly, and two of Stewart's "favorites"—Chris Matthews and Rush Limbaugh—another frequent target of Jon's satire, Jon Stewart does not explicitly set out to correct, preach, teach, refute, or outshout people, ideas, or issues. Stewart's number one purpose, as it has always been, is humor; a close second, though, would have to be exposure of the banality—the silliness—of what networks offer as "news stories," investigative reporting, analysis of current events, or even just so-called factual information. *The Daily Show with Jon Stewart* is, as philosopher Brad Frazier puts it, a "nightly irony bath."[28] In fact, by the time he dissects any given network news broadcast, Jon's audience starts to realize that, in Jon Stewart's world—and perhaps in ours—just about every "news" broadcast is more fiction than fact. He has, at one time or another, said with regard to *The Daily Show* that it's "The mistrusted name in news"; it's "All the news our sponsors approve of"; "More people get their news from *The Daily Show with Jon Stewart* . . . than probably should"; and "*The Daily Show*—the only news program with credibility left to lose." In the early days of Jon's tenure, as had been the case during Craig Kilborn's time, the voice-over at the start of the show would tell us that *The Daily Show* is "The Most Important News Show—Ever!" Yet, despite the most blatant acknowledgments that his show is "fake," Jon Stewart has amassed an enormous audience who *trust* his take on current events and the ways in which his team of "correspondents" serve to highlight the absurdities of mainstream reporters providing pseudo-information about our world. He may be a comedian, and his point of view may be that there is humor to be found nearly anywhere, but Jon Stewart is, in his viewers' perspective, also somehow more authentic than what the talking heads of network news read from their teleprompters.

One reason Stewart's take on the news media is so incisive may be that, more often than not, he allows the sources to speak for themselves in the very same news clips that network news stations air. *The Daily Show* demonstrates, again and again, how deeply misleading, and often flat-out false, are the major networks' representations of national and international issues, crises, and, of course, political campaigns. The comedy comes in when Stewart pilots his audience toward embarrassing moments as spoken by sources like politicians as well as by the "real" news reporters. But despite Jon's own arguments that *The Daily Show* is intended simply as comedy, the fact is that it has become much more than that. In fact, under the direction of Jon Stewart, *The Daily Show* has drawn the attention not only of audiences watching for humor, but of a growing crowd of people who watch specifically for Stewart's insightful analysis of current events, people in the news, and people who purport to *present* the news. As it happens, Jon Stewart—one of the "world's most beautiful people"—was about to win the prestigious Peabody Award for journalistic excellence. The fake news show that everyone was talking about had stolen the network news broadcaster's thunder with its coverage of the 2000 presidential elections.

A MOST DECISIVE "INDECISION 2000"

What do I do? I write jokes.[29]

A lot of important things were happening as the 20th century vaulted into the 21st. There was a combination of fascination and fear over the concept of "Y2K"—the moment when, as the name of the century changed, the electronic devices throughout the world would cease to function. Doomsday prophets foretold of the fiery (or icy) destruction of the world. And in the United States, one of the stranger presidential campaigns and elections was taking place.

From 1992 until 2000, Bill Clinton was the U.S. president, and many in America believed that Clinton's vice president of eight years, Al Gore, would be elected president at the end of Clinton's term. In fact, that's precisely what happened. Sort of. In the end, George W. Bush was elected president. Sort of.

All through 2000, the two presidential candidates had campaigned aggressively, staging debates, running both positive and negative advertisements, and filling the American electorate's eyes and ears with promises and slogans. Jon Stewart and his crew of "correspondents" jumped right on the campaign trail, "reporting" on what the candidates were up to. *The Daily Show with Jon Stewart* featured, most nights, at least a few minutes of their running feature, *Indecision 2000*. Jon and his gang covered some of the speeches, the primaries leading up to the general election, and the election itself. Remarkably, *The Daily Show* actually sent correspondents to both the Republican and Democratic national conventions, and even more remarkably, the correspondents were able to get interview time with a few politicians at each headquarters. "We didn't get very much access," Jon told Charlie Rose, "but we're fake anyway."[30]

This was just a little over a year after Jon took over *The Daily Show*. Already he and his co-comedians were confusing public figures—as well as other media outlets—about whether the Comedy Central show should be taken *seriously*. For some, however, there was no doubt. On November 2, 2000, *The Daily Show* embarked on a landmark night of live broadcasting; Jon Stewart and his crackerjack team of "correspondents" and "analysts" covered the presidential election between Texan George W. Bush and Vice President Al Gore. The election of Bush in 2000 was tainted by allegations that the Republicans had "stolen" the election from candidate Al Gore. For many weeks, postelection, the nation was bombarded with news footage about missing or faulty ballots, recounts that were halted, restarted, and then halted again, and the ultimate decision by the U.S. Supreme Court that the recounts be ended and that George W. Bush be declared the victor. By calling the ongoing coverage "Indecision 2000," Stewart had had the opportunity to highlight countless examples of double-talk, media inaccuracies, false debates, empty predictions, and much more. It was a remarkable undertaking for at least two big reasons: first, it was a completely different take on our national elections. It was irreverent, funny, insightful in ways that network pundits were not. Second, incredibly, *The Daily Show* was awarded the prestigious Peabody Award for its coverage. The award, named for George Foster Peabody, recognizes those television and radio stations and broadcasts that have, in the view of the award officials, distinguished themselves for their excellence and for their outstanding service to the industry and the public. Recipients of the Peabody Award are a highly select group. There are only around 30 award winners picked from more than 1,000 entries.[31] Remarkably, the Peabody panel of scholarly judges chose a *comedy* show as one of the best news and analysis shows on television.

It had been a momentous year for Jon Stewart—newly married, respected for his work on television and even in a few movies, recipient of the internationally coveted Peabody Award, co–executive producer of at least a half-dozen television movies or specials, including *The Daily Show Fourth Anniversary Special* in which he acknowledged his predecessor Craig Kilborn's two-year stint. In addition, in 2000, during his appearance on a celebrity episode of Regis Philbin's *Who Wants to Be a Millionaire*, Jon won $125,000 for Alzheimer's disease research. Jon even quit smoking in 2000. The lingering question was how was he ever going to exceed his own track record?

Chapter 9

EXCEEDING HIS OWN
TRACK RECORD

I didn't realize it at the time, but after you cut out smoking, drinking and drugs, you feel much better.[1]

I get up in the morning, I go to work, I come home, my wife and I have dinner, we do a crossword puzzle, we go to bed, I get up . . .[2]

It was going to be pretty tough for Jon Stewart to top the year 2000. *The Daily Show* wasn't just going strong, it was also steadily gaining recognition from all corners and so was its host. *Indecision 2000: Election Night—Choose or Lose* was supposed to have been a spoof on the network coverage of the election. But as Stewart told interviewer Charlie Rose, a year or so later, the 2000 election was, in fact, "a turning point because for the moment, we could pretend that we were in the midst of a relevant situation."[3] By mid-2001, not even three full years into his hosting duties, Jon Stewart was about to be catapulted onto a much larger "stage." For his "coverage" of the 2000 presidential election—a fake piece of journalism!—Jon Stewart was nominated for the American Comedy Award for Funniest Male Performer in a TV Special. It was a fitting acknowledgment not only of Jon's show, but of Comedy

Central's choice of Stewart as host of *The Daily Show*. Jon and his *Daily Show* colleagues also won the Emmy Award for Outstanding Writing for a Variety, Music or Comedy Program. Incredibly, *The Daily Show* was also nominated for a second Emmy for outstanding *series*. Jon could scarcely believe the rush of accolades coming his way. "This is a very fortunate run . . . that I'm on right now," he told Rose. "I definitely have an appreciation for that."[4] Fortunate run, indeed. Just a month

Jon Stewart and his wife, Tracy, celebrate at the Governor's Ball after the 55th Annual Primetime Emmy Awards on September 21, 2003, at the Shrine Auditorium in Los Angeles. His show The Daily Show with Jon Stewart *won for both outstanding writing for a variety, music, or comedy program and outstanding variety, music, and comedy series. (AP Photo/Kevork Djansezian)*

before his interview with Charlie Rose, Jon Stewart had been named by *Time* magazine as the country's best talk show host in their "America's Best" issue.[5] Jon Stewart had "beat out" Letterman, Leno, Koppel, Conan . . . all of them!

Before the year was out, Jon coproduced another half-dozen TV specials for a few of his talented writers and "correspondents"—for example, Steve Carell (*Steve Carell Salutes Steve Carell*), Mo Rocca (*Mo Rocca's Back to School Special*), and Stephen Colbert (*Stephen Colbert Again: A Look Back*)—who by then were working on some of their own projects.

SEPTEMBER 20, 2001: A TURNING POINT LIKE NO OTHER

Then, catastrophe struck—not just for Jon Stewart, but the entire United States and, in many ways, the entire world. On September 11, 2001, terrorists hijacked four passenger airplanes. American Airlines Flight 11 and Flight 175 crashed into the Twin Towers of the World Trade Center in New York City, killing thousands of people. Two additional planes, American Airlines Flight 77 and United Airlines Flight 93, were crashed into the Pentagon and into a field in Pennsylvania. At least 3,000 people died horrible deaths as a direct consequence of the attacks. Most of the southern end of Manhattan was engulfed in smoke, debris, toxic waste, soot, and the bodies of the dead. The nation was stunned, and New Yorkers reeled, overcome with grief and fear. Buildings had to be razed down, businesses were shut down, and many had no electricity or water. Hospitals were overrun with the dead, the dying, and the badly wounded. Not surprisingly, regular television programming was disrupted to allow for round-the-clock news broadcasts and updates. Like most regularly scheduled television programs, *The Daily Show* was off the air as Jon and his staff first took care of their families and themselves. They also had to figure out what kind of show they could possibly do when they returned to the airwaves.

Nine days later, on September 20, 2001, *The Daily Show with Jon Stewart* taped its first show since 9/11, and for the first few minutes of the broadcast, Jon Stewart refused to do something he had devoted his career to mastering; he refused to be funny.

He began by telling viewers that this was the first show since the tragedy of 9/11, and that he could find no other way to start than by asking the question he'd already asked of his studio audience: "Are you okay?" He added, "We pray that you are and that your family is."[6] Jon then apologized for being yet another talk show host on yet another TV show that was going to start off on such a somber note. But the fascinating thing was that although this was a deeply moved, humbled, and hurting Jon Stewart, he actually managed to talk to his audience in a way that mixed honesty and empathy. Only after several minutes did Jon mix in a degree of gentle humor. The audience laughed—quietly—but they laughed, when Jon told them, "They said to get back to work, and there were no jobs available for a man in the fetal position under his desk crying . . . so we come back here." Jon explained that it would not be the usual kind of show, but that they had looked in "the vault" to come up with some material "that might make you smile." Clearly, it was painful for Jon to have to attempt to be funny in the face of indescribable sadness and suffering, but it might have been more painful for him had he not been able to "come back here" to an audience so full of respect for him that they were trusting him to restore some—any—semblance of sanity.

But what could he say? He told his audience that, while some had expressed sympathy for his having to return to the show so soon after 9/11, he saw it as a "privilege." And then he treated everyone to a stirring "lesson" in how and why *The Daily Show* can do what it does. Fighting back tears, he said, "Even the idea that we can sit in the back of the country and make wisecracks, which is really what we do. We sit in the back and throw spitballs. But never forgetting the fact that it is a luxury in this country that allows us to do that." None of Jon's viewers had ever seen or heard him speak so seriously. It was as though he were talking with a group of family members, trying to sort his thoughts out while trying not to cry as he said, "I wanted to tell you why I grieve. But why I don't despair." At this point, Jon could not continue and took a moment to compose himself. He told a story about when he was five years old and how, when Martin Luther King was killed, he and his classmates were told to sit under their desks. For reasons they did not understand, they were given cottage cheese for lunch (because the cafeteria had been shut down), and the kids all thought it was fun because they didn't understand what had happened. But afterward, the entire country had to find ways to repair itself and to grow stronger. "The reason I don't despair is that, this attack happened. It's not a dream. But the *aftermath*, the recovery, is a dream realized. And that is Martin Luther King's dream." At this point, Jon could not completely stifle a sob. He mused, "The view from my apartment was the World Trade Center. And now it's gone. They attacked it. This symbol of American ingenuity, and strength, and labor, and imagination and commerce, and it is gone." There was no mistaking it; Jon was crying. "But you know what the view is now? The Statue of Liberty. The view from the South of Manhattan is the Statue of Liberty. You can't beat that." At that point, Jon went to commercial as the audience's quiet applause began to swell into a fitting tribute to a man who had just spoken in terrible pain from his heart. It was a profound turning point like no other Jon Stewart had been through. There would be many more laughs, jokes, and compelling guest interviews. But more effectively than he had ever done before, Jon had shown his audience a depth of feeling and insight that distinguished him from countless other "talking heads" of network news, cable news opinion shows, and even most of his fellow comedy talk show hosts. Questioned about his willingness to do his show so soon after 9/11, Stewart responded, "My guess is, even at Auschwitz, people were telling jokes. It's human nature to find light in darkness."[7]

As if to add an exclamation point, in February 2002, after being invited at the last minute to host the Grammy Awards (Whoopee Goldberg had dropped out just a few days before air time), Jon mined the new post-9/11 security measures for humor. At the start of the show, Jon walked onto the stage where he was confronted by a pair of very large security guards and a metal detector. Jon was "forced" to strip down to his boxer-shorts and stood nearly naked on stage in front of thousands of musicians and millions of television viewers. For everyone, it seemed, it was a relief to laugh out loud.

HUMOR AND POLITICS

I will never understand in a million years why people will always say to humorists or people that are doing jokes, "Where do you draw the line?" We're making jokes about sh** that other people do.[8]

Most of America had difficulty moving past the national upheaval following September 11, 2001. New Yorkers continued to dig themselves out—both literally and figuratively—from the disaster. Already, rescue workers who had been on the scene moments after the Twin Towers fell were experiencing some of the symptoms of illness that would ultimately be attributed to the airborne toxins emanating from the buildings' collapse. Families that had lost loved ones still mourned, and community leaders did their best to rally citizens, to encourage them to return to work, to play, to as much of a normal life as possible. New York City mayor Rudy Giuliani did his best to lead a physically and emotionally devastated city. On a national stage, President George W. Bush vowed to retaliate against al-Qaeda, the terrorist organization that had engineered the horror of 9/11. He and other political figures around the country saw the events of 9/11 as both a call to arms and a terrible moment that could, if Americans stayed strong, become perhaps the most unifying experience in our history. At the same time, Bush and the others repeated the refrain that New Yorkers—and all Americans—should return to living their lives as normally as possible. To do so, they said, would show al-Qaeda and all other terrorists that America could not intimidated.

Slowly, tentatively, and nervously, people went back to work, began to plan vacations, attended events at their children's schools, ate out at the local restaurants, and of course, watched a lot of television. They wanted not only to see the latest news, but also to be distracted and entertained. Jon Stewart delivered. On October 1, just three weeks after 9/11, *The Daily Show* featured "correspondent" Stephen Colbert's report on Mayor Giuliani's appearance at the United Nations. For many New Yorkers—and Americans around the nation—Giuliani had become a hero. For weeks, nearly every news broadcast following 9/11 featured at least a few clips of Giuliani speaking to New York City residents, to other New York politicians, and to national leaders. His appearances had become so frequent that some were beginning to feel that he was perhaps taking too much credit for all of the amazing rescue and rebuilding efforts that had been taken on by the police, firefighters, volunteers, doctors and nurses, and others. Colbert's "report" was also a glowing account of the "Churchillian" leadership of Mayor Giuliani, who according to Colbert, demonstrated "the greatness that makes this great man so great." After a few minutes, Jon interrupted him to show a clip from earlier in the year in which Colbert had called the mayor "the city's head Philistine" and made fun of Giuliani's attempts to police the world of art and free expression.⁹ Jon and his team of writers and correspondents had taken the mayor—and the president—at their word: he had gone back to work, finding humor within the chaos of current events. A little over a year later, while speaking at Harvard University's Kennedy School of Government, Stewart responded to a question about Rudy Giuliani. "What do I think of him? That is a complicated issue . . . What he did for our city was magnificent . . . you have to put it in the context of that day . . . feeling like the world was ending, and he, carrying himself with dignity and with courage, made us feel like we were going to survive . . . And that forgives, for me, a lot of sins. That showed me his heart. And do I agree with him all the time? God, no."¹⁰

A year or so later, Rudy Giuliani was Jon's guest on *The Daily Show,* and the two had a little fun together. Although Stewart had never made a secret of his criticism of the former New York City mayor, it was clear immediately that the two liked each other and that Giuliani's appearance would be entertaining. When Jon asked Giuliani if he was flattered by rumors about him replacing Dick Cheney on George W. Bush's presidential ticket, Giuliani replied that he wasn't. "I'm a big supporter of Vice President Cheney. He's a good friend of mine." Jon's eyes widened as he asked, "Is he really?" Giuliani said, "I've known him for twenty-five years . . . I think he's been a great Vice President," to which Jon replied, looking even more amazed, "Really?" They were having fun, and so was the audience. But then Giuliani got serious for a moment and told Jon, "I believed in [President Bush and Vice President Cheney] before September 11, 2001, and from that day on, my admiration for how they dealt with the worst attack in the history of this country has only grown." It was going to be difficult for Jon to make that funny, so he did what he does best—he made it funny. He sat up straight, looked very sober, and said, "Boy, that's a tough one to make a joke with." The audience and Rudy Giuliani laughed hard.¹¹

Jon kept his hand in political humor throughout 2002. *The Daily Show* continued with its "Indecision" series, this time with *Indecision 2002: Election Night.* Once again, the show was nominated for Emmy Awards, and Jon's star status kept growing. From the start of 2002, it seemed that every media outlet wanted at least a little piece of Jon

Stewart. *The New Yorker*, a well respected and popular magazine, pro-
filed him.[12]

Within 10 weeks, beginning in January, in addition to the daily tap-
ing of his own show, Jon was the featured guest on *Last Call with Carson
Daly* (NBC),[13] *Live With Regis and Kelly* (ABC),[14] *The Rosie O'Donnell
Show* (Syndicated),[15] *The Tonight Show with Jay Leno* (NBC),[16] *Denis
Miller Live* (HBO),[17] *Larry King Live* (CNN),[18] *The Late Show with David
Letterman* (CBS),[19] and the host, for the second time, of *The Grammy
Awards* (CBS).[20] No matter what channel audiences watched, they
were going to see Jon Stewart. Lorne Michael of NBC's *Saturday Night
Live* jumped onto the bandwagon and recruited Jon to be the host of
the March 9 show.

Like most major celebrities, Jon was making the rounds on the talk
show circuit. But he was also in demand for his thoughtful insights on
contemporary issues. In the spring of 2002, Jon was asked to moderate
a panel called "September 11th: How It Changed Us" at Pace University's Michael Schimmel Center for the Arts in New York City.[21] He
appeared on CNN's *Inside Politics* to discuss *The Daily Show*'s unique perspective on American politics.[22] No one was surprised when, in July, Jon
was nominated for another Emmy for best "Individual Performance in
a Variety or Music Program" for the previous year's work on *The Daily
Show with Jon Stewart*. The man was busy. And he was going to get busier.

In August, the animated video, *The Adventures of Tom Thumb and
Thumbelina* (Hyperion Pictures) was released, and Jon played the voice
of Godfrey. He was back in the movies, and Godfrey wasn't going to
be the only character he'd play. Actor and director Danny DeVito had
other plans for Jon, casting him in the role of Marion Frank Stokes
in the movie *Death to Smoochy,* a movie that became Jon's standard
joke about how bad an actor he really is. Starring Robin Williams and
Edward Norton (along with DeVito), Jon Stewart's character was the
hypocritical program director at Kidnet, a network station that airs
children's TV shows. When show host Rainbow Randolph (Robin Williams) is busted for taking bribes from parents to get their children on
the show, Stokes is ordered, by the station's owners, to replace Randolph with someone "squeaky clean." Stokes and producer Nora (Catherine Keener) go through their list of potential replacements, including
"Buggy Ding Dong" (Vincent Schiavelli) who they reject because he's

a heroin addict, and Square Dance Danny (unseen) because he's a "wife-beater." Finally, they decide to hire a local guy Sheldon Mopes (Edward Norton) who dresses up as a rhinoceros named Smoochy. In his wine-grape-colored costume, Smootchy entertains the people of New York City by promoting good health, healthy attitudes, and positivity—things that Stokes and Nora consider pointless and unprofessional.

Sporting what may be his most comical haircut, Stewart as Marion Frank Stokes is a slimy operator who has his hands in whatever pot of money he can dip into. When a bitter and slightly deranged Randolph tries to exact revenge on Smoochy, he is ultimately defeated by members of an Irish mob family, by Stokes (who has washed his hands of this has-been), and by Randolph's own conversion to decency moments before he shoots Sheldon and Nora. Ultimately, it is Randolph who saves Smoochy's life when some of Randolph's former associates, including the notorious Merv Green (Harvey Fierstein) plot to kill Sheldon/Smoochy as he performs at an ice show. In the meantime, Stokes, and an unscrupulous agent, Burke Bennet (Danny DeVito) who were in on the plot to kill Smoochy, are confronted and taught a lesson by the Tommy (Pam Ferris), the matriarch of the local Irish mob. Tommy has taken kindly to Sheldon when he gives a job to Spider Dunn (Michael Rispoli), a punch-drunk ex-boxer she takes care of.

Stewart frequently refers to *Death to Smoochy* when he jokes with guests about his lacking of acting talent. He once told an interviewer from *Premiere* magazine that he has no particular fear of being misunderstood from his role in movies. "Listen, you know, I was in *Death to Smoochy*. I'm not afraid of movies."[23] But, in fact, his Frank Stokes was quite convincing as the conniving sleazeball who would do anything to satisfy his greed, and Jon had proven once again that he could be a good sport even on the big screen.

PUNCTURING BALLOONS WITH GRACE, ELEGANCE, AND HUMOR

Boy, I never want to be part of something called "good television."[24]

By the time Jon Stewart turned 40 on November 28, 2002, he was a bona fide television star, a much sought-after stand-up comedian, a frequent guest on talk shows of all kinds, an executive producer for dozens of television specials, a husband, and the host of one of the hottest talk shows on TV. He seemed unstoppable. How much bigger could he get?

The following year, Jon continued his string of appearances on talk shows such as the highly respected *NOW with Bill Moyers* (PBS) where host Bill Moyers got Jon to talk about everything from comedy to politics to his status as one of the most respected people on television. In October 2003, Jon also did something he'd done only three times before; he and *The Daily Show* went through the writing and rehearsals but did not tape the show. Instead, they went live to "cover" the California gubernatorial recall election—the one in which Arnold Schwarzenegger became California's governor. During a commercial break, the show's executive producer, Ben Karlin, actually walked out onto the set to hand Jon a note saying that Arnold Schwarzenegger was now Governor Schwarzenegger. When the show came back from commercial, Jon had to ad-lib for a few minutes about "Ah-nuld" and then ran out of time. Apologizing to his guest, Arianna Huffington, Stewart told her, "On a fake program like ours, it's difficult to cram real news in."[25]

In 2003, *The Daily Show with Jon Stewart* won another couple of Emmy Awards, one of which Jon was keeping under plastic wrap on his desk after cutting himself on it. The Television Critics Association gave Jon the Award for Individual Achievement in Comedy. The *GQ* magazine named Jon Stewart as a "Man of the Year" winner,[26] and *The Daily Show* was the cover story in *Entertainment Weekly*.[27] Perhaps the biggest news regarding *The Daily Show* is that it was now a weekly broadcast *internationally* on CNNi (CNN international). Jon Stewart had gone global. Back home in the United States, Jon had garnered the respect and admiration of some of the nation's top political correspondents as well as politicians themselves. Broadcast journalist and commentator Peter Jennings described Jon as "an essential character in the national political landscape."[28] Two years prior, Jennings had been part of a debate in New Hampshire between a group of top journalists and some high-profile politicians. Included in the event were Sam Donaldson (ABC), Walter Isaacson (managing editor of *Time*), and Congressman Jerrold Nadler (D-NY). For a moderator, the group had agreed upon someone they believed would bring both insight and good humor to the event: Jon Stewart, the guy who, as a nine-year-old kid on a trip with his elementary school band, contemplated spitting out of a hotel window at a Nixon campaign van.[29]

When Jon Stewart and John Edwards shared their moment of hilarity, Stewart's audiences were in on his playful ambush of the senator. To prepare for *The Daily Show*'s "fake" election night coverage in November 2002, Jon jokes with his audience that he starts drinking before the polls close and assures his laughing viewers that it doesn't matter; "We have actually no news gathering capabilities."[30] The truth is, of course, that Jon and his staff have formidable news gathering skills, perhaps as much as most network news shows. Declaring time after time that *The Daily Show* is comedy and not real news, Stewart and his audience become co-conspirators; both Jon and his viewers know full well that there is as much truth to be found in a half-hour of *The Daily Show* as there is in the average network news broadcast. *The Daily Show* is "fake" only in the sense that its stated agenda is comedy. It may be a fake news show, but its unique perspective on what is generally understood as "the news" is quite real. Senator Edwards's confusion was, no doubt, a result of that ambiguity: *The Daily Show* may not take itself very seriously, but *Daily Show* audiences surely do. Senator Edwards laughed, Jon Stewart laughed, the audience laughed, and once again, Jon had punctured another not-so-little political balloon.

In a strange way, in that moment, Jon had added a new layer of credibility to his celebrity. He could write and tell jokes about virtually anything and anyone, but, as Peter Jennings put it, "There's nothing mean about him. And in a society where there's so much mean talk, someone who punctures the balloons with grace and elegance and humor is just a blessing."[31] For his graceful humor, Jon and his *Daily Show* crew were awarded another Emmy, and during the postshow press conferences, when he asked why his half-hour show needed a couple of dozen writers, Jon joked with the reporters that "It's a very impressive feat to fake the news for twenty minutes a night."

Jon was at the top of his game as 2004 rolled around. He'd helped to write and produce countless TV specials and movies, and *The Daily Show*, as a writer for *Newsweek* put it, had "got everyone by the throat."[32] Not only were celebrities now clamoring to get a guest spot on *The Daily Show*, Jon's interviewees were, increasingly, coming from the world of national politics, scholarship, and even the military. That summer, Jon's guest was former U.S. president Bill Clinton—the first of six appearances Clinton made between 2004 and 2010. It would not be the last time a former president would sit and talk with Jon. Former president Jimmy Carter joined Jon in late 2005 and enjoyed his experience so much, he, too, returned several more times.

When U.S. military troops landed in Iraq, *The Daily Show* launched a segment called "Mess O'Potamia" in which, each week, Jon and his correspondents would follow the escalating war. Between its coverage of the war in Iraq and its coverage and analysis of yet another presidential election—this time the Peabody Award-winning feature titled *Indecision 2004: Prelude to a Recount*—*The Daily Show with Jon Stewart* had risen to such heights of respectability, the Democratic National Committee announced, in early 2004, that it planned to invite Stewart and his team to cover the Democratic National Convention. It was incredible. The basic cable television show that people tuned into for fake news and jokes was now considered a rightful contender to report on the serious events of a national political party. People like General Wesley Clark, Bill Clinton, Jimmy Carter, and Bob Dole—leaders from both the Democrat and Republican parties—agreed that Jon Stewart and *The Daily Show* were influential on a national level. Jon could scarcely believe it. To him, the purpose of the show, and of his career, was to be funny, not to be politically influential. "I'm nobody," he has said, despite the fact that in 2004, *The Daily Show with Jon Stewart* won another Peabody Award for their coverage of the presidential election.

To make certain that audiences did not forget that he was a comedian, Jon continued to make stand-up appearances at venues around the country. He also produced comedy specials for comedians and *Daily Show* correspondents Stephen Colbert, Steve Carell, and Mo Rocca. He appeared on Comedy Central's special, *Richard Pryor: I Ain't Dead Yet*, and had been voted funniest person in America (behind Chris Rock) by *Entertainment Weekly*. The year 2004 also saw *The Daily Show* win another pair of Emmys and another nomination by The Television Critics Association for the Award for Individual Achievement in Comedy. In the fall of 2004, Jon was interviewed at length on CBS's *60 Minutes*. As Jon put it, he was feeling healthy and happy. He'd been married to Tracey for four years, and overall, he said, "It's a very contented and warm feeling."[33] He was invited that spring to share some of that warmth in his commencement speech to the graduating class at his alma mater, the College of William and Mary, where he was also awarded an honorary doctorate. Standing before them in his flowing green and black doctoral robes, Jon told the new graduates, "When I spoke earlier about the world being broke[n], I was somewhat being facetious, because every generation has their challenge. And things change rapidly, and life gets better in an instant." He told stories about himself, about how "mediocre" a student he had been and about how mediocre he still was in so many ways. But, he told them, "Love what you do. Get good at it. Competence is a rare commodity in this day and age."[34]

In the summer of 2004 Jon's life, and Tracey's, did, in fact, get "better in an instant": on July 3, Tracey gave birth to their son, Nathan Thomas Stewart. "Nate," as Jon calls him. Tracey was pursuing her career as a veterinary assistant, and Jon was pursuing his usual slew of projects. But with the birth of Nathan, Jon had been cast in his most profound role as a dad. But, the presidential elections were looming, and after the 2000 election debacle in which the U.S. Supreme Court had brought a halt to the recount of errant votes, the 2004 contest between President Bush and Senator John Kerry (D-MA) promised to be, at the very least, interesting. *The Daily Show with Jon Stewart*, once again, featured all kinds of jabs and pokes and comical observations about the candidates, and Jon's correspondents were stationed at various hot spots (including the usual green-screen "hot spot" on *The Daily Show* set itself). And that's not all Jon and his team did. With Jon at the lead, they had embarked upon a project of a very different kind: they were writing a textbook.

The brainchild of Stewart, *Daily Show* producer Ben Karlin, and *Daily Show* head writer, David Javerbaum, *America (The Book): A Citizen's Guide to Democracy Inaction*,[35] published in 2004, extended Jon's show's running commentary on the government's—and the media's—ineffectiveness. A large, hardcover volume, complete with a traditional student-issue stamp on the inside cover, *America* looked exactly like textbooks that fill the shelves, lockers, and backpacks of American middle and high school students. With a foreword miraculously written by Thomas Jefferson 178 years after his death, *America*'s subject matter includes hilarious discussions of the founding of the U.S. government, the branches of government, a brief history of the electoral process, and an examination of "Democracy's Valiant Vulgarians," the media.

As satirically edgy as the book is, in his foreword, "Jefferson" reminds readers that the Constitution and governance, in general, are "imperfect" and that citizens now must "work as hard as we did on keeping what we think is a profoundly excellent form of government supple, evolving and relevant."[36] Stewart and his coauthors had created a comical look at America that wasn't at all mean and that was, in fact, respectful. But *mostly*, it was funny, providing "students" with discussion questions, including "If you lived in a monarchy, would you rather be the king or a slave? Why or why not?" (15) and classroom activities, including "Found a country" (33). There are charts, maps, "reviews" of the Constitution including one by "Alexander Hamilton": "The *Constitution* grabs you right from the Preamble and doesn't let go until the last Article . . . the must-ratify document of the summer!" (29).

Perhaps the most controversial feature of all can be found in the chapter on the judicial branch of the government. That's where Jon and his collaborators included a page of cut-outs of black Supreme Court Justice robes followed by a page depicting the nine justices without a stitch of clothing on any of them! (The photographs are "doctored" and are not actually of the justices.) While this raised more than a few eyebrows, the reviews of the book were generally good. One reviewer wrote that as Jon "mocks nearly everything about our past and present, he gets it right more often than not, which is another way of saying that despite the obvious fiction, few books have been as true in spirit."[37] Even when Jon and his *Daily Show* gang were most irreverent, he had, by then, garnered enough respect for critics to take at least the book's subtext seriously. Or as *TV Guide* put it, Jon was "winning big laughs without losing his individual voice."[38]

LIARS, SPINNERS, AND BOASTERS

"Jon Stewart is allergic to liars, spinners and boasters."[39]

When Peter Jennings had said that Jon Stewart knew how to pop balloons with grace and good humor, he had not yet seen Jon's less gentle side. But audiences were about to experience precisely that. For at least

30 minutes in 2004, Jon's grace and elegance, and even his humor, took a leave of absence, and it would prove not only to show television audiences a markedly different side to Jon, it would also demonstrate the media power Stewart had amassed. The show was called *Crossfire* (CNN)—and "was" is the operative word for the show that Stewart was on his way to marking for death.

To set the stage, hosts Paul Begala and Tucker Carlson typically invited two guests—one from "the left" and the other from "the right"—to discuss current issues with the hosts. As the show began on October 15, 2004, Paul Begala reminded the audience that whereas normally the show had two guests, this day's show would have only one—Jon Stewart. The audience applauded enthusiastically. Either Jon had a lot of fans in the room, or the crowd couldn't wait to see co-host Tucker Carlson, a frequent target of Stewart's disdain on *The Daily Show*, attempt to skewer Jon. Whatever was going to happen, it was going to happen in real time, as the show was airing live.

When the applause died down, Stewart turned to Carlson and said, "Let me ask you a question," but Carlson interrupted, saying, "Let me ask you a question first." Carlson's question was about who Stewart thought was the best democratic candidate for president, and was John Kerry really the best choice. Stewart responded by pointing out that the democratic primary elections process was how these choices are determined. There was a little more back and forth about this before Jon sat forward with elbows on the little table and told his hosts, "I made a special effort to come on this show today because I have, privately amongst my friends, and also in occasional newspapers, television show, mentioned this show as being, uh, bad." The audience roared with laughter, and both Begala and Carlson were visibly surprised. Stewart continued, "And I felt that that wasn't fair, and I wanted to come here and tell you . . . it's not so much that it's bad, as it's hurting America."

What followed was a discussion in which Paul Begala said little while Jon made a few points above and around Tucker Carlson's frequent interruptions. What Jon had come on the show to say was that the debate format of *Crossfire* offered a wonderful opportunity to ask tough questions and to get to real issues with political figures (the usual guests), but that the hosts of *Crossfire* were, in Stewart's words, "partisan hacks." When Carlson argued that his show did a valuable service for audiences, something he wished Jon would do, it was Jon's turn to look surprised, replying, "If you want to compare your show to a comedy show . . ." Stewart then asked both Carlson and Begala about the fact that after events like presidential debates, the two headed for "Spin Alley"—referring to various meeting areas reserved for the members of the news media after political events so they could conduct interviews of candidates and other politicians. Critics of this practice argue that these "interviews" just become opportunities for politicians to promote themselves and other members of their political party. But Carlson wanted to press the point that when *The Daily Show* had hosted Senator Kerry for an interview, Jon Stewart had not asked hard questions. He accused Jon of being Kerry's "butt-boy" because one of Stewart's questions to Kerry had been to ask how the senator was holding up under Republican suggestions that he was "flip-flopping" on issues.

The audience was laughing, but Jon was not. He stared at Carlson and responded, "It's interesting to hear you talk about my responsibility. I didn't realize that the news organizations look to Comedy Central for their cues on integrity." The audience laughed even louder, and Tucker Carlson muttered something about how Stewart could at least have asked tougher questions to Kerry. Jon continued, "If your idea of confronting me is that I don't ask hard-hitting enough news questions, we're in bad shape, fellas." By this point, the cameras were no longer following Begala at all; it had become a showdown between Carlson and Stewart. After Jon made a few more remarks about how *Crossfire* did its audiences a disservice by catering to conservative points of view, Carlson, looking increasingly unsettled, his voice becoming more high-pitched, said, "I'm sorry, I think you're a good comedian. I think your lectures are boring." He added that Stewart's failure to take advantage of the opportunity to grill Kerry proved that Stewart was just "sniffing Kerry's throne." The gloves had come off, and Jon, obviously fed up, turned to Carlson, inched his chair a little closer to him, and told him, "The show that leads into me is puppets making crank phone calls! What is wrong with you?" Carlson, turning for a moment toward the audience, and then back to Stewart, complained, "I thought you were going to be funny! Come on!" The audience made the sounds that people make when they suspect they are about to see a schoolyard fight. Jon stared for a long couple of seconds and said, "No. No, I'm not going to be your monkey." When Tucker Carlson began to interject, Jon continued, "I watch your show, and it kills me. It is so painful to watch—."

At this point, whatever Paul Begala might have had to say was lost in the laughter of the audience. Tucker Carlson then made a tactical error. Hoping to regain the approval of the audience but, instead, giving them more cause to rally behind Jon Stewart, Carlson asked in his highest-pitched voice to that point, "What's it like to have dinner with you? It must be excruciating. Do you, like, lecture people like this when you come over to their house?" Before Jon could really answer, Carlson sat back as though to sum things up, but the audience was clearly cheering for Jon's rejoinder. Instead, Carlson told Jon as though it would be the last word, "I do think you're more fun on your show." As music came up on the set, Jon responded, saying, "And you're as big a dick on your show as you are on any show." The audience's laughter and applause for Stewart was much louder than the theme music.

Now here is the truly amazing part. Less than three months after the Jon Stewart appearance, CNN decide to cancel *Crossfire* and to end its professional relationship with none other than Tucker Carlson. While there were, no doubt, other factors contributing to CNN's decision, there can be little doubt that Stewart's clobbering of Tucker Carlson and his pointed attack on the weaknesses of *Crossfire* itself were significant contributing factors. It was an indisputable indication of the kind of influence Jon Stewart could wield. In a moment of authentically real television, Jon had schooled Tucker Carlson. He may not have been particularly elegant and certainly not all that humorous in his performance, but he had nevertheless burst the very big balloon of a show and a host that he considered to be lying, spinning, and boasting. For Jon's ability to articulate so clearly the problems inherent in mass media's coverage of current events, the National Council of Teachers of English (NCTE), in 2005, made Jon the 30th recipient George Orwell Award for Distinguished Contribution to Honesty and Clarity in Public Language.

Chapter 10

KILL OR BE KILLED

I don't know if stand-up is a requirement for anything in life. I feel weird that it's what I'm most trained for . . .[1]

The 77th Annual Academy Awards featured Chris Rock as host, and while some viewers found his jokes to be a little too edgy, most viewers, and critics, thought that Rock had succeeded masterfully in poking fun at Hollywood and its celebrities. Certainly the audience at the Academy Awards themselves had a terrific time, laughing hard at Chris Rock's humor even when it was directed at them. The following year, for the 78th Academy Awards extravaganza, Hollywood tapped Jon Stewart to be host, and he was excited to be chosen for the March 5th event. Of course, while the two-time Grammy presenter was, as he put it, "tickled"[2] to be picked as the Academy's man of the hour, it was going to be tough to follow the February 4th event: the birth of Jon and Tracey's daughter, Maggie Rose Stewart. Nate had a baby sister, and the Stewarts had a full house of kids and pets, including a pair of pit bulls named Shamsky—after former NY Mets outfielder Art Shamsky— and Monkey, along with a cat named Stan. Shamsky and Monkey also contributed to the Stewart household by lending their names to the Shamsky Monkey Trust, a business entity through which the Stewarts bought their Tribecca apartment in New York City.

Now, a month after Maggie Rose made her entrance, Jon would be making his on the Oscar stage, watched by a few hundred million people. Quickly, the tabloids and magazines were interviewing Jon about the gig, and Jon was responding with his customary humor. An interview he did for *Premier* magazine featured the headline question: "*The Daily Show's* Jon Stewart is one of the funniest people in America, but can he kill at the Oscars?"[3] When he was asked whether he was nervous about hosting the Oscars, Jon joked, "Listen, I get nervous for contestants on *American Idol*. You don't need to egg me on in terms of anxiety." But Jon wanted to make it clear that the Oscars gig was a stand-up comedy opportunity, not an extension of his role as talk show host. "I'm not doing my show on the Oscars. I'm not bringing the desk . . . I accepted their invitation to host the Oscars. It's not an invitation to do *The Daily Show* in front of people getting movie awards." So, on March 5th, as the announcer brought everyone to attention with the words, "Ladies and Gentleman, please welcome your host for the 78th Annual Academy Award . . ." the audience watched the big screen as they heard, "Mr. Billy Crystal!" There, in the midst of a field, Billy Crystal poked his head out of a tent wearing only his underwear, and said, "Oh, I can't do it right now. I'm busy." Then, in keeping with the theme of the year's multinominated movie, *Brokeback Mountain*—the story of two cowboys who are gay—Chris Rock poked his head out and said, "I'm busy too!"

The announcer introduced several other "hosts," including Steve Martin, David Letterman, and Whoopee Goldberg, all of whom turned the hosting duties down. Jon Stewart, appearing in bed, tells Halle Berry, beside him, that he'd just had a dream about being invited to host the Oscars. Moments later, it was George Clooney in bed with him, which ultimately prompts Stewart to get up and get moving to host the show. Finally properly introduced, Jon stepped to the microphone in front of thousands of celebrities and millions of viewers and introduced himself as "the fourth male lead from *Death to Smoochy*." For the rest of the evening, Jon was occasionally funny, but did not "kill"—some critics went so far as to say he bombed. He wasn't going to worry. He'd once told a reporter, "You can't avoid offending people"; sometimes audiences just don't like a comedian's material.[4]

Back on more familiar turf, Jon and his *Daily Show* crew got back to work on *Indecision 2006: Midterm Midtacular*, back to winning Emmys and Television Critics Association Awards for the show, and Jon continued his remarkable string of producing TV specials including *Night of Too Many Stars: An Overbooked Event for Autism Education*. He was also featured, briefly, in a short documentary film entitled *Wordplay* focusing on the creators and consumers of crossword puzzles—including those that compete in the Annual American Crossword Puzzle Tournament in Stamford, Connecticut. The film highlights the role that Will Shortz, who holds a university degree in "Enigmatology" and has been editor of the *New York Times* crossword since 1993, has played in promoting crossword puzzles as a test of intellectual prowess. Among those who are featured as true lovers of crosswords are former president Bill Clinton and film producer, director Ken Burns, and Jon Stewart. When we first encounter Stewart—he is in his Comedy Central office doing a *New York Times* puzzle. He looks up and says, "My name is Jon Stewart, and I tell dumb jokes for money." About the puzzle on which he is working, he says, "I'm so confident, I'm going to do [the puzzle] in glue-stick!" During an interview on *The Daily Show*, three years earlier, Stewart told his guest, Will Shortz, "Will, as you know, I'm a bit of a crossword afficionado."[5] Stewart has a particularly interesting relationship with Shortz; on June 30, 1999, during a taping of the television program *The View*, Jon told the studio audience that he had asked Shortz to create a crossword puzzle for him in which the answers to various clues would spell out Stewart's marriage proposal to Tracey. Tracey solved the puzzle by accepting.

That year, Stewart was also invited to play the voice of Zeebad in the animated film, *Doogal*. In this production, the title character, Doogal (voice of Daniel Tay), is a cute dog that loves to eat candy. He also ends up going on a mission to save the world by stopping Zeebad (voice of Jon Stewart), the evil sorcerer, from freezing the entire earth. Zeebad—who is a coil-spring and is able to shoot a freeze-ray from his moustache—possesses the power of three enchanted diamonds.

Doogal's three friends and co-adventurers are a guitar-playing rabbit named Dylan (voice of Jimmy Fallon), a shy and loyal snail named Brian (voice of William H. Macy), and an opera-singing cow named Ermintrude (voice of Whoopi Goldberg). After hopping onto a magic train, they journey over mountains, dodge the licking flames of lava-pits, and sail make their way across the ocean. It is a journey as much about friendship and trust as it is about rescuing the planet, and it is the power of their friendship that ultimately defeats the evil Zeebad.

Jon's Zeebad may not have had any friends, but Jon was piling up professional friendships, receiving invitations to appear on an ever-increasing number of talk shows. Ellen DeGeneres interviewed him on her show, *Ellen* (ABC). Howard Stern did his customary raunchy interview on *Howard Stern on Demand* (Sirius Satellite Radio) and Jon spent an hour with fellow comedian and respected interviewer David Steinberg on *Sit Down Comedy with David Steinberg* (US). The country's most popular fake news anchor was the real deal—so much so that an article in the *Columbia Journalism Review* framed contemporary journalism as "Before Jon Stewart" and after.[6] It seems Jon Stewart was killing comedy audiences and serious audiences alike.

KILLED . . . AND STILL KILLING

In early 2007, Tina Fey killed Jon Stewart. There could be no doubt; the evidence was overwhelming, as was the blood and gore. At the end, although Jon had temporarily regained some of his sight and made a valiant effort to stave off Fey's relentless attacks, Tina's cunning and brute strength were too much for the diminutive Stewart. Tired of the skirmish, despite being egged on by the crowd, Fey ultimately lifted *The Daily Show* anchor and drop him onto the barbed end of—fittingly—an enormous ship's anchor that happened to be there. Impaled and broken, Jon Stewart expired. A tragic and violent end for Jon.

Fortunately, Jon could enjoy the pride a celebrity feels when he or she is transformed into a "claymation" action figure and is "booked" for *Celebrity Deathmatch* (MTV) with a carefully selected opponent. Launched on New Year's Day, 1998, *Celebrity Death Match* rapidly became a favorite among MTV viewers. The "Jon Stewart vs. Tina

Fey" episode had now joined the company of claymation death match pairs like Arnold Schwarzenegger vs. Sylvester Stallone, Jay Leno vs. David Letterman (both were defeated simultaneously by an electrified dragon), and Conan O'Brien vs. Bill Maher (Conan was the victor), and Ashley Simpson vs. her old nose. As frivolous and as adolescent as critics accused *Celebrity Deathmatch* of being, MTV fans knew that Jon Stewart had, despite his ghastly defeat, achieved an even higher status among the hippest audiences. In fact, the "Death Match" served as a wonderful and ironic symbol: Jon had "died"—comedian-speak for "bombed on stage"—precisely because he was killing—comedian-speak for "making audiences laugh hysterically"—audiences around the country and around the world.

Jon continued to "kill" throughout 2007, once again being nominated for the Television Critics Association Award for Individual Achievement in Comedy. *The Daily Show* won another Emmy for Outstanding Variety, Music, or Comedy Program and was nominated—again—for Outstanding Writing for a Variety, Music, or Comedy Program. Jon himself was nominated for an Emmy for Outstanding Individual Performance, and it surprised no one that Comedy Central rushed to secure a contract renewal with their best asset. Jon agreed to continue hosting *The Daily Show* for another three years.

Jon was now "killing" with intellectuals, too. In 2007, The Blackwell Philosophy and Popculture Series—a collection of books filled with scholarly essays on popular culture icons—published *The Daily Show and Philosophy: Moments of Zen in the Art of Fake News*.[7] The contributing writers included professors and scholars from throughout the United States, and the essays included titles like "Amusing Ourselves to Death with Television News: Jon Stewart, Neil Postman, and the Huxleyan Warning,"[8] "Public Discourse and the Stewart Model of Critical Thinking,"[9] and "Stewart and Socrates: Speaking Truth to Power."[10] In an essay entitled "*The Daily Show's* Exposé of Political Rhetoric," Professor of Philosophy Liam P. Dempsey argues that *The Daily Show with Jon Stewart* creatively undermines politicians' "attempts at rhetorical manipulation," rendering them "(literally) laughable." Dempsey goes on to highlight Jon Stewart's talent for pointing out "misuses of reason in political life."[11] Was there a limit to what Jon could accomplish now that he had become one of "America's anchors" and, quite possibly, one of "the most trusted names in the news"?[12]

AMERICA'S MOST TRUSTED NEWSCASTER/THE MOST ANNOYING MAN ON TELEVISION[13]

I understand that what we do is inherently annoying.[14]

It's fair to say that what, to its host, is simply a comedy show that takes jabs at news media and newsmakers, *The Daily Show with Jon Stewart* is, to a growing community of sharp-eyed viewers, a cultural phenomenon. Despite his own self-characterization as "the duodenum of the American news system,"[15] Stewart has been referred to as "the era's preeminent political comic"—one who is highly skilled at "winning big laughs without losing his individual voice."[16] Academics across the nation are discovering, in both *The Daily Show* and in Jon Stewart himself, subjects of study worthy of scholarly research and publication.[17]

One of the ways in which Stewart is both trusted and "annoying" is his approach to what is considered important by the typical news media. Obviously aware of the events around the world that shape our lives, Stewart nevertheless finds gaping holes in the coverage of "news" by the people supposedly responsible for informing the public. As one writer from *Time* magazine puts it, Stewart has complained that "[T]he national conversation has become dominated by the loudest, craziest 15% to 20% of Americans—the Koran burners, the flag burners, the truthers, the birthers, the town-hall screamers, the folks who compare opponents to Hitler or the Taliban—and that they're rewarded with attention from journalists and politicians who should know better."[18] To Stewart, the excessive attention paid by news media to the sensational stories, coupled with the shallowness of the media's coverage of significant social, political, and economic issues, all serve to make America "look ridiculous."[19] He has complained that networks such as CNN are noisier than they are informative, referring to them as "grits without salt," and that "CNN feels like an opportunity squandered."[20] Still, Stewart was, just a few years into his *Daily Show* hosting duties, a little puzzled by how much trust his growing audience was placing in him. When Bill Moyers observed to him that he was never sure if Stewart was doing satire or a modern kind of journalism, Jon told him, "Well then that either speaks to the sad state of comedy or the sad state of the news. I can't figure out which one."[21] By 2007 and into 2008, the lines between Stewart's *Daily Show* comedy and the serious side of news reporting were getting blurred even as the comedy itself was becoming even more outrageous.

It was time for *The Daily Show* to take on another presidential election, this time called *Indecision 2008: Election Night—America's Choice*. This was a tame title compared to the 2007 recurring segment on the campaign entitled *Clusterf@#k to the Whitehouse*, so-named because, by late 2007, there were 13 pairs of candidates from 13 different parties running for the presidency. In addition, there were over 60 write-in candidates including "Average Joe" Schriner (Ohio), Jonathan "The Impaler" Sharkey from the "Vampire, Witches, and Pagan Party" of New Jersey, and Cris Ericson from the Marijuan Party of Vermont. By the spring of 2008, the field had been narrowed to three candidates: Senator John McCain (R-AZ), Senator Barack Obama (D-IL), and Senator Hillary Clinton (D-NY). The latter two candidates were vying for a ticket for the Democrats, but it took until early June 2008 for Clinton to concede the Democratic Primary votes to Obama.

The 2008 election looked to be such a complicated mess. Jon Stewart and Stephen Colbert joined forces, and their shows, to present live coverage of the actual election. Before that, however, *The Daily Show* spent a few episodes looking more closely at the various frontrunners. In May 2008, Stewart did what would have seemed like a hatchet job on Senator McCain's long list of physical ailments that might preclude his surviving office, *if* Jon had been making things up. He wasn't. Clip after clip of doctors and medical experts served to amass a list of health problems that included kidney stones, skin cancers, intestinal polyps, an eye lens implant, degenerative arthritis, and the removal of over 30 lymph nodes from McCain's neck. There was more, as NBC's chief medical editor, Dr. Nancy Snyderman, was quick to point out, listing multiple surgeries and, on top of it all, vertigo. Stewart was wide-eyed, amused but also showing how alarming it was to hear how fragile McCain seemed to be. But the next clip showed a commentator on *Fox News* saying, "McCain is fit as a fiddle! Is 71 [years old] the new 30?"

Jon stared ahead, feigning even deeper surprise and consternation, and said, "I guess that means *death* is the new 50!"[22]

But for at least a brief moment, when the 2008 election results were certain, Jon Stewart and Stephen Colbert sat side-by-side at the end of a long day of live coverage of the vote. Colbert watched as Stewart announced, "At 11:00 at night, Eastern Standard Time, the President of the United States is Barack Obama." The audience erupted in cheers. Jon Stewart was the bearer of incredible news, and his various correspondents were upset. One by one, they emerged from stage left and stage right, echoing Jason Jones's bewildered confusion, "Jon, we're a little confused. What are we supposed to cover now?" Jon assured them that there was still a world out there and abruptly got up and told them to "Follow me to freedom!" They trooped out of the studio, up a few flights of stairs, through a backstage area, and then, finally through the door and out to the roof where they felt the sunshine (despite the fact that it was nighttime!) and breathed the newly refreshed air now that Obama had been elected. That is, until Stephen Colbert observed that Bush still had another two and a half months to be president. The gang trudged back to the studio. Jon and Stephen retook their seats, thanked the audience, and wished them a good night. And it was a good night, one that would earn *The Daily Show* yet another Emmy for its fake news coverage of the election. Jon had killed, and it didn't end there.

After a lackluster performance two years earlier at the 78th Annual Academy Awards, the Academy passed Jon over for the 79th edition, selecting Ellen DeGeneres instead. But in 2008, Stewart was back, and this time, his performance as host earned him an Emmy nomination. The awards kept on coming. In 2009, *The Daily Show*'s international broadcast was nominated for a British Academy of Film and Television Arts (BAFTA) TV Award for Best International Show. Perhaps the most unique "award" Jon Stewart received in 2009 was when, on April 21, the President of Liberia, Ellen Johnson Sirleaf, formally made Jon an African Chief, and presented him with African Chief's garb, including a hat that Stewart immediately wore. Jon looked as pleased, if not more so, than when he'd found out five years earlier that astronomers had named an asteroid after him: 116939 Jonstewart (2004 GG39). Fittingly, according to various astronomy websites, Jon's asteroid is one that measures zero centimeters in diameter![23]

FILIBUSTER KILLER AND SANITY RESTORER

I'm attempting to scratch an itch.[24]

Late in 2010, Jon Stewart went to Washington, D.C., and Washington, D.C. came to Jon Stewart. But first, *The Daily Show* was about to make an appearance on *Earth*, or more accurately *with Earth* in Jon Stewart and his collaborators' sequel to their fake textbook, *America (The Book): A Citizen's Guide to Democracy Inaction.* The new book, titled *Earth (The Book): A Visitors' Guide to the Human Race*, is filled with fake science, fake statistics, fake religion, and fake apocalyptic scenarios that, unfortunately, seem less fake all the time. *Publisher's Weekly* called *Earth* "laugh-out-loud, rollicking social satire,"[25] while a reviewer for *The Christian Science Monitor*, who summed up *Earth* as a "pseudo-document for discovery in the future by vaguely imagined aliens" seemed unsure of whether to treat the book as a humorously serious text or a seriously humorous one when he added, "it is an idea that stretches credulity, even in a book that does not need to feel 'real.'"[26] One person who found Jon Stewart quite credulous, however,

President Barack Obama chats with Daily Show *host Jon Stewart during a commercial break in taping in Washington, D.C., on October 27, 2010. (Roger L. Wollenberg / POOL/epa/Corbis)*

was the president of the United States, Barack Obama, who stopped by, on October 27, 2010, to chat with Jon Stewart on *The Daily Show*. Even so, after Jon told his audience who his guest would be, he began the show with the "new segment: Let's keep the President Waiting." For two minutes, he scribbled on his papers, looked around, flicked a paper-triangle football from his desk, sang "la la la" and then showed a clip from the "Pasta Roundup" before finally introducing Obama.

While Tucker Carlson might have complained about Stewart's relatively gentle questions, Jon's audience seemed to understand that their favorite fake news guy was actually speaking with the president who was visibly pleased to be on *The Daily Show* and talking to Jon. As Obama strode out to join Jon at the desk, he offered an enthusiastic handshake and a warm greeting to Stewart. Reaching below his desk, Jon produced, for the president, "Mug-Force One." Obama laughed, and the interview began.

To his credit, Jon's questions were, if gentle, also just edgy enough to keep the audience highly entertained as they awaited the president's replies. Echoing Obama's own campaign slogans, Jon started by asking, "You're two years into your administration . . . are we the people we were waiting for?" Obama chuckled as Stewart continued, "You ran on very high rhetoric—'hope and change' and the Democrats this year seem to be running on 'Please, baby, one more chance!'" Again, Obama chuckled while Jon concluded the question that hinted at the possibility of the Congressional midterm election actually weakening of its Democratic stronghold: "Now, how did we go, in two years, from 'hope and change' and 'we are the people we've been looking for' to 'you're not going to give them the keys, are you?'" It was a funny—and interesting—moment. Jon had just asked the president how his base of power had slipped so much in such a short time. Obama responded by listing a number of accomplishments his administration had made over the previous 18 months, including "things that some folks don't even know about." Before he could continue, Jon sat up in amused surprise and asked, "Oh? What have you done that we don't know about? Are you planning a surprise party for us, filled with jobs and healthcare?" The audience roared in laughter, and the president laughed right with them. Jon's confidence in cajoling President Obama was fueling his audience's appreciation of just how far their *Daily Show* hero had come. Responding to Jon's point that at times Obama's administration seemed "legislatively timid," the president leaned forward and said, "Jon, I love your show. But, this is something where I have a profound disagreement with you, and I don't want to lump you in with a lot of other pundits . . ." Moments later, Jon tried to explain his point, and to volley a turn of phrase, "I'll tell you what I mean, and I don't mean to lump you in with other Presidents . . ." The audience laughed, Obama laughed, and Jon had "killed" again.

As the interview drew to a close, the president made a few points about the ways in which the filibuster operates in Congress, and how obstructive it can be. As if taking his cue from those remarks, a few weeks later, Stewart spent nearly nine minutes blasting the Congress for its opposition to adopting the Zadroga bill, which had been designed to provide health care coverage to all first responders at the September 11, 2001, attacks on New York's World Trade Center. Republicans in Congress had used the filibuster to prevent passage of the bill, but, as Senator Chuck Schumer (D-NY) said, after Stewart's rant, "This bill has long been a huge priority for us in New York, but Jon's attention to this helped turn it into the national issue it always should have been." White House press secretary Robert Gibbs agreed, telling a roomful of reporters that Jon's words may have helped turn the tide with regard to the bill. "I think he has put the awareness around this legislation. He's put that awareness into what you guys cover each day, and I think that's good."[27] The bill was ultimately passed, in large part because of public pressure. ABC's Ted Koppel had once told Jon, "You make your living making us laugh fundamentally about serious things."[28] It was the idea of mixing serious things with comedy that prompted Jon, Stephen Colbert, and dozens of others to take on one of the largest projects any of them had imagined. On October 30, 2010, with a crowd of over 200,000 excited people on hand at the National Mall in Washington, D.C., and with tens of millions of television viewers around the country and abroad, Stewart and Colbert treated the crowd to a day of speeches, performances, and comedy at what they dubbed, The Rally to Restore Sanity and/or Fear. As if he had not proven, again and again, that he could play with the big shots in media and politics, Jon Stewart had raised his game once more. On CNN's *Reliable Sources*, journalist Howard Kurtz described *The Daily Show* as being "perhaps the most important program for political satire on television" with Jon Stewart being among the most influential commentators in the country.[29]

COUNTERACTING THE "24-HOUR POLITICO-PUNDIT-PERPETUAL-PANIC CONFLICTINATOR"[30]

We live in hard times, not end-times . . . If we amplify everything, we hear nothing.[31]

Sometimes the light at the end of the tunnel isn't the Promised Land. Sometimes it's just New Jersey.[32]

On August 28, 2010, at the Lincoln Memorial in Washington, D.C., 240 members of the clergy, former Alaska governor Sarah Palin, Major League Baseball's Albert Pujols, a few members of the U.S. Military, members of the Boy Scouts of America, and a handful of others joined talk show host Glenn Beck for his "Restoring Honor" rally. Beck had put together the program to ask Americans to return to religious values, to pray, and to recognize that the nation had begun to lose its religious heritage. A frequent target of *The Daily Show* for his self-aggrandizing style and his carelessness with facts, Beck played the role of a national evangelist. Estimates of the size of the crowd ranged from 70,000 or 80,000 to Beck's own estimates of nearly half a million. It was in response to this rally that Jon Stewart and Stephen Colbert staged their own event. But their event, "The Rally to Restore Sanity and/or Fear," served the purpose of reminding people that rational, truthful conversations among informed individuals and groups would, in the end, do more to "restore" sanity in the country than would the polemics of self-proclaimed national spokespeople.

Jon's rally began with a musical performance by John Legend and The Roots. The guys from the popular show *Mythbusters* (Discovery Channel) then came on and got the entire crowd of around a quarter million people to do the "wave"—no easy trick considering that many of the attendees were holding some hilarious rally signs, such as "According to Glenn Beck math, there are 17 million people here!" and "It's a sad day when our politicians are comical and I have to take our comedians seriously!" One little boy held up a sign reading, "Glen Beck brainwashed my grandparents!! I want them back Glen!!" A young woman's sign read, "My comedy channel: Fox News. My News Channel: Comedy Central."[33]

Also present were Sam Waterston from *Law & Order*, Sheryl Crow, Kid Rock, Kareem Abdul-Jabbar, Tony Bennet, and many of the correspondents from *The Daily Show* itself. Performing in a kind of singer-parody were Yusaf Islam (formerly known as Cat Stevens), the Ojays, and Ozzie Osbourne. Colbert came out wearing a skintight jumpsuit, but later changed into a suit and tie for a mock debate with Jon. Star Wars robot R2D2 came rolling out at one point, as did an enormous paper mache effigy of Stephen Colbert. Correspondent (and substitute *Daily Show* host in the summer of 2013) John Oliver pranced across the stage in a Peter Pan costume, and Jon and Stephen reappeared in matching red, white, and blue suits to sing together. In contrast to Beck's crowd, which had remained relatively and respectfully quiet, Stewart's crowd was clearly having the time of their lives, singing, swaying, cheering, and laughing. Jon's closing speech, however, had everyone's attention. First he told everyone, "I'm really happy you guys are here, even if none of us are quite sure why we're here." But the truth was, and is, that Jon knew precisely why he was there and why he and Colbert had scrambled to get the rally together. It was to assure people that in fact there was already a great deal of sanity in the nation and that people should not simply believe the media outlets that make their money on transforming every event into an unsolvable crisis. With a voice hoarse from a day of joking, talking, singing, and cheering, Jon told the crowd, "We hear every damn day about how fragile our country is, on the brink of catastrophe, torn by polarizing hate, and how it's a shame that we can't work together to get things done, when the truth is, we do! We work together to get things done every damn day!"

During the press conference that followed immediately after the rally, both Stewart and Colbert looked exhausted but happy. Reporters took turns asking questions, and Stewart did most of the answering. But it was clear that the two men were talked out. Finally, when one reporter asked what was next for them, Jon said quietly, "I'm going to go hug my children."

Chapter 11

JON, JUDAISM, AND JEWISH HUMOR

In the public square, Stewart may be the perfect Jewish ambassador for our times: smart but not arrogant, extremely funny but not mean—a valedictorian, most popular, best-looking and class clown all wrapped into one.[1]

Let's face facts: very few people would confuse me with Maimonides.[2]

I was born in New York City, but I was raised in New Jersey, part of the great Jewish emigration of 1963.[3]

The fact that one chapter in this biography of Jon Stewart focuses on his relationship with Judaism might suggest that Stewart is a religious man; he is, by his own frequent admissions, decidedly not. But Stewart's Jewish heritage has played a significant role in his life, his comedy, and in his public persona. Rabbi Moshe Waldoks, coeditor of *The Big Book of Jewish Humor*, notes that "Stewart brings a sharpness of wit and a clear desire to never let the audience forget who he is by bringing his Jewishness up again and again."[4] At start of the Washington, D.C., press conference following his "Rally to Restore Sanity and/or Fear," the moderator asked that reporters give their names and their affiliations before asking their questions. Jon pretended to think that the instruction was meant for him and murmured, "Jon Stewart: reform Jew." Even more to the point, Jon Stewart, the comedian, is part of a long-standing tradition of Jewish comics who have made audiences laugh for generations—people like Don Rickles, George Burns, the Marx Brothers, Henny Youngman, Jack Benny, and Milton Berle, all the way to the current funnymen: Jerry Seinfeld, Amy Schumer, Richard Belzer, Louis Black, and, of course, Jon Stewart. At the 2005 Emmy Awards, Jon told the audience, "When I first said that I wanted to put together a late-night comedy-writing team that would only be 80 percent Ivy League-educated Jews, people thought I was crazy. They said you need 90, 95 percent. But we proved 'em wrong."[5]

When Jon was five years old, his parents enrolled him a Yeshiva kindergarten in nearby Trenton, New Jersey. Like any good kindergarten program, the Yeshiva class provided instruction in basic reading, math, telling time, tying shoes, learning how to measure things, and how to count by 2s, 5s, and so on. In addition, the Yeshiva's Judaic program involves teaching children the Hebrew alphabet, how to pronounce Hebrew words, and to recite basic Jewish prayers. Perhaps more than most mainstream kindergarten programs, those offered at Yeshivas strongly encourage students to see reading and learning as among the noblest goals, along with developing a deep identification with Judaism and Jewish culture. Stewart spent just one year at the Yeshiva before his parents switched him to a secular elementary school, but since that time, Jon has been clear about self-identifying as Jewish and about his support for Jewish culture. Of course, Jon Stewart wouldn't be Jon Stewart if he didn't also find humor in his own Jewishness and in the unique place that the Jewish people occupy in the world. About his college experiences in Virginia, Jon said, "I met these guys from Danville, Virginia, who were nice sweet guys, but who would just say, 'So, you're a Jewish fella. We've never met a Jewish fella like you before.'"[6]

Stewart talks about Jewish holidays, examines media reports about Israel, occasionally speaks in a mock Yiddish accent, and tells jokes that highlight stereotypical perceptions about Jewish people, one of which is that every Jewish person takes on the suffering of all the trials and tribulations of the Jewish people throughout history. For instance, during the Jewish high holy day of Yom Kippur, Jews traditionally fast for 24 hours and do not work; instead they attend religious services at the synagogue throughout this "day of atonement." In 2003, on Yom Kippur, Stewart was working as usual, doing *The Daily Show* and poking fun at himself. With regard to Yom Kippur, Stewart told his audience that he was, in fact, fasting, not for religious reasons, "but because I don't want to let a day go by where I can't feel worse about myself."[7]

In some ways, Stewart's personality may come through most authentically when he is joking about Judaism and its impact on his early life and how it now informs his public identity. At the beginning of one *Daily Show,* Jon acknowledged the NCAA basketball tournament, March Madness, and sent a shout-out, and a good luck wish, to his "peeps" from the Yeshiva University basketball team. Yeshiva University, first established in 1896 for the education of both religious and secular Jews in New York City, offers a full array of organized sports teams for its students. The teams—including a well-established basketball program—compete with other university teams around the city. None of these teams, however, play at the level of those who regularly make the NCAA tournament, and moments after wishing his "peeps" at Yeshiva University good luck, his invisible producer spoke into his invisible earpiece, prompting Jon to say, "I'm sorry, I'm just being told that they're not in it this year—the Yeshiva team. I'm sorry, I'm getting more word; they've never been in it. Uh, they're tiny little people."[8] The audience laughed, Jon looked comically embarrassed, and everyone in the room knew that Jon had made a good-hearted joke about the Yeshiva team—not because he was mocking them, but because it was an opportunity to reinforce—with good humor—his connection to an aspect of his Jewish heritage. (In an interesting coincidence, the address of the original Yeshiva school was Pike Street on the Lower East Side of Manhattan. When Stewart attended the College of William and Mary, he was briefly in the fraternity, Pi Kappa Alpha, otherwise known as the "Pikes.")

It's something of a puzzle to sort out Jon Stewart's complex collection of references to his Jewishness, Judaism, and the state of Israel. On the one hand, as noted, he regularly makes mention of him being a Jew, of Jewish holidays, events, people, and history. On the other hand, some argue, Stewart's true attitudes about Judaism and Israel are, at the very least, ambiguous, and at worst, harmful. One critic, who considers Stewart "perhaps the most famous Jewish television personality working today," complains that Stewart's evident "detachment" from Judaism only makes it that much easier for people to justify anti-Jewish sentiments.[9] For example, during his *Jon Stewart: Unleavened* television special, he told the audience, "My girlfriend's not Jewish, and I am. But it doesn't, really, it doesn't present a problem, which is really nice. 'Cause I'm a Jewish guy, but I'm not a serious Jew."[10] As with virtually every topic he addresses, Stewart's Jewish references occasionally provoke his audiences, and not all those who generally enjoy his humor find his jokes about Judaism funny. One writer for *The Philadelphia Jewish Voice* described Jon Stewart's connection to Judaism as "very tenuous" and complained that "It is Stewart's own exceptional talent and obvious intellectual curiosity that make his vulgar Jewish references all the more embarrassing."[11]

Some writers have pushed their criticism of Stewart's so-called Jewish humor to a much harsher level. Michael Savage, on his radio show *Savage Nation*, ranted as though directly to Jon Stewart, "You wonder why there's anti-Semitism, Jon? Jon, you wonder? You wonder why Jews like you cause anti-Semitism, Jon? You can't figure it out?" Stewart had, a few days earlier, spoken about logical inconsistencies in the protests opposing the Park 51 project. The proposed project (originally to be called Cordoba House) was to build a 13-story Islamic community center that would be open to all as a way to promote interfaith dialogue and understanding. Because the proposed site is just two blocks from Ground Zero, where the World Trade Center was destroyed by Islamist terrorists, many considered the idea of the Islamic center as an affront to those who died and as a kind of victory for the terrorists. According to Savage, ideas like Stewart's are "the product of inbreeding. It is only the product of inbreeding."[12] What Stewart had actually said was that the debate had created profound confusion. On the one hand, those opposed to building the community center were arguing that it would be a monument to terrorism, and on the other hand, there were people who argued that not to build it would indicate a fear of terrorism and of Islam, which would just further encourage Islamist terrorists to see us as weak. Some pundits had argued that people shouldn't even talk about the controversy; the arguments themselves would encourage terrorists to see us as vulnerable and ineffectual. Framing the entire issue in this way, argued Stewart, meant that "the jihadists are the only ones . . .

who can't lose!"[13] Stewart went on to propose an alternative to the Park 51 project: "the 'No Talk Endless Half-Invisible Mosque Downtown Center.' They won't know *what* we're talking about!" Savage, in chastising Stewart for his jokes about the controversy, then told his audience, "Now you understand why he's only a comedian . . . Now you understand why your children get the kind of education they get because they actually rely upon a comedy for their ideas."

Such criticisms have not deterred Stewart from finding humor in religion in general and in Judaism in particular. He once quipped that religion has "given people hope in a world torn apart by religion." At the 2011 Republican Jewish Coalition Forum, Republican presidential candidates were asked about their political views on Israel. *The Daily Show* created a segment to cover the "highlights" of the event called "The Matzorian Candidate." Stewart introduced this segment by asking his audience, "Did you know that not all Americans celebrate Christmas?" As the audience laughed, he continued, "It's true! Many American Jews celebrate a completely different holiday." Then, to drive the irony home, Stewart deliberately mispronounced the word "Chanukah" as "Choww . . . come we don't get to celebrate Christmas?"[14]

It might seem to some that Jon Stewart's critical remarks about one or another Jewish person are an indication of his ambivalence about being Jewish, but nothing could be further from the truth. A more careful consideration of things he says tell a much more complex story. Soon after Jon took over *The Daily Show*, there were news stories about a number of ultra-Orthodox Jewish protesters in Israel[15] who had tried to intimidate a group of Reform rabbis, some of whom were women, as they prayed at the Western Wall. Stewart's analysis of the controversy included his observation that the protestors, who were "desperately fearful of biblical cooties, got all Jewier-than-thou when they discovered that a handful of Reform Jews who actually allow their women to do something other than breed and cook also had the chutzpah to be praying nearby." He added that the protestors, in their outrage, acted as though they were better Jews than those who identify as Reform, as though "the Word was handed to them directly, right before [God] handed us big noses and took away all our athletic ability."[16]

The Jewish Republican Coalition Forum is intended to allow the top Republican presidential candidates to reflect on how, if elected president, they would implement policies in support of Israel. Stewart, not surprisingly, saw the forum somewhat differently. In his interpretation, the event was an annual "celebration" in which "Jews commemorate the miracle of incredibly religious Christian presidential candidates fighting over who loves Jews more."[17] Stewart was referring, in part, to the position taken by a large number of evangelical Christians that Israel must be protected and preserved because they believe that it will be the locus of divine activity for the second coming of Jesus. In fact, the Reverend John Hagee, founder of the organization Christians United for Israel, has called support of Israel "God's foreign policy."[18] In other words, for evangelical Christians, Israel's role in the Christian end-of-the-world scenario is part of God's plan, as are the terrible and destructive natural disasters that have left, for example, places like Haiti in ruins. In response to the ideas like these, Jon Stewart used his *Daily Show* voice to tell evangelist Pat Robertson to "Shut your piehole!"[19] It's not surprising, then, that anything short of all-out support of Israel by Jon Stewart would be met by disapproval of the evangelical Christian community.

There are Jewish detractors who believe Jon Stewart is a self-hating Jew, a Jewish anti-Semite, or worse. As some have noted, he dropped his Jewish-sounding name of Leibowitz in favor of the more ambiguous Stewart.[20] Danielle Berrin, writing for the JewishJournal.com, observes that many of Stewart's Jewish fans wonder, "How could the Jew who makes Jewish 'cool' be so indifferent to Judaism?"[21] Others point out that he doesn't seem to be publically supportive of Israel and that he often mocks Jewish holidays by claiming not to know what they are. But during a stand-up act in 1996, Stewart told his audience, "I'm a Jewish guy. I've been to Israel; I'm really glad it's there."

On occasion, Stewart has joked about eating bacon (proscribed by Jewish law). He has on various occasions referred to himself as "Jewey Von Jewstein" or "Jewy Jewman" and made jokes about Jewish noses, circumcision, Jewish athletes, and Jewish families—his own included. On an episode of *The Daily Show* during Passover, on April 9, 2012, Stewart told his viewers, "As the father of mixed-faith children who are exposed to both Christian and Jewish holidays, I can't help but feel that we Jews are getting our asses kicked out here." To offset the advantage that, he says, the Easter holiday has over Passover, Stewart jokes that the Jewish holiday needs a kind of mascot to compete with the Easter Bunny, something like "Passover Pete, the guitar-playing, pizza-eating lion."

In fact, he makes the kinds of jokey remarks about Jews and Judaism that non-Jewish comedians attempt only gingerly. But to see Jon Stewart as anti-Jewish is to ignore the fact that he consistently identifies himself as Jewish, and clearly has an appreciation for his Jewish heritage. Part of that appreciation is represented in how he manages to incorporate a great deal of his "Jewishness" in his humor. As blogger Danielle Berrin observes, Jon Stewart's satirical view of Jewish life is actually evidence of his close identification with Judaism. She suggests that Jewish people "can participate in Stewart's jokes because there's a shared reference point; Jews aren't laughing at Stewart, they're laughing with him."[22] The same could be said for Jon's non-Jewish audience— and guests. They do not necessarily need to be in on the particulars of a humorous remark to "get it." When Mindy Kaling (*The Mindy Project*, *The Office*) joked with Jon about background music she might choose, Jon joked that for him, it would most likely be Klezmer music—a reference to the unique-sounding music associated with eastern European Jews. Kaling's laughter was genuine, and so was the audience's, whether any of them knew what Klezmer music was. Because *Jon* said it, others just seem to *know* it's funny.

He also isn't afraid to touch on commonly sensitive topics, such as religious intermarriage. For example, while interviewing former British prime minister Tony Blair, Stewart told his guest, "My wife is Catholic. I'm Jewish. It's very interesting; we're raising the children to be sad." It's hard to imagine Stewart raising children without humor and laughter, but his joke about his "sad" children points to his willingness to see humor even in traditionally "touchy" areas. As film critic Saul Austerlitz once put it, on *The Daily Show*, "Stewart plays the Jewish court jester, offering gleefully impolite, impolitic observations from an outsider's perspective. The frame of reference for Stewart's jokes, and those of his correspondents, is often a Jewish one."[23] And despite his frequent gentle mocking of his own Jewishness, Stewart is quick to show discomfort about news stories that cast Jewish people in, to say the least, an unflattering light. In highlighting a story about the lawsuit that some shareholders of AIG—the multibillion dollar insurance company—filed against the Federal Government over the terms of its multibillion dollar bailout, Stewart watched the monitor as the man behind the suit was put on screen. With his fingers crossed and in a prayerful pose, Stewart said, "Who is the greedy [bleep] behind this lawsuit—please don't be a Jew, please don't be a Jew, please don't be a Jew."[24] Unfortunately for Stewart, the man behind the lawsuit was former CEO of AIG, Hank Greenberg, who is Jewish. Jon then reacted with mock exasperation, in a poke at himself, he added that perhaps Greenberg was really not Jewish but had changed his last name from "Stuart"—a reference to Stewart's own name change from Liebowitz to Stewart.

What may fool some viewers about Jon Stewart's public references to Judaism and Jewish traditions is that Stewart often seems to undermine his own knowledge of those traditions. On one show in 2009, Stewart's *Daily Show* guest was Seth Rogen. Stewart told his audience that with Rogen—also Jewish—on the program, "Our show . . . will be kosher for Passover." But then he quickly turned what was already a funny joke into a different kind of self-mocking joke in which he pretended to have no idea what he was talking about. "Is it Passover now? Does anybody know?"[25] He has referred to the traditional Jewish celebration of the week-long festival of Sukkot, in which celebrants build and then eat, sleep, and socialize in a temporary structure of wood, branches, and leaves, as "the holiday with the huts."

The Jewish jokes are not reserved for just Stewart himself, however. He often pokes good-natured fun at Israel and the complicated politics that dominate news stories about the Middle East. When President Obama spoke about Israel at the 65th Session of the United Nations General Assembly, he told those assembled, "Those of us who are friends of Israel, must understand that true security for the Jewish State requires an independent state of Palestine." As the news cameras then panned to the empty seats of the Israeli delegation, the image of those seats appeared on the screen to Stewart's right. Stewart peered "into" those empty seats, did a couple of double-takes, and then remarked, "I know we are not necessarily a tall people, but . . ." As it turns out, the press reported, the Israelis were not in attendance because of their observance of the Jewish holiday of Sukkot. Stewart seemed surprised (not really) and said, "Wow. Sukkot. I'm Jewish and I didn't know . . .

I thought that Sukkot was like Jewish Arbor Day." Then, getting the word from producers through his pretend earpiece, he added, "I'm actually told that Jewish Arbor Day is called Tu B'Shevat. Um . . . we have a lot of holidays."[26] On the one hand, Jon Stewart would like his audiences to believe that while he is Jewish, he is a bit like an outsider to his own heritage. On the other hand, even his Jewish outsider position serves to reinforce the significance of Stewart's connection to, and appreciation of, his Jewish roots. When his "senior Middle East correspondent," the British John Oliver, reports "from the Middle East," he tells Jon that one way to keep the Israelis from building houses in disputed territories is to invent more Jewish holidays to keep the Israelis home. He proposes holidays like "Bagelmania" and the "entire month of 'Choctober," and is disappointed when Jon reminds him that Jewish holidays aren't just made up for convenience; they have been a part of the Jewish culture for thousands of years. But Stewart also makes it clear that self-deprecating humor among Jews has also had a very long history. And he is not alone. Fellow comedian Adam Sandler has made famous a song-parody whose first line is "Put on your yarmulke, it's time to celebrate Chanukah!" When Sandler came on *The Daily Show* in November 2011, he and Stewart greeted each other by saying "L'shana tova!"—the traditional Jewish expression for "happy new year" following Rosh Hashanah. While this greeting seemed to amuse both of them, it was also a moment of closeness between two men whose "Jewishness" have long been an integral part of their comedy.

Particularly revealing of Stewart's sense of humor regarding Judaism is the chapter on religion in his best-selling book, *Earth (The Book): A Visitor's Guide to the Human Race*. Regarding Jewish prayer, he gives an example: "Please protect me from violent pogroms/offensive stereotypes/negative reviews of my new Broadway show or novel/negligence lawsuits from my podiatry practice."[27] To be fair, Stewart pokes fun at the prayers of Protestants, Catholics, Muslims, Scientologists, Wiccans, Buddhists, and, as one further bit of ribbing, Reform Jews, which, elsewhere in the book, Stewart wryly suggests are not actually very Jewish at all.

When he writes about religious holidays, focusing on the month of December as his example, Stewart presents a humorous list of Jewish holidays that become the holidays of the world. For instance, the eight-day holiday of Chanukah (sometimes spelled "Hanu-kah") becomes "Hânâkâ" in "Japanese Judaism, which then becomes "Ha'a'nu-u-ka'a"—the "Polynesian" Jewish celebration. "Charmo-nukkah" is from the "Blues Judaism"; "Guernica" is from "Abstract Judaism"; and Christmas is listed as a holiday for both Christians and Reformed Jews.[28]

In many ways, Stewart's jokes about Judaism and his own Jewish identity are part of a tradition of Jewish humor that casts an ironic look at its own customs, rituals, and history. Regarding Chanukah, Stew-art explains that it is a "celebration the birth of our savior, Hanukkah Harry." Joke-writing and joke-telling, in fact, are one of the many tal-ents typically—perhaps *stereotypically*—credited to Jewish people. At the 2005 Emmy Awards ceremony, where Stewart received the Emmy for Outstanding Variety, Music, or Comedy Series, he told the audience, "When I first said that I wanted us to put together a late-night com-edy writing team that would only be 80 percent Ivy League-educated Jews, people thought I was crazy. They said you need 90, 95 percent. But we proved 'em wrong." The jokes and satirical observations, the pretended ignorance about Jewish holidays and practices, and even his correspondents' occasional good-natured participation in "making fun" of Judaism all serve to further foreground Jon Stewart's *connections* to his Jewish heritage. As one writer put it, "Judaism, in Stewart's world, becomes a cool kids' club everyone is desperate to join."[29]

Some of that "coolness" comes from Stewart's willingness to joke about—and in doing so, also demystify—even Judaism's darkest moments in history. About Nazi Germany, Stewart writes that it "was so destructive to Judaism not only for the loss of life, but because many who survived began to view the practice of Judaism as somewhat of a health hazard." He goes on to say, "Up to now, being the Chosen Ones has brought nothing but trouble. In the New Judaism, all Chosen Ones will receive a value pack worth hundreds of dollars in discounts at participating vendors . . ."[30] In his book, *Naked Pictures of Famous People* (1998), Adolph Hitler is "interviewed" by television personality, Larry King. At the start of the "interview," Stewart writes that Hitler is enjoying a traditionally Jewish favorite: a fresh bagel. Hitler tells King, "I don't know what I was so afraid of. These are delicious!!!"(140). The fearless one, here, is Jon Stewart. Knowing full well that joking about Hitler might be seen as the ultimate insult to the Jewish people, Stewart is more interested in mastering his subject matter than being intimidated by it. With regard to the Jewish religion—in fact, religious faith in general—Stewart may empty upon it what one writer calls a "bucket of derision," but he does so in a way that is "as comedically deft as it is religiously shrewd."[31]

But there is a somewhat more complicated side to Stewart's relationship to Judaism and to Israel. It could be argued that his jokes about religion are indicative of a kind of comfort zone he feels—he can make jokes in safety because he is a member of the group. But as his viewers have long realized, Stewart's role on *The Daily Show* is not simply to tell jokes and funny stories. His status as a trusted "newsman" often casts him the role of deep truth-teller. When he opines about something, more often than not, his point of view seems quite rational, thoughtful, and nearly always controversial. In late 2012, in response to the Israel–Gaza conflict, many network newscasters and analysts focused their broadcasts on the question of "who won?" and not much more. Viewers were treated to video clips of members of Hamas and of Israel's government declaring victory. American politicians and leaders, including President Obama, were quick to point out that an end to the conflict would benefit the United States. On *The Daily Show*, Jon Stewart characterized the winner–loser discussion among news anchors by asking, "Did anybody *lose* this . . . thing? Did anybody *lose*? Did anybody actually lose in this bloody conflict that killed over 150 people?"[32]

Stewart has been criticized fairly often for "failing" to challenge guests on matters of anti-Semitism or anti-Israeli attitudes. In perhaps one of the more dramatic omissions, during his January 14, 2013, show, Stewart opted not to ask his guest, Roger Waters (of Pink Floyd fame), about his publically anti-Israel activities. Waters had announced, on the Internet, that he would be serving as a "juror" on the Fourth Russell Tribunal on Palestine as a way to "shed some light on the Israeli occupation of Palestine." Waters goes on to say that "the main conclusions are that there have been lots and lots of violations of international law by the Israeli government in complicity with the government of the United States . . . Israel acts with impunity outside the courts of international law."[33] It is unlikely that Stewart was unaware of Waters's activities on behalf of the Palestinians; he had, after all, praised Waters for his various charitable activities about which Stewart had obviously done research. Waters himself did not bring up his involvement on the Russell Tribunal. As the interview segment came to a close, Stewart praised Waters for his involvement in raising money for victims of Hurricane Sandy, "You, the archetypal rock 'n' roller, are just out there doing good in the world." But for supporters of Israel and for many Jewish people throughout the United States, Stewart choosing not to challenge Waters only fueled more questions about Stewart's relationship to, and genuine support for, Judaism and Jewish causes. Not surprisingly, the answer to those questions is that it's complicated. But not everyone gets the kind of "pass" that Stewart may have given Waters. In October 2010, during a radio interview with comedian Pete Dominick, CNN anchorman Rick Sanchez complained that "Jon Stewart's a bigot." When Dominick asked who Stewart is bigoted against, Sanchez replied, "Everybody else who's not like him." Sanchez had been making a point about the ways in which he, as a Cuban American, had experienced oppression and prejudice in America. Dominick suggested that perhaps Stewart could understand the plight of someone from an oppressed group since Stewart is Jewish. Sanchez's response was, "Please, what are you kidding? . . . I'm telling you that everybody who runs CNN is a lot like Stewart, and a lot of people who run all the other networks are a lot like Stewart, and to imply that somehow . . . the people in this country who are Jewish . . . are an oppressed minority? Yeah." CNN's reaction was swift; Sanchez was fired. A few days later, Sanchez called Stewart and apologized. Somehow, without even having been there, Jon Stewart had once again been an agent provocateur. It was, and is, a role that continues to define him.

Chapter 12

A LONG MOMENT OF ZEN

Oprah: So, you don't think you'll be doing *The Daily Show* in 20 years?

Jon: I don't want to be. I love my wife, and we want more kids. I'm not going to disappear, but I don't want to work this hard.[1]

When the producers of the 2011 movie *The Adjustment Bureau* (Universal) approached Jon to play a role, he was asked to take on the part of someone about whom he knew a great deal: Jon Stewart. In the story, David Morris (Matt Damon) is a young, charismatic politician running for U.S. Senate. One day he gets a brief glimpse of how his—and everyone's—destiny is controlled, and who controls it. The problem is, Morris wants to control his own destiny, especially when he meets and falls in love with a lovely dancer named Elise Sellas (Emily Blunt). The men of The Adjustment Bureau have other plans for David and do whatever is necessary to keep David and Elise apart. The situation seems hopeless, but David is determined to outwit the agents of destiny to be with the woman he loves.

In a life-imitates-art moment, David Morris appears on *The Daily Show with Jon Stewart* and is interviewed about his political life by Jon. It is somewhat disorienting to see Matt Damon, in character as David Morris, on the set of *The Daily Show* where Damon *as Damon* has been interviewed several times. The decision to have Stewart appear as "himself" reflects an interesting connection between the real Jon Stewart, who seems so wise to the concerns of contemporary young people, and the movie Jon Stewart who interviews a young man now wise to the ways in which the world "really" works. It's a mind-blowing situation: Jon Stewart the fake news icon plays the role of the fake Jon Stewart. It was exactly the kind of fakery, of course, that the real Jon Stewart finds so enjoyable.

Meanwhile, the real Jon Stewart was still very much in the fake news reporting game. After all, with the 2012 elections approaching, Jon and his crew of writers were busy studying every inch of footage of events like the Republican candidates debate on November 10, 2011, in Rochester, Michigan. Most of the network newscasts focused on trying to pick the "winner" of the debate. Serious-faced pundits from Fox News, ABC, NBC, CNN, CNBC, and scores of smaller stations around the country, consulted experts, columnists, campaign managers, and people on the street (some of whom seemed not to know that there was to be an election) to "determine" who came out on top of the debate and whom they thought would be the likely Republican nominee. The next day, *The Daily Show* took on the same task, but without the consultants, experts, commentators, analysts and spin doctors. Instead, Jon did what he does so well: he played the tape, watched with us, and celebrated the comedy material being offered up by the candidates. In fact, he began this particular segment—which he would call *Indecision 2012: Mercy Rule Edition*—by "calling" the nomination. "Mitt Romney!" he declared to his audience. "It's over!" (Less than two months later, at the Iowa Caucus, Stewart would prove prescient, as Romney came out on top, albeit by a slim margin.)

The debate itself seemed tailor-made for Stewart to skewer. The candidates had undergone "spontaneous combustion," he explained. "Eliminating" the candidates' chances, one by one, he first dismissed Romney's "chief rival in the campaign," Herman Cain ("the guy's in the middle of a scandal involving his treatment of women"). Stewart replayed the moment in which Cain refers to former speaker of the U.S. House of Representatives Nancy Pelosi (D-California), the highest ranking female official in U.S. history, as "Princess Pelosi." Turning his lasers on Newt Gingrich, Stewart pretended to wonder why "Newt" can't win the nomination. He then explained that all of Gingrich's ideas and theories are delivered with his typical "dickishness," and pointed out that people aren't going to want to vote for the Pilsbury Doughboy's "angrier know-it-all brother." Next on the hit list: Ron Paul, whose views, for the most part, conflict with the Republican mainstream. "The guy's for gay marriage, legalizing drugs, and against military spending . . . He's certainly capable of winning his party's nomination. But the Republicans ain't his party." Michelle Bachman's candidacy was, Stewart observed, finished ever since she claimed, in contradiction with known medical fact, that a vaccine for human papillomavirus (HPV) causes mental retardation. Continuing to play on candidate Rick Perry's memory lapse about a third federal agency whose budget he would cut, Stewart said, "that leaves three people, John Huntsman, Rick Santorum, and uh, uh, oh, . . . the Transportation Department?" About Huntsman, Stewart riffed, "Why can't the handsome, Mormon, ex-governor beat Mitt Romney? 'Cause he *is* Mitt Romney . . . just not quite." Why, Stewart joked, vote for a less popular version of the same guy. As for Rick Santorum, Stewart suggested that he was an even more inferior version of Mitt Romney and John Huntsman, leaving only Rick Perry to put over the hot coals of satire.

Candidate Rick Perry (R-TX) had experienced a moment of brain freeze that may well have undermined any credibility he'd had to that point. In vowing to eliminate three specific federal agencies as a step toward balancing the budget, he was then only able to name two. The name of the third agency eluded him, despite the half-hearted attempts to help him from candidate Ron Paul (R-MA) who stood at the adjacent podium. From Stewart's perspective, what brought the house down was the way Perry, upon conceding that he could not remember the third agency, blithely muttered "Oops." Stewart jumped all over that.[2] In fact throughout the segment, Stewart kept making lists of three items and each time would "forget" the third item in the list.

Perry's forgetfulness became a running joke for Stewart. As recently as May 6, 2013, following stories about a large-scale National Rifle

Association (NRA) convention in Texas, Stewart showed clips with various speechmakers from that convention. In one clip, Texas senator Rick Perry appears with an assault rifle, shooting at—and hitting—a number of targets. When he has emptied the clip, he turns to the camera with a grin. Then, he strides onto the NRA convention stage, exclaiming, "Yeah! Welcome to Texas, ladies and gentlemen!" Jon Stewart's response was, "Wow! If that dude doesn't have a CMT show by tomorrow . . . lock, stock, and . . . um . . . um." He'd "forgotten" the third term in the familiar list. In another clip from the same convention, several speakers chided President Obama and "the government" for promoting a "politics of emotion." Moments later, one speaker—Glenn Beck—told the NRA audience that the only thing stopping their mothers and sisters from being sexually assaulted was a gun. Stewart commented, "You are aware that fear is an emotion, right? Along with, uh, there's three of them, I think. There's guilt and fear and . . . um . . . um . . . I forget the third. Oops."[3]

Not even his own show is exempt from *Daily Show* irony. After claiming that the show is actually written by monkeys, Stewart went on to "quote" the staff of monkeys as having complained, "Are we not sentient beings who deserve more than the relentless grind of ephemeral, topical, humor pabulum?"[4] In echoing the type of criticism often leveled at *The Daily Show* by talk show hosts (Bill O'Reilly, Rush Limbaugh, Sean Hannity, Ann Coulter, Glenn Beck, to name a few), Stewart reminds them—and us—that he is "onto" them. And by including his audience in this satirical "admission" of doing just what the pundits say he does, Jon's audience trusts him all the more. Indeed, one of Jon Stewart's most notable talents is his ability to deconstruct the complaints that people like O'Reilly, Coulter, and Hannity make about him. Stewart repeatedly reminds these individuals as he reminds us that they are actually taking seriously a program that is blatantly and unabashedly intended to be both fake and funny. Strangely enough, Stewart's gift of self-deprecation has helped garner a fiercely loyal audience who recognize that *The Daily Show*'s best moments are those that simply tell—or show—the truth about the ways in which the purported truth-tellers (i.e., broadcast journalists and pundits) consistently get it wrong.

In another bit of satirical horseplay, Stewart illustrated the ways in which so-called political analysts will go on the air to make claims and predictions that are based on little more than the fact that they are permitted to tell them. In one *Daily Show* episode, Stewart showed several clips of expert analysts predicting the winner of the 2012 presidential election. Republican hopeful, Newt Gingrich, told viewers, "The odds are very high I'm going to be the nominee." Then, it turned out he wasn't; Romney—or as Stewart put it, "Rominee"—was nominated and Gingrich became a nonfactor in the election. But on October 26, 2012, Fox News, one of Stewart's favorite targets, featured Gingrich incorrectly predicting the outcomes of the election. This time, he told Fox's viewers that the victor will be Romney by a 53 to 47 percent margin, that Romney would receive over 300 electoral votes, and that the Republicans would "pick up the Senate." In fact, Obama's winning margin was 50.6 percent to Romney's 47.8 percent. Obama ended up with 332 electoral votes to Romney's 206, and Democrats "took" the Senate by a 53 to 45 seat margin. Gingrich, looking certain of his own predictive skills, added, "I base that on years and years of experience," to which Stewart then added, with raised brows and an incredulous smile, "of being wrong!"[5]

The Daily Show did not ignore the Democratic presidential contender, President Obama himself. One other truly remarkable aspect of Jon Stewart's craft as a host and interviewer: his ability to have conversations with virtually anyone while maintaining an atmosphere of good humor, intelligence, and respect, all of which reflects meticulous preparation for his conversation with each guest. After the second 2012 presidential candidate's debate between Mitt Romney and President Barack Obama, Stewart and his staff went to work, studying miles of video and reams of transcripts. They were of course looking for those golden moments when one or the other candidate said or did something peculiar, absurd, or just plain funny. Even more intensely, they were also looking at the ways in which the media outlets covered the debates, the ways in which the network news media declared either Obama or Romney the winner or the loser, and the assortment of analysts who spun the debates this way and that. As the nation's leading "fake news" show, *The Daily Show with Jon Stewart* was expected to skewer the fakery issuing from the variously more "reliable" news sources. In the first debate, by most accounts, Obama did poorly, and Romney came off as the more impressive candidate. The second debate—set up as a "town hall" interaction with a select audience of undecided voters—featured a resurgent President Obama and a less-impressive version of Mitt Romney. Following both debates, the media's fact-checkers scrambled to point out one or the other candidate's mistakes. Stewart, in a post-debate interview with President Obama himself, took a different tack. After an exchange of genuinely warm greetings between Obama and Stewart, the obviously relaxed president seemed ready and willing to discuss whatever topics Stewart was about to serve up. So, with a mischievous glint in his eye, Stewart held up two large photographs, both of President Obama and First Lady Michelle Obama. In the first, taken moments after the conclusion of the first debate, Mrs. Obama looked displeased as her husband, the president, strolled over to her. In the second, taken moments after the second debate, President Obama is seen walking toward a beaming first lady who was clearly delighted with her husband's second debate performance. Stewart then asked the president, "Do you know which debate was which?" The audience roared with laughter, and Obama himself looked amused as he replied, "Cute. Cute, Jon."[6] It was a striking moment not only of humor and satire, but of an amazing familiarity and rapport that Jon Stewart has developed with some of the most important people in the world.

That familiarity—and interest in international issues—prompted Jon to take on yet another fascinating project. This one would, for the first time since taking over The Daily Show, require him to be on hiatus from the show for the entire summer of 2013. The project was a film entitled Rosewater, and Stewart was the director. An ambitious production, Rosewater was born, in a sense, in 2009.

Iranian journalist Maziar Bahari had agreed to chat with Daily Show correspondent Jason Jones in a segment entitled Behind the Veil: Minarets of Menace. Bahari, cheerful and helpful, answered Jones's questions about how Iranians really felt about Americans. Shortly after that interview, Bahari was arrested and put in prison for 118 days where interrogators tortured him. One of those interrogators was a man who, according to Bahari, smelled of rosewater. Bahari was accused of revealing secrets to an American spy, and the "spy" in question was Jason Jones.

As 2014 has dawned, Jon Stewart and The Daily Show have, without question, changed the way people think about how the major news media outlets present current events and the analysis of those events and issues. Over the years, Jon and his team have created, in the words of *Newsweek* senior writer Devin Gordon, "a place that is extraordinarily funny and that doesn't insult [viewers'] intelligence" and that *The Daily Show* "is one of the few places, including network news, that seems like it's giving you the truth."[7]

"THAT'S OUR SHOW! HERE IT IS, YOUR MOMENT OF ZEN"

One of the nightly features of *The Daily Show* is the "moment of Zen" that Stewart offers viewers. Begun before Jon's tenure, during Craig Kilborn's stint as *Daily Show* host, the "moment" is usually a bit of video, showing someone famous doing or saying something absurd or just an event that Jon and his writers have isolated for a contextless second look. When Jon announces this moment, his expression is almost reverent, as though this last bit of footage is going to feature something from the media that is simply too indescribable to say more about. There is no additional captioning required, no last bit of clever—or cynical—commentary. With this setup, Jon's audience gets a last taste of all that Jon Stewart considers utterly ridiculous: a moment of stupidity, an inexplicable remark, or even a brief glimpse at something that might otherwise have been overlooked. (In a 2007 NBC *Nightly News* broadcast, and as a gesture of respect toward Stewart, host Brian Williams ended the program with his own "moment of Zen": a painstakingly intricate sand painting completed by a group of monks, and then obliterated by a toddler as he blithely stomped his way through it.) Jon's audiences are reminded, once more, that Stewart overlooks virtually nothing. Selecting the footage for the "moment of Zen" is part of a much more complex preparatory process that further distinguishes Jon Stewart from assorted network talk show hosts. The use of note cards has become a common denominator among the late-night talk show hosts, but the ways in which these cards are utilized is telling. Whereas Jay Leno and David Letterman frequently look at their cards, telling guests, "It says here that you once appeared in . . ." or "I see that your favorite co-star is . . .," Jon Stewart rarely actually reads from his cards, opting instead to shuffle them around his desk as he looks his guests in the eye during conversation. The other hosts seem to have been provided with bits of information about their guests' latest exploits, movies, vacations, love affairs, or political events. Stewart's note cards are more of a symbolic prop, a kind of Plan B—if the conversation fizzles out, Jon's got stuff on those cards to restart the discussion. The conversation never fizzles.

After spending the day in his *Daily Show* office writing, bouncing ideas around with his writers, watching hours of video, reading and rereading portions of a book written by his guest, reviewing a slew of newspaper and magazine articles on his guest's latest activities, playing for a few minutes with one of his dogs who might be hanging out on the office couch, doing his daily *New York Times* crossword puzzle, and fine-tuning what will become that night's program, Jon is prepared

Jon Stewart and "The Boss," Bruce Springsteen, perform at the MusiCares Person of the Year concert honoring Springsteen at the Los Angeles Convention Center, February 8, 2013, in Los Angeles, California. (Photo by Kevin Mazur/WireImage/Getty Images)

for the show as though he'd studied for the SATs. But there is no way to prepare, completely, for what inevitably happens when Jon and his guests get down to it. Typically, in the middle of an interview, Stewart will ask his guest, "Can I ask you a question?" And the subsequent questions—some call them challenges—are occasionally the kind that a guest cannot answer without playing into Stewart's crafty hand. The status of the interviewee is rarely if ever a factor in Stewart's willingness to suddenly cut to the chase. In an exchange with Alan Greenspan (Fed), Stewart pointed out that, "When you lower interest rates, it drives money to stocks and lowers the return people get on savings." Greenspan confirmed this, and Stewart then asked, "So they've made a

Jon Stewart with his family as they watch the New York Knicks face the Boston Celtics in an NBA basketball game at Madison Square Garden in New York, on January 4, 2009. Comedian Whoopi Goldberg is seated at left. (AP Photo/Kathy Willens)

choice—'We would like to favor those who invest in the stock market and not those who [save]' . . ." Greenspan was visibly uncomfortable and shifted in his seat as he replied, "That's the way it comes out, but that's not the way we think about it." The quick-thinking Stewart came right back to say, "Explain that to me. It seems that we favor investment, but we don't favor *work*. The vast majority of people work." The only thing Greenspan was able to do, at that point, was to suggest that Stewart reread the book that Greenspan had, presumably, come onto the show to promote.[8]

With an impressive knowledge of the night's material, as well as of his guest's agenda for the evening, Jon Stewart reminds his viewers every night that a "fake news" show need not—indeed must not—be overlooked as mere comedy. On a good night (which, according to ratings, accolades, and the extent to which *The Daily Show* is referred to, dissected, and complained about by someone on network news or commentary, is nearly every night), Jon Stewart provides his audience with a half-hour long "moment" of Zen. But for the real Zen moments, Jon Stewart always comes back to what, besides comedy, he loves most: his wife, his son, his daughter, his dogs, and his cat.

Oprah: What kind of daddy do you want to be?
Jon: The kind who stays.[9]

Appendix

MY GUEST TONIGHT . . .

The *Daily Show with Jon Stewart* has been called "the hot destination for anyone who wants to sell books or seem hip, from presidential candidates to military dictators."[1] On the opposite end of the "temperature spectrum," Stewart's show has also been called "the coolest pit stop on television."[2] Over the years, Stewart has played host to U.S. presidents and vice presidents, kings, prime ministers, Nobel laureates, high-ranking military officers, Pulitzer Prize winners, and even the occasional player from his favorite baseball team, the New York Mets.

Most talk show "interviews" are actually a form of staging for the guests. By and large, the advantage of appearing on these shows is two-fold: for the guests, they get to promote their latest projects and achievements, which keeps their producers and directors happy; for the hosts, big-name guests—particularly movie stars and supermodels—increase viewership, which keeps big-name sponsors happy. On average, the typical audience size for Jay Leno's *The Tonight Show* is around 3.8 million viewers; *Late Night with David Letterman* draws around 3 million viewers. How do these numbers compare to Jon Stewart's numbers? *The Daily Show with Jon Stewart* attracts somewhere around 1.8 million viewers per show, a startling number for a show on a basic cable

channel. *The Daily Show* now has about as many viewers as Jimmy Kimmel and Conan O'Brien. But numbers tell only a small part of the story
about Jon's guests.

To be fair, Jon interviews his share of show biz personalities. He's
played host to pop megastars like Jennifer Lopez and Pink; he's chatted with Colin Farrell and Halle Berry. He's put up with a cranky visit
from Hugh Jackman (someone Jon once deemed his least favorite
interviewee) and thoroughly enjoyed a conversation with Heidi Klum.
But in nearly all cases, Jon Stewart's guests are (a) typically not provided with questions in advance, (b) surprised by at least one or two
of Jon's questions, and (c) aware that Stewart will have learned a great
deal about them, read their books, updated himself on their current
activities, and, very often, prepared himself to push his guests beyond
their comfort zones. It is a testament to the respect and affection that
Jon Stewart's guests feel toward him and to his enormous popularity
that so many of even his most prestigious and busiest guests—including incumbent President Obama, as well as members of Congress, and
renowned scholars—return for more conversations with the diminutive
host who once said he "aspires" to be "schmuck of the decade."[3]

The comprehensive list of Jon Stewart's *Daily Show* interviews is stag-
gering, and far too long to list here. In the first half of 2011 alone, Stewart conducted close to 90 interviews. Since his *Daily Show* debut, Jon
has interviewed hundreds of people on issues such as the global economy, international relations, the environment, health, and medicine—
all topics that, as his guests learn, Stewart has meticulously prepared to
discuss. The vast majority of those interviewed by Stewart seemed to
genuinely enjoy their encounter with Jon (with at least a few notable
exceptions: Lynn Cheney, Jim Cramer, and Hugh Grant).[4] Although
the portion of each interview that survives editing may be relatively
small (typically three to eight minutes), the actual conversation may
go on for 15 minutes to as long as an hour. The entire interview, then,
is put up on *The Daily Show* website.

These are people that Jon spends his days and years getting to
know—their work(s), relationships, histories, awards, quirks, and
more. Remarkably, although it would be impossible for anyone to read
so many large books in so short a time, Jon manages to read *enough*
of every book discussed on *The Daily Show* that he is able to refer to

passages and sections of the books that go beyond his own notes. It is a testament to Jon's staff that he always seems thoroughly briefed with regard to his guests' activities and achievements.

Stewart has become an expert at turning the tables on guests who have reputations for intimidating others. When Lynne Cheney appeared on *The Daily Show*, Stewart threw her off-balance when he challenged her views, and those of her husband, Dick Cheney, on gay rights and gay marriage. He also disputed some of Cheney's claims about the war in Iraq. First, though, he greeted her cheerfully as she walked on stage holding a gift for Jon—a toy version of Darth Vader from *Star Wars*—which she plopped onto the desk between them. On previous occasions, Stewart had referred to her husband, Dick Cheney, as "Darth Vader" and this was Lynne Cheney's acknowledgment of those barbs. Stewart thanked Cheney and then told her, "We're pleased you're here . . . surprised" to which Cheney responded, "I've never watched your show. How is it?"[5] The rest of the interview was, as Stewart said several times during it, a little "uncomfortable." Responding to a question about whether husband Dick was the type to admit he was wrong at home, Cheney stopped him, saying, "What kind of question is that?"

So, taking the bait, Stewart asked whether she thought that Americans had been told at the start of the Iraq war that it would be much easier than it actually turned out to be, a none-too-subtle reference to the oft-stated White House reassurance that the mission in Iraq would be a slam dunk. Looking irate, Cheney responded tersely, "No." But Stewart's audience knew she had been lured into a waiting trap. Referring to the 9/11 attack on the World Trade Center and then the following six years, Cheney reminded Stewart that there had not been another attack in those years, and, she added, "I think this administration, my husband and the President, deserve a lot of credit for that." Not one person in the studio audience applauded; the silence was palpable, and Cheney realized that she was not on friendly ground.

At the end of the interview, Jon's guests usually stick around as the show goes to commercial. This time, Cheney simply walked off the set immediately after the interview, clearly none too happy with having been outthought by Stewart. Despite telling Cheney that he felt a bit awkward asking her about some of these issues, it was clear that Stewart was not at all intimidated. He had proven to his fans, once more, that he always came to the table prepared.

In his March 12, 2009, interview of CNBC financial analyst Jim Cramer, Jon Stewart did something unusual—he blasted his guest. On his program, *Mad Money with Jim Cramer*, for which the program's slogan is "In Cramer We Trust," the host repeatedly suggested that Bear Stearns stock was one he recommended and that it was a safe investment. It was decidedly not, and many people lost a great deal of money. While no one—Stewart included—claimed that people should have blindly followed Cramer's advice, Stewart argued that the whole *Mad Money with Jim Cramer* show, along with its slogan, were misleading at best, and dangerous at worst. Cramer and Stewart began an on-air feud in which Cramer would complain that Stewart had made fun of him, and Stewart would replay the videos of those moments. Of course, every time Cramer complained, it meant that *The Daily Show* was getting free publicity on network TV. Ultimately—and somewhat unbelievably— Cramer appeared on Stewart's show to be interviewed. During a semi-polite extended interview, Stewart and Cramer exchanged points about the financial crisis and the forecasters who got it wrong. But the dams broke when Cramer suggested that all he had done was to try to make financial analysis entertaining for his audience. Stewart erupted: "I understand that you want to make finance entertaining, but it's not a [expletive] game. When I watch that . . . I can't tell you how angry it makes me because it says to me . . . You knew what the banks were doing and yet were touting it for months and months—the entire network was. And so now to pretend that this was some sort of crazy, once-in-a-lifetime tsunami that nobody could have seen coming is disingenuous at best and criminal at worst."[6] In his role as fake news broadcaster, Jon Stewart had, for a brief moment, spoken the words so many of his viewers would have liked to have said.

Here, then, are a few selected lists of guests Jon has had on *The Daily Show* over the past decade and a half or so.[7]

Presidents and Vice Presidents
Joe Biden (D), 45th U.S. vice president
Jimmy Carter (D), 39th U.S. president

Bill Clinton (D), 42nd U.S. president
Al Gore (D), 43rd U.S. vice president
Barack Obama (D), 44th U.S. president

Members of the United States Congress (Past and Present)

Dick Armey (R-TX)
Evan Bayh (D-IN)
Kit Bond (R-MO)
Henry Bonilla (R-TX)
Barbara Boxer (D-CA)
Bill Bradley (D-NJ)
Eric Cantor (R-VA)
Hillary Clinton (D-NY)
James Clyburn (D-SC)
Tom Coburn (R-OK)
Tom Daschle (D-SD)
Jim DeMint (R-SC)
John Dingell (D-MI)
Christopher Dodd (D-CT)
Bob Dole (R-KA)
Dick Durbin (D-IL)
John Edwards (D-NC)
Barney Frank (D-MA)
Al Franken (D-MN)
Dick Gephardt (D-MO)
Kirsten Gillibrand (D-NY)
Chuck Hagel (R-NE, currently U.S. secretary of defense)
Gary Hart (D-CO)
Tim Kaine (D-VA)
Ted Kaufman (D-DE)
Ted Kennedy (D-MA)
John Kerry (D-MA, currently U.S. secretary of state)
Dennis Kucinich (D-OH)
Joe Lieberman (R-CT)
Trent Lott (R-MI)

John McCain (R-AZ)
Zell Miller (D-GA)
Carole Mosley-Braun (D-IL)
Rand Paul (R-KY)
Ron Paul (R-TX)
Nancy Pelosi (D-CA)
Harry Reid (D-NV)
Marco Rubio (R-FL)
Bernie Sanders (I-VT)
Rick Santorum (R-PA)
Chuck Schumer (D-NY)
Alan Simpson (R-WY)
Louise Slaughter (D-NY)
Fred Thompson (R-TN)
Elizabeth Warren (D-MA)
Anthony Weiner (D-NY)

U.S. Supreme Court Justices (Past and Present)
Sandra Day O'Connor (Retired)
Sonia Sotomayor

U.S. Governors (Past and Present)
Evan Bayh (D-IN)
Rod Blagojevich (D-IL)
Chris Christie (R-NJ)
John Corzine (R-NJ)
Mario Cuomo (D-NY)
Mitch Daniels (R-IN)
Howard Dean (D-VT)
Jennifer Granholm (D-MI)
Mike Huckabee (R-AR)
Gary Johnson (L-NM)
Thomas Kean (R-NJ)
Jim McGreevey (D-NJ)
Deval Patrick (D-MA)

Tim Pawlenty (R-MN)
Rick Perry (R-TX)
Marc Racicot (R-MT)
Bill Richardson (D-NM)
Tom Ridge (R-PA)
Buddy Roemer (R-LA)
Arnold Schwarzenegger (R-CA)
Arlen Specter (D-PA)
John Sununu (R-NH)
Henry Waxman (D-CA)
Christine Todd Whitman (R-NJ)

Military

Lieutenant General William B. Caldwell
General Wesley Clark
Robert Gates (U.S. secretary of defense)
Admiral (Dr.) Connie Mariano (First Filipino American to become
    a rear admiral in the U.S. Navy; the first female director of the
    White House Medical Unit; and the first military woman to be
    appointed as the White House physician)
General Stanley McChrystal (former U.S. and NATO Force Com-
    mander)
General Richard B. Myers
Sgt. 1st Class Leroy Petry (Medal of Honor recipient)
Captain Richard Phillips (captain of the U.S. cargo ship *Maersk Ala-
    bama* in 2009. On April 8, 2009, his ship was attacked by four So-
    mali pirates. To spare his crew, Captain Phillips offered himself as a
    hostage.)
General Hugh Shelton (commander in chief of the U.S. Special Op-
    erations Command, including Delta Force, Navy SEALS, and other
    top secret special mission units. General Shelton was chairman of the
    Joint Chiefs of Staff under both Presidents Clinton and George W.
    Bush)
Howard Wasdin (former SEAL Team Six Sniper)

Muppets
Kermit the Frog
Miss Piggy

New York Mets (Past and Present)
Ron Darling
Willie Mays
Mike Piazza
David Wright

Nobel Laureates
Jimmy Carter (39th U.S. president)
Leymah Gbowee (Author)
Barack Obama (44th U.S. president)

Prime Ministers and Kings (Past and Present)
His Majesty King Abdullah II bin Al-Hussein (Jordan)
Prime Minister Tony Blair (United Kingdom)
Prime Minister Gordon Brown (United Kingdom)
President Ellen Johnson Sirleaf (Liberia)
President Pervez Musharaf (Pakistan)
President Mohamed Nasheed (Maldives)

Pulitzer Prize–Winning Authors
Robert A. Caro—*Master of the Senate*
Steve Coll—*The Bin Ladens: An Arabian Family in the American Century*
Doris Kearns Goodwin—*No Ordinary Time: Franklin and Eleanor Roosevelt: The Home Front in World War II*
Paul Ingrassia—(for journalism, *Wall Street Journal*)
Jon Krakauer—*Into Thin Air: A Personal Account of the Mount Everest Disaster*
John Meacham—*American Lion: Andrew Jackson in the White House*
Edmund Morris—*The Rise of Theodore Roosevelt*
David Nasaw—*Andrew Carnegie*

Daniel Okrent—*Great Fortune: The Epic of Rockefeller Center*
Jack Rackove—*Original Meanings: Politics and Ideas in the Making of the Constitution*
David Remnick—*Lenin's Tomb: The Last Days of the Soviet Empire*
Marilynne Robinson—*Gilead*
Stacey Schiff—*Vera (Mrs. Vladimir Nabokov)*

Comedians

Louie Anderson
Greg Bear
Joy Behar
Richard Belzer
Sandra Bernhard
Elayne Boozler
David Brenner
George Carlin
Adam Carolla
Dave Chappelle
Margaret Cho
Louis C. K.
Sascha Barron Cohen
Billy Connolly
David Cross
Billy Crystal
Larry David
Ellen DeGeneres
Jimmy Fallon
Craig Ferguson
Will Ferrell
Tina Fey
Judah Friedlander
Jeff Garlin
Janeane Garofalo
Ricky Gervais
Tom Green
David Alan Grier

Kathy Griffin
D. L. Hughley
Eric Idle
Dom Irrera
Kevin James
Jimmy Kimmel
Robert Klein
Martin Lawrence
Denis Leary
Richard Lewis
Bernie Mac
Norm MacDonald
Bill Maher
Steve Martin
Mike Meyers
Mark McKinney
Dennis Miller
Tracy Morgan
Kevin Nealon
Bob Newhart
Conan O'Brien
Patton Oswalt
Cheri Oteri
Greg Proops
Colin Quinn
Michael Richards
Andy Richter
Don Rickles
Chris Rock
Joe Rogan
Adam Sandler
Rob Schneider
Amy Sedaris
Jerry Seinfeld
Gary Shandling
Molly Shannon

Martin Short
Wanda Sykes
Tracey Ullman
Damon Wayans
Marlon Wayans
Shawn Wayans
Kristen Wiig
Robin Williams
Steven Wright

Other Notable Guests

Akbar Ahmed (former ambassador of Pakistan to Great Britain)
Madeleine Albright (former U.S. secretary of state)
Matthew Alexander (military interrogator, "Matthew Alexander" is a
    pseudonym)
Alli Allawi (former Iraqi minister of Trade and Minister of Defense)
Kofi Annan (former secretary-general of the United Nations)
John Ashcroft (former U.S. attorney general)
Jed Babbin (former U.S. deputy undersecretary of defense)
James Baker (former chief of staff under President Ronald Reagan)
Melody Barnes (director of the Domestic Policy Council)
Dan Bartlett (Assistant to the President for Communications under
    George W. Bush)
Ishmael Beah (former Sierra Leone child-soldier)
Josh Bernstein (survival expert)
Lisa Beyer (vice president, Communications, International AIDS Vac-
    cine Initiative)
Jeff Bezos (founder and president of Amazon.com)
Ken Blackwell (vice chairman of the Republican National Commit-
    tee's Platform Committee)
Michael Bloomberg (108th mayor of New York City)
John R. Bolton (former U.S. ambassador to the United Nations)
Cory Booker (mayor of Newark, NJ)
Bob Bradley (manager of Egypt's national soccer team)
Donna Brazile (vice chairwoman of the Democratic National Committee)
Zbigniew Brzezinski (former U.S. National Security Advisor)

Warren Buffet (business magnate)

Richard Burt (former U.S. ambassador to the Federal Republic of Germany)

Herman Cain (former Republican presidential candidate)

Rosalynn Carter (former first lady)

Rajiv Chandrasekaran (national editor, *Washington Post*)

Zaki Chehab (founder and editor-in-chief of ArabsToday.net)

Lynne Cheney (former director of the National Endowment for the Arts)

Warren Christopher (former U.S. secretary of state)

Steven Chu (U.S. secretary of energy)

Richard A. Clarke (former National Coordinator for Security, Infrastructure Protection, and Counter-terrorism for the United States)

Clarence Clemons (musician)

Tom Coughlin (head coach, NY Giants)

Ivo Daalder (U.S. ambassador to NATO)

Bill DeBlasio (New York City mayor)

R. A. Dickey (professional baseball player)

Landon Donovan and Bob Bradley (U.S. soccer player and coach)

Shaun Donovan (U.S. secretary of housing and urban development)

Arne Duncan (U.S. secretary of education)

Jon Favreau (former speech writer for President Obama)

Louis Freeh (former FBI director)

Bill Gates (founder of Microsoft)

Rudolph Giuliani (former mayor of New York City)

Tom Goldstein (publisher of SCOTUSblog)

Jane Goodall (anthropologist)

Austan Goolsbee (chairman of the Council of Economic Advisers and the youngest member of President Barack Obama's cabinet)

Alan Greenspan (former chairman of the Federal Reserve)

Efraim Halevy (former director of Israel's Mossad and former director of the Israel National Security Council)

John R. Hall (dean of Westminster Abbey)

Hugh Hefner (publisher, *Playboy* magazine)

Anita Hill (Professor of Social Policy, Law, and Women's Studies, Brandeis University)

Kambiz Hosseini and Saman Arbabi (creators, hosts, and producers of *Parazit*, the popular Iranian political comedy show that airs on Voice of America's Persian News Network. During the interview, the two joked to Jon Stewart that they regard him "as the prophet" of what they do)

Gigi Ibrahim (journalist and socialist activist; Ibrahim was one of the leaders of the takeover of Tahrir Square during the Egyptian Revolution in 2011)

Lisa P. Jackson (administrator of the U.S. Environmental Protection Agency)

Wyclef Jean (musician)

Boris Johnson (mayor of London)

William Kamkwamba (Malawian inventor)

Mark Kelly (former NASA shuttle commander, author)

Ray Kelly (New York City police commissioner)

Gary Locke (U.S. secretary of commerce)

Jennifer Lopez (singer, actress)

Elon Musk (CEO of SpaceX)

Ray Nagin (former mayor of New Orleans)

Grover Norquist (president of Americans for Tax Reform)

Michelle Obama (first lady of the United States)

Colin Powell (former U.S. secretary of state)

Prince Zeid Ra'ad (Jordan's ambassador and Permanent Representative to the United Nations since 2000)

Condoleezza Rice (former U.S. secretary of state)

Susan Rice (U.S. ambassador to the United Nations)

Cecile Richards (president of Planned Parenthood)

J.K. Rowling (author of the Harry Potter series of books)

Donald Rumsfeld (former U.S. secretary of defense)

Roxanna Saberi (American journalist, convicted of spying by the Iranian government and sentenced in April 2009 to eight years in an Iranian prison. On May 11, 2009, an appeals court reduced her sentence and she was released.)

Jehan Al Sadat (former first lady of Egypt)

Kathleen Sebelius (former U.S. secretary of health and human services)

Will Shortz (puzzlemaster)

Bruce Springsteen (musician)

Morgan Spurlock (documentary filmmaker: *Supersize Me*)

Ringo Starr (musician)

Michael Steele (former Republican National Committee chairman)

Chesley "Sully" Sullenberger (retired airline captain, aviation safety expert, and accident investigator)

George Tenet (former CIA director)

Desmond Tutu (South African archbishop, social activist)

Neil deGrasse Tyson (Frederick P. Rose director of the Hayden Planetarium at the Rose Center for Earth and Space)

Kurt Vonnegut (author)

Bassem Youssef (the "Jon Stewart" of Egypt, host of *El Bernameg*)

NOTES

INTRODUCTION

1. Interview with Maureen Dowd, *Rolling Stone*, November 2006.

2. Bill Moyers's *NOW*, from the introduction to his television interview with Jon Stewart, July 11, 2003.

3. "Jon Stewart," *The Biography Channel*, A & E Television, 2007.

4. "Celeb-Fools Stupid Asinine Ridiculous Unpatriotic Hollywood Celebrities, Stars, Fools," http://celebfools.tripod.com/id5.html. Retrieved April 14, 2010.

5. Interview on *Fresh Air*, "Jon Stewart: The Most Trusted Name in Fake News," NPR, October 4, 2010.

6. "Jon Stewart Intelligence Agency," http://www.jonstewart.net /bio/quotes.html. Retrieved January 11, 2009.

7. Paul Harris, "The Observer Profile: Jon Stewart," *The Observer*, February 26, 2006, http:www.guardian.co.uk/media/2006/feb/26/broad casting.oscars2006. Retrieved October 2, 2010.

8. See *Wordplay* (2006), directed by Patrick Creadon.

9. "On-line Poll: Jon Stewart Is America's Most Trusted Newsman," *The Huffington Post*—Eat the Press, August 22, 2009, http://www .huffingtonpost.com/2009/07/22/time-magazine-poll-jon-st_n_242933.html. Retrieved October 29, 2011.

10. "John Stewart: The Most Trusted Man in Fake News," NPR Books (online), October 4, 2010, http://www.npr.org/templates/story /story.php?storyId=130321994. Retrieved August 13, 2011.

11. Moyers's *NOW*.

12. Shira Ovide, "Yes, Jon Stewart Is the Most Powerful Economic Force in the U.S.," *The Wall Street Journal*—Deal Journal, November 4, 2010, http://blogs.wsj.com/deals/2010/11/04/yes-jon-stewart-is-the-most-powerful-economic-force-in-the-us/. Retrieved January 21, 2011.

13. Terrance MacMullan, "Jon Stewart and the New Public Intellectual," in *The Daily Show and Philosophy: Moments of Zen in the Art of Fake News*, ed. Jason Holt, The Blackwell Philosophy and Popculture Series, William Irwin, Series Editor (Malden, MA: Blackwell, 2007), p. 57.

14. *The Daily Show with Jon Stewart*, October 21, 2008.

15. "Encore: Interview with Jon Stewart," *Larry King Live* (CNN), December 28, 2010.

16. Ibid.

17. Ibid.

18. Jody Baumgartner and Jonathan S. Morris, "*The Daily Show* Effect: Candidate Evaluations, Efficacy, and American Youth," *American Politics Research* 34 (2006): 360.

19. Ovide, "Yes, Jon Stewart Is the Most Powerful Economic Force in the U.S."

20. Michael Gettings, "The Fake, the False, and the Fictional: The Daily Show as News Source," in *The Daily Show and Philosophy: Moments of Zen in the Art of Fake News*, ed. Jason Holt, The Blackwell Philosophy and Popculture Series, William Irwin, Series Editor (Malden, MA: Blackwell, 2007), p. 17. [Gettings writes: "Most fictions aren't intended to deceive, and this is true of *The Daily Show* just as it is of *Billy Budd*."]

21. Stewart claims that Easton "only spoke to me once because I bombed so badly at one gig" (Interview with Dave Itzkoff, *Maxim*, November 2000, p. 116).

CHAPTER 1

1. Chris Smith, "The Man Who Should Be Conan," *New York Magazine*, January 10, 1994, p. 36.

2. Nathan Laskin died on August 8, 2000, in Stamford, Connecticut.

3. Willy S. Thomas, "An American in China: 1936–1939—A Memoir" (2005), http://willysthomas.net/TientsinBuildings.htm. Retrieved October 11, 2011.

4. Jon Stewart, *Jon Stewart: Unleavened*. Busboy Productions, HBO Downtown Productions, 1996. http://www.imdb.com/title /tt04777021. Retrieved May 11, 2012.

5. Interview with Marlo Thomas in: Marlo Thomas, "The Only Jew in the Neighborhood," *Growing Up Laughing: My Story* (New York: Hyperion, 2010), p. 362.

6. There is no truth to the story, found on the D2TV.wordpress .com website, "Ernie Kovacs Was Jon Stewart's Great-Grandfather." The writers admit as much but point to the close connections between Kovacs's and Stewart's television personae. (http://d2tv.wordpress.com /2011/04/19/tv-on-dvd-ernie-kovacs-was-jon-stewarts-great-grandfa- ther/. Retrieved November 11, 2011). But as one writer put it, Kovacs was "doing in the 50s and 60s what Jon Stewart is doing now—looking around at the TV landscape and pointing out its failures and excesses by making fun of it." (David Bianculli, "Ernie Kovacs: The King of Early Television Comedy," *NPR.org*, April 18, 2011, http://www.npr .org/2011/04/18/135511104/ernie-kovacs-the-king-of-early-television- comedy. Retrieved October 19, 2011.)

7. Dorothy Denneen Volo, *Daily Life during the American Revolu- tion* (The Greenwood Press Daily Life through History Series) (West- port, CT: Greenwood, 2003), pp. 208, 255, 276–77.

8. Jeremy Gillick and Nonna Gorilovskaya (November/Decem- ber 2008). "Meet Jonathan Stuart Leibowitz (aka) Jon Stewart: The Wildly zeitgeisty Daily Show Host." Moment: Independent Journal- ism from a Jewish Perspective. November/December 2008, http:// www.momentmag.com/Exclusive/2008/12/JonStewart.html. Retrieved July 2, 2010.

9. Ibid.

10. Randolph Portugal, "No Joke: Stewart's Dad Taught at College," *The Signal*, September 15, 2009, http://www.tcnjsignal.net/2009/09/15 /no-joke-stewart's-dad-taught-at-college/. Retrieved March 6, 2013.

11. Quoted in A. J. Jacobs, "Jonny on the Spot," *Entertainment Weekly*, January 8, 1999, p. 62.

12. Warren Kalbacker, "20 Questions: Jon Stewart," *Playboy*, March 1995, p. 124.

13. "Oprah Talks to Jon Stewart," The O Talks Collection, *Oprah* (magazine), June 2005, http://www.oprah.com/magazine/Oprah-Inter views-Jon-Stewart/8. Retrieved July 31, 2011.

14. Quoted in: Rob Tannenbaum, "How I Became a Man," *Details*, January 1999, http://jon.happyjoyfun.net/tran/1999/99_0100details .html. Retrieved November 8, 2011.

15. Executive profile: Don Leibowitz CCP. *Bloomberg Businessweek*, n.d., http://investing.businessweek.com/research/stocks/private/person .asp?personID=36145128. Retrieved August 1, 2012.

16. *eLuminate.org* newsletter, http://www.eluminate.org/Newsletters /Newsletters-05-06-2012.html#Link2. Retrieved September 9, 2012.

17. "TCNJ Featured in the Princeton Review's 'The Best 378 Colleges' 2014 Edition," August 7, 2013, News.pages.tcnj.edu/2013/08/07tcnj-featured-in-the-princeton-reviews-the-best-378-colleges-2014-edition/ Retrieved August 8, 2013.

18. RateMyProfessor.com, January 15, 2009, http://www.ratemy professors.com/ShowRatings.jsp?tid=1163045. Retrieved May 1, 2011.

19. Randolph Portugal, "No Joke: Stewart's Dad Taught at College," *The Signal* (The College of New Jersey Student Newspaper), September 15, 2009, http://www.tcnjsignal.net/2009/09/15/no-joke-stewart's-dad-taught-at-college/. Retrieved December 4, 2010.

20. "Oprah Talks to Jon Stewart," O, *the Oprah Magazine*, June 2005, p. 188.

21. Kalbacker, "20 Questions: Jon Stewart," pp. 108–9, 124–25.

22. Obituary in *The Times*, Trenton, June 9, 2013, Obits.nj.com/obit uaries/Trenton/obituary.aspx?pid=165245750. Retrieved June 30, 2013.

23. Interview with Diane Ravitch, *The Daily Show with Jon Stewart*, March 3, 2011.

24. *The Daily Show with Jon Stewart*, December 14, 2011.

25. Valerie Strauss, "Jon Stewart Tries to Talk to Arne Duncan," The Answer Sheet, *The Washington Post* (online), http://www.washington post.com/blogs/answer-sheet/post/jon-stewart-tries-to-talk-to-arne-dun can/2012/02/16/gIQATPNVJR_blog.html. Retrieved August 1, 2013.

26. Marian Leibowitz (primary contributor), "Coping with Stress: Teacher Proven Strategies." Learning Institute Videos for Teachers (n.d.), http://www.amazon.com/Coping-Stress-Teacher-Proven-Strategies/

dp/B0012A49R2/ref=sr_1_3?ie=UTF8&qid=1354977484&sr=8-3& keywords=Marian+leibowitz

27. Marian Liebowitz, "Instruction for Process Learning," in Arthur L. Costa and Rosemarie M. Liebman, eds., *Supporting the Spirit of Learning: When Process Is Content* (Thousand Oaks, CA: Corwin, 1997), pp. 47–54.

28. Nancy Olson, "On Gifted and Talented: A Conversation with Marian Leibowitz," *Educational Leadership*, a publication of the Association for Supervision and Curriculum Development, 1980, pp. 259–260.

29. Ellen Jin R Kaufman, "Zachary's First Visit to the U.S. Mainland," *A Life to Remember* (blog), Summer 2010, http://pearlsofseren dipity.blogspot.com/2010/07/zacharys-first-visit-to-us-mainland.html. Retrieved March 10, 2014.

30. Jessica Pressler, "Jon Stewart's Unfunny Brother Is Testifying about the 'Flash Crash' Right Now," *New York News and Features*, May 11, 2011, http://nymag.com/daily/intel/2010/05/jon_stewarts_ unfunny_brother_i.html. Retrieved December 2, 2011.

31. "Jon Stewart vs. Larry Leibowitz: Brother of *Daily Show* Host Is President of the NYSE," *The Daily Bail*, May 13, 2010, http://dailybail .com/home/jon-stewart-vs-larry-leibowitz-brother-of-daily-show-host- is.html. Retrieved May 29, 2011.

32. "Executive Profile: Lawrence Leibowitz," *Bloomberg Businessweek*, http://investing.businessweek.com/research/stocks/people/person .asp?personId=1375584&ticker=NYX:US. Retrieved August 9, 2011.

33. "High Frequency Trading," CBS *60 Minutes*, October 10, 2010.

34. Christian Plumb, "Jon Stewart's Brother Says Mom 'Pretty Happy with Both,'" Summit Notebook, *Reuters* U.S. edition, March 29, 2010, http://blogs.reuters.com/summits/2010/03/29/jon-stewarts-brother-says- mom-pretty-happy-with-both/. Retrieved January 31, 2011.

35. "Jon Stewart vs. Larry Leibowitz: Brother of *Daily Show* Host Is President of the NYSE."

36. Michael Corkery, "Daily Show: Jon Stewart's Big Brother Speeds Up NYSE," *Deal Journal*, March 29, 2010, http://blogs.wsj.com /deals/2010/03/29/daily-show-jon-stewarts-big-brother-speeds-up- nyse/. Retrieved April 19, 2011.

37. Matthew Leibowitz, *LinkedIn*, http://www.linkedin.com/profile/ view?id=9650564&authType=NAME_SEARCH&authToken=UsUJ& locale=en_US&srchid=3307924311394803263153&srchindex=3&

srchtotal=17&trk=vsrp_people_res_name&trkInfo=VSRPsearchId%3
A33079243111394803263153%2CVSRPtargetId%3A9650564%2CV
SRPcmpt%3Aprimary. Retrieved November 19, 2012.

38. Matthew Leibowitz, "The Book of Mormon: Real Religious
(Musical?) Discourse," *The Wesleyan Argus*, October 17, 2011, http://
wesleyanargus.com/2011/10/17/the-book-of-mormon-a-step-towards-
real-religious-discourse/. Retrieved November 28, 2011. Somewhat
ironically, it is Jon Stewart's remarks about the play that have been featured on television commercials for *The Book of Mormon*, where he is
quoted saying the show is so good, "it makes me angry."

39. "The Ram Report," Hightstown High School, 1994, https://
www.youtube.com/results?search_query=jon+stewart+ram+report.
Retrieved June 15, 2012.

CHAPTER 2

1. Jon Stewart, quoted in Marlo Thomas, *Growing Up Laughing:
My Story and the Story of Funny* (New York: Harper Collins, 2010),
chapter 51, unpaginated.

2. Clark Collis, "Jon Stewart," *Entertainment Weekly*, December
11, 2009, p. 69.

3. Michiko Kakutani, "Is Jon Stewart the Most Trusted Man in
America?" *The New York Times*, August 17, 2008, p. AR1.

4. According to most sources, Stewart is somewhere between 5'6"
and 5'7" tall.

5. The May 2011 Nielson Ratings indicate that *The Daily Show
with John Stewart* had an average of 2.3 million viewers per night, over
a half-million more viewers, for example, than any prime-time program
on Fox News. (See "Jon Stewart's Ratings Are Now Higher Than All
of Fox News," June 4, 2011, http://www.politicususa.com/jon-stewart-
fox-ratings.html. Retrieved September 9, 2011.)

6. "Scarecrows in the Village," http://www.lawrencevillemain
street.com/events/scarecrows.htm. Retrieved March 9, 2011.

7. "Washington Crossing," Pennsylvania Historical and Museum
Commission, http://www.ushistory.org/washingtoncrossing/history/faqs
.htm. Retrieved March 1, 2011.

8. "A Brief History of Lawrence Township," http://www.law
rencetwp.com/history.html. Retrieved July 11, 2011.

9. Rob Tannenbaum, "How I Became a Man," *Details*, January 1999, http://jon.happyjoyfun.net/tran/1999/99_0100details.html. Retrieved March 19, 2011.

10. Maria Speidel, "Prince of Cool Air," *People*, April 4, 1994, pp. 99–100.

11. "Jon Stewart Intelligence Agency," http://www.jonstewart.net/bio/quotes.html. Retrieved January 9, 2009.

12. Stewart, quoted in Thomas.

13. Tad Friend, "Is It Funny Yet?" *The New Yorker*, February 11, 2002, http://jon.happyjoyfun.net/tran/2002/02_0211newyorker.html. Retrieved April 4, 2010.

14. "20 Questions: Jon Stewart," *Playboy*, March 1995, p. 124.

15. "Oprah Talks to Jon Stewart," p. 188.

16. Tannenbaum, "How I Became a Man."

17. Eric Fundin, "Jon Stewart," YouTube, June 6, 2007, http://www.youtube.com/watch?v=D4nT5FpWm9k. Retrieved September 1, 2011.

18. Sam Wood, "TV's Mrs. Noah, 86, of *Captain Noah and His Magical Ark*, dies," *Philadelphia Inquirer*, June 24, 2011, http://articles.philly.com/2011-06-24/news/29699450_1_puppeteer-captain-kangaroo-first-mate. Retrieved July 9, 2011.

19. Ed Condran, "Stand-Up Comedy Lifts Jon Stewart Out of His 'Daily Show' Seat," *The Morning Call*, Lehigh Valley's Newspaper, November 26, 1999, http://articles.mcall.com/1999-11-26/features/3274686_1_stewart-jokes-stand-up-jon-stewart. Retrieved February 14, 2012.

20. Ibid.

21. Jeremy Gillick and Nonna Gorilovskaya, "Meet Jonathan Stuart Leibowitz (aka) Jon Stewart: The Wildly Zeitgeisty *Daily Show* Host." *Moment: Independent Journalism from a Jewish Perspective*, November/December 2008, http://www.momentmag.com/Exclusive/2008/12/Jon Stewart.html. Retrieved July 2, 2010.

22. The Jewish Center at Princeton, New Jersey, http://www.thejewishcenter.org/about/egalitarianism.asp. Retrieved August 10, 2011.

23. Lauren F. Friedman, "Jon Stewart's Shout-Outs to the Tribe," *The Jewish Daily Forward*, September 30, 2010, http://blogs.forward.com/the-shmooze/131761/. Retrieved May 21, 2011.

24. *The Daily Show with Jon Stewart*, June 12, 2001.

25. Stewart, quoted in Thomas.

26. Biography Resource Center, Farmington Hills, Mich.: Gale, 2008, http://galenet.galegroup.com/servlet/BioRc. Retrieved September 2, 2009.

27. Prairie Miller, "Playing by Heart: Interview with Jon Stewart," Star Interviews, Rye, March 8, 1999, http://proquest.umi.com.ez.lib .jjay.cuny.edu/pqdlink?did=494615531&Fmt=3&clientid=31967&RQT= 309&VName=PQD. Retrieved February 19, 2011.

28. Chris Smith, "The Man Who Should Be Conan," *New York Magazine*, January 10, 1994, p. 38.

29. Allison Adato, "Anchor Astray," *George*, May 2000, p. 99.

30. Marshall Owens, "Jon Stewart Recalls Life as a Local Boy," *The Daily Princetonian*, March 23, 2000, http://dailyprincetonian.com/news/2000/03 /jon-stewart-recalls-life-as-a-local-boy/. Retrieved June 22, 2011.

31. "20 Questions: Jon Stewart."

32. "Jon Stewart Intelligence Agency."

33. Tannenbaum, "How I Became a Man."

34. Stewart, quoted in Thomas.

35. Randolph Portugal, "No Joke: Stewart's Dad Taught at College," *The Signal*, The College of New Jersey Student Newspaper, September 15, 2009, p. 2.

36. David Rensin, "Playboy Interview: Jon Stewart," *Playboy*, March 2000, p. 149.

37. Warren Kalbaker, "20 Questions: Jon Stewart," *Playboy*, March 1995, p. 124.

38. "Oprah Talks to Jon Stewart," p. 188.

39. "20 Questions: Jon Stewart," p. 125.

40. Marshall Owens, "Jon Stewart Recalls Life as a Local Boy," *The Daily Princetonian*, March 23, 2000, http://www.dailyprincetonian.com /2000/03/23/490/. Retrieved April 16, 2011.

41. David Rensin, "Playboy Interview: Jon Stewart," *Playboy*, March 2000, p. 64.

42. Ibid.

43. Owens, *The Daily Princetonian*.

44. Ibid.

45. Rich Tucker, Editor, *The Daily Princetonian*, March 9, 2000, http:// www.dailyprincetonian.com/2000/03/09/428/. Retrieved April 16, 2011.

46. Fred Schepisi, Director, *I.Q.* (Paramount), 1994.

47. Paul Harris, "The Observer Profile: Jon Stewart," *The Observer*, February 26, 2006, http:www.guardian.co.uk/media/2006/feb/26/broad casting.oscars2006. Retrieved October 2, 2010.

48. Interview with Jon Stewart, *Movie Talk*, July 1999, http://www .hollywood.com/movietalk/celebrities/jostewart/html/sound.html. Retrieved December 20, 2011.

49. *Chrysalis*, 1978 (Lawrence High School Yearbook).

50. Jen Ortiz, "Jon Stewart: The Strange and Fascinating Career Path of America's Most Influential Newsman," *Business Insider* (The Wire), http://www.businessinsider.com/jon-stewart-daily-show-fox-2011-6?op=1. Retrieved June 22, 2011.

51. Selma Litowitz died in 2005 from complications associated with Parkinson's disease. (See: Nicole Kukawski, "'Parkinsong' Concerts Honor Alumna," *TCNJ* Magazine, Summer 2006, p. 20.)

52. "The Parkinsong Story," Parkinsong: to Benefit Parkinson's Disease Research. http://www.parkinsong.com/Story/Story.htm. Retrieved December 9, 2013.

53. *ParkinSong 1: 38 Songs of Hope*, Megaforce, 2004.

54. Interview with Ted Koppel, *Upclose* (ABC), November 12, 2002.

55. Ibid.

56. "Frequently Asked Questions," Brody Jewish Center, Hillel, January 10, 2012, http://bjcatuva.hillel.org/home/aboutus/frequentlyasked questions.aspx. Retrieved March 16, 2012.

CHAPTER 3

1. Chaunce Hayden, "Jon Stewart: Steppin' Out," *The Jon Stewart Resource*, December 20, 1993, http://jon.happyjoyfun.net/tran/1990/93_1223steppingout.html. Retrieved November 11, 2009.

2. Stewart's Commencement Address, College of William and Mary, May 21, 2004, http://web.wm.edu/news/archive/index.php?id=3650. Retrieved June 20, 2010.

3. Comment by Stewart on surviving the millennium and other pressures. "Jon Stewart Intelligence Agency," http://www.jonstewart .net/bio/index.html. Retrieved March 10, 2008.

4. Al Albert, *Willliam and Mary Men's Soccer* (Charleston, SC: Arcadia Publishing, 2010), p. 6.

5. Brian Kilmeade, *The Games Do Count* (New York: It Books, 2005), p. 13.

6. "Jon Stewart Intelligence Agency."

7. "Who Is W&M," http://www.wm.edu/admissions/whoiswm /index.php. Retrieved May 31, 2013.

8. www.pikes.org. Retrieved June 3, 2012.

9. "About Pike," www.pikes.org/AboutPike.aspx?pid=3. Retrieved June 3, 2012.

10. Ibid.

11. The members of all chapters of Pi Kappa Alpha are known as "Pikes."

12. Jeremy Gillick and Nonna Gorilovskaya, "Meet Jon Stuart Leibowitz (aka) Jon Stewart, the Wildly Zeitgeisty *Daily Show* Host," *Moment—Independent Journalism from a Jewish Perspective*, November/ December, 2008, p. 29.

13. Phil Rosenthal, "Watch Out, Conan; Heeeeeeeere's Jon!" *San Diego Union-Tribune*, January 31, 1994, p. B2.

14. Stephen Colbert, University of Virginia 2013 commencement Speech, May 19, 2013, http://www.huffingtonpost.com/2013/05/18 /Stephen-colbert-university-of-virginia_n_3298839.html. Retrieved June 19, 2013.

15. Jennifer Gonzalez, "A Third of Students Transfer before Graduating, and Many Head toward Community Colleges," *The Chronicle of Higher Education*, February 28, 2012, http://chronicle.com/article/A-Third-of-Students-Transfer/130954/. Retrieved May 19, 2012.

16. William and Mary website: http://wm.edu/about/history /chronology/1618to1699/index.php. Retrieved November 1, 2012.

17. Stewart's Commencement Address.

18. Ibid.

19. According to the 2011 update of the Jewish Virtual Library, Jewish people make up approximately 1.2 percent of the total population. For the sake of comparison, Virginia's Muslim population is estimated to be around 2.4 percent of the total population, the Catholic population makes up approximately 14 percent, and White Evangelicals make up nearly 33 percent. (See http://www.beliefnet.com/Faiths/2004/11/State-By-State-Percentage-Of-White-Evangelicals-Catholics-And-Black-Protestants.aspx, www.islam101.com/history/population2_usa.html, and www.jewishvirtuallibrary.org/jsource/US-Israel/usjewpop.html)

20. "About Hillel," College of William and Mary website: http://wmpeople.wm.edu/site/page/hillel/abouthillel. Retrieved December 2, 2011.

21. Stewart's Commencement Address.

22. The College of William and Mary official website: http://www.wm.edu/about/index.php. Retrieved November 19, 2011.

23. According to Yale University alumnus Richard Moll, who first created the list of "Public Ivy League" colleges in the 1980s, there were at first eight Public Ivies. He has since revised the list to 10. In addition to the College of William and Mary, the other nine "public Ivy" colleges are Miami University of Ohio, University of California, University of Michigan, University of North Carolina at Chapel Hill, University of Texas at Austin, University of Vermont, University of Washington, University of Georgia, and University of Virginia. Others have, over the years, added colleges to this list, including Rutgers University, Ohio State University, the University of Colorado, and the University of Illinois. For more information on the Public Ivy League colleges, see for example, the website "YOUNIVERSITYTV," http://www.youniversitytv.com/news-general/5196-what-is-the-public-ivy-league-list.

24. The College of William and Mary official website: http://www.wm.edu. Retrieved October 19, 2012.

25. The William and Mary Alumni Association website, http://www.wmalumni/?page=notable_alumni. Retrieved May 2, 2012.

26. "John Stewart Intelligence Agency." http://www.jonstewart.net/bio/index.html. Retrieved March 10, 2008.

27. Maureen Dowd, "America's Anchors," October 31, 2006, http://www.Rollingstone.com/news/coverstory/jon_stewart_stephen_colbert_americas_anchors. Retrieved August 30, 2010.

28. Biography Resource Center, Farmington Hills, MI, Gale, 2008, http://galenet.galegroup.com/servlet/BioRc. Retrieved September 2, 2009.

29. "Jon Stewart Intelligence Agency."

30. Gillick and Gorilovskaya, "Meet Jon Stuart Leibowitz."

31. Quoted in Allison Adato, "Anchor Astray," *George*, May 2000, http://home.earthlink.net/~aldato/anchor.html. Retrieved March 29, 2011.

32. *The Daily Show with Jon Stewart*, February 4, 2010.

33. Among the edgy jokes the two exchanged, Weiner first introduced himself as "Richard Sweat." Stewart followed by saying that he'd

known Weiner for many years, had gone to the beach with him and, he added, "I could, let's face facts, destroy your political career." Weiner countered by asking, "You know the concept of mutual assured destruction, Jon?" Stewart answered, "You believe you have pictures of me . . ." to which Weiner responded, "I've got stuff." Ironically, it was Weiner who had pictures—inappropriate images of himself that he'd texted to various women over the years, the exposure of which led directly to his resignation.

34. *The Daily Show with Jon Stewart*, May 30, 2011.

35. Weiner first ran for New York City mayor in 2005.

36. "Jon Stewart Intelligence Agency."

37. Stephen Birmingham, *Our Crowd: The Great Jewish Families of New York (Modern Jewish History)* (New York: Syracuse University Press, 1996), p. 149.

38. Rob Tannenbaum, "How I Became a Man," Interview with Jon Stewart, *Details*, January 1999, http://www.jon.happyjoyfun.net/tran/1999/99_0100details.html. Retrieved March 28, 2011.

39. Gillick and Gorilovskaya, "Meet Jon Stuart Leibowitz."

40. Brian Kilmeade, "Jon Stewart: Soccer," *The Games Do Count: America's Best and Brightest on the Power of Sports* (New York: Regan Books, 2004), p. 12.

41. Gillick and Gorilovskaya, "Meet Jon Stuart Leibowitz."

42. Al Albert, *William and Mary Men's Soccer* (Mount Pleasant, SC: Arcadia Publishing, 2010), p. 55.

43. David Handelman, "The Cat in the Hats," *TV Guide* (large edition), December 11, 1999.

44. Jon Stewart's ('84) Commencement Address, May 20, 2004, http://web.wm.edu/news/archive/index.php?id=3650. Retrieved January 30, 2010.

45. Jon Stewart's Commencement Address.

46. "Not Always Famous: 5 Celebrities' Weirdest First Jobs," The Savvy Intern, April 2, 2013, http://www.youtern.com/thesavvyintern/index.php/2013/04/02/not-always-famous-5-celebrities-weird-first-jobs/. Retrieved August 22, 2013.

47. Interview with Ted Koppel, *Upclose* (ABC), November 12, 2002.

48. Ibid.

49. Jon Stewart's Commencement Address.

CHAPTER 4

1. *NPR Weekend* interview with Jon Stewart, WNYC, October 3, 1998.

2. Kalbacker, "20 Questions: Jon Stewart," pp. 108–109, 124–125.

3. Ibid.

4. Bill Brownstein, "Comic Stewart Sees Fearful Future," *The Montreal Gazette*, October 8, 1992, quoted at *The Jon Stewart Resource*: http://jon.happyjoyfun.net/tran/1990/92_1008gazette.html. Retrieved December 30, 2009.

5. Interview with Marlo Thomas. Marlo Thomas, "The Only Jew in the Neighborhood," *Growing Up Laughing: My Story* (New York: Hyperion, 2011), p. 369.

6. Quoted in Brooke Gladstone, *NPR Weekend*. "John Stewart," October 3, 1998.

7. *Paul Colby's The Bitter End*, http://www.bitterend.com/. Retrieved December 19, 2012.

8. Interview with Ted Koppel, *Up Close* (ABC News), November 12, 2002.

9. Thomas, *Growing Up Laughing*.

10. *Paul Colby's The Bitter End*.

11. Quoted in Barry Koltnow, "Jon Stewart Lives by His Sharp Wit," *Dallas Morning News*, July 9, 1999, p. B3.

12. Interview with Ted Koppel.

13. "The Treasures of MacDougal Street," *Untapped Cities*, November, 26, 2012, Http://untappedcities.com/2012/11/26/the-treasures-of-macdougal-street/. Retrieved July 10, 2013.

14. Lloyd Jack, "Not Easy Becoming a Comic Jon Stewart Has Climbed from Comedy Cellar to Comedy Central and, Now, a Hilton Headliner," Philly.com (Philadelphia Inquirer on line), http://articles.philly.com/1999-11-26/entertainment/25496487_1_jon-stewart-show-hilton-casino-resort-hbo-s-young-comedians. Retrieved January 29, 2000.

15. Interview with Ted Koppel.

16. Jack, "Not Easy Becoming a Comic Jon Stewart Has Climbed from Comedy Cellar to Comedy Central and, Now, a Hilton Headliner," Philly.com.

17. "About Carolines," http://www.carolines.com/about-us/. Retrieved February 19, 2013.

18. "We Want Answers!" Interview with Jon Stewart, *Maxim*, November 2000, p. 112.

19. Interestingly, "short attention span theater" is the term given by Jessica Helfand, author of *Screen: Essays on Graphic Design, New Media and Visual Culture* (Princeton, NY: Princeton Architectural Press, 2001) to the phenomenon of the younger generation's demand for faster delivery of information, entertainment, and communication on their various electronic devices.

20. "Molt," Jonathan K. Bendis and Steven Start, Producers.

21. "You Wrote It, You Watch It," *Clicker: The Internet Television Guide*, http://www.clicker.com/tv/you-wrote-it-you-watch-it/ http://www.clicker.com/tv/you-wrote-it-you-watch-it/. Retrieved July 30, 2011.

22. Bill Brownstein, "Comic Stewart Sees Fearful Future," *The Montreal Gazette*, October 8, 1992, quoted at *The Jon Stewart Resource*: http://jon.happyjoyfun.net/tran/1990/92_1008gazette.html. Retrieved December 30, 2009.

CHAPTER 5

1. *Philadelphia Inquirer* interview, April 22, 2007.

2. Interview with Ted Koppel, *Up Close* (ABC News), November 12, 2002.

3. Kalbacker, "20 Questions: Jon Stewart," pp. 108–109, 124–125.

4. *Mixed Nuts*, Nora Ephron, Dir., TriStar Pictures. http://www.imdb.com/title/tt0110538/. Retrieved December 20, 2010.

5. *Variety* Staff, Review of *Mixed Nuts*, December 31, 1993, http://variety.com/1993/film/reviews/mixed-nuts-1200435509/. Retrieved March 2, 2009.

6. Jon Stewart, "Oprah Talks to Jon Stewart," *The O Talks Collection*, http://www.oprah.com/omagazine/Oprah-interviews-Jon-Stewart/7. Retrieved January 6, 2013.

7. Ibid.

8. Ibid.

9. "WYNX," http://www.imdb.com/title/tt0660241/. Retrieved March 12, 2011.

CHAPTER 6

1. "John Stewart Intelligence Agency," http://www.jonstewart
.net/bio/index.html. Retrieved March 10, 2008.

2. *The First Wives Club*, Full Cast and Crew, http://www.imdb.com
/title/tt0116313/fullcredits#cast. Retrieved December 20, 2010.

3. "Kissing Cousins," http://www.imdb.com/title/tt0657272/. Retrieved March 12, 2011.

4. *News Radio*, "Twins," Director Tom Cherones, episode #3.18
(1997).

5. Jon Stewart, *Jon Stewart: Unleavened*, Busboy Productions,
HBO Downtown Productions, 1996. http://www.imdb.com/title/tt04
777021 Retrieved May 11, 2012.

CHAPTER 7

1. A. J. Jacobs, "Jonny on the Spot," *Entertainment Weekly*, January 8, 1999, p. 55.

2. *Playing by Heart*, William Carrol, Dir., Hyperion Pictures.
http://www.imdb.com/title/tt0145734/. Retrieved May 3, 2011

3. Rob Vaux, *Flipside Movie Emporium*, August 1, 2002, "Playing
by Heart," Rotten Tomatoes, http://www.rottentomatoes.com/m/play
ing_by_heart/. Retrieved October 19, 2012.

4. G. Allen Johnson, "What a Cast! What a Waste!" *San Francisco
Chronicle*, January 22, 1999, http://www.sfgate.com/news/article/What-
a-cast-What-a-waste-3099164.php. Retrieved October 19, 2012.

5. *The Faculty*, Robert Rodriguez, Dir., Dimension Films. http://
www.imdb.com/title/tt0133751/. Retrieved March 24, 2011.

6. Dave Itzkoff interview with Jon Stewart, *Maxim*, November
2000, p. 116.

7. Rob Gonsalves, "The Faculty," *EFilmCritic.com*, January 13, 2007.
http://www.efilmcritic.com/review.php?movie=725&reviewer=416.
Retrieved May 1, 2012.

8. *Half Baked*, Full Cast and Crew, http://www.imdb.com/title/
tt0120693/fullcredits#cast. Retrieved March 22, 2011.

9. *Elmopalooza!* (Tom Trbovich, director). Children's Television
Workshop (CTW), 1998.

10. Terry Kelleher, "Picks and Pans: Elmopalooza!" *People*, February 16, 1998, http://www.people.com/people/archive/article/0,,201244 70,00.html. Retrieved May 9, 2011.

11. Tony Scott, "Review: Elmopalooza!" *Variety*, February 18, 1998, http://variety.com/1998/tv/reviews/elmopalooza-1200452885/. Retrieved May 9, 2011.

12. *Big Daddy*, http://www.imdb.com/title/tt0142342/. Retrieved March 30, 2011.

13. "Big Daddy Reviews at Metacritic.com," *Metacritic*, http://www.metacritic.com/movie/big-daddy. Retrieved April 22, 2011.

14. "Razzie Awards: Incinerating Cinematic Sins for Over Three Decades," http://www.razzies.com/forum/1999-razzie-nominees-and-winners_topic5534.html. Retrieved April 22, 2011.

15. "Razzie Awards," 2013. http://www.imdb.com/event/ev0000 558. Retrieved July 2, 2013. (The other two actors given Worst Actor in two consecutive years were Sylvester Stallone and Pauly Shore.)

16. Paul Harris, "The Oscar for Best Satirist Goes to . . ." *The Observer*, Sunday February 26, 2006, http://www.guardian.co.uk/media/2006/feb/26/broadcasting.oscars2006. Retrieved August 2, 2011.

17. *Wall Street*, http://www.imdb.com/title/tt0707115/. Retrieved March 30, 2011.

18. *Dr. Katz, Professional Therapist*—306, Episode #25, "Guess Who," Season 3, January 5, 1997.

19. *Dr. Katz, Professional Therapist*, Episode #6, "Guess Who," Season 3, http://www.imdb.com/title/tt0565068/. Retrieved February 24, 2011.

20. Interview with Ted Koppel, *Up Close* (ABC News), November 12, 2002.

21. Peter Keepnews, "Late-Night Hosts in Search of Their Niches," *New York Times*, October 3, 1999, http://www.nytimes.com/1999/10/03/arts/television-radio-late-night-hosts-in-search-of-their-niches.html?src=pm. Retrieved March 23, 2010.

CHAPTER 8

1. Interview with Marlo Thomas. Marlo Thomas, "The Only Jew in the Neighborhood," *Growing Up Laughing: My Story* (New York: Hyperion, 2010), p. 369.

2. Thomas Goetz, "Reinventing Television: The Wired Interview with Jon Stewart," *Wired,* September 2005, pp. 102–5.

3. Jon Stewart's guest appearance on *The Daily Show,* September 12, 1996.

4. Ibid.

5. Ibid.

6. *The Daily Show,* December 16, 1998.

7. Ibid.

8. Randy Newman, "Short People," *Little Criminals,* Warner Bros, 1977.

9. "The 50 Most Beautiful People in the World," *People,* May 10, 1999.

10. "We Want Answers!" Interview with Jon Stewart, *Maxim,* November 2000, p. 112.

11. Quoted in Bruce Fretts, "In Jon We Trust," *Entertainment Weekly,* October 31, 2003, p. 35.

12. Sharilyn Johnson, "Jon Stewart Almost Quit Daily Show Over 'Asshole' Coworkers," *Third Beat Magazine,* December 10, 2012, http://www.third-beat.com/2012/12/10/jon-stewart-almost-quit-daily-show-asshole-coworkers-and-secrets-revealed-conversation-stephen-colbert/#sthash.s2pIXeE0.dpuf. Retrieved August 24, 2012.

13. Jon Stewart, College of William and Mary Commencement Address, May 20, 2004.

14. Jason Holt, "Introduction: Great Book or the *Greatest* Book?" in *The Daily Show and Philosophy: Moments of Zen in the Art of Fake News,* ed. Jason Holt, The Blackwell Philosophy and Popculture Series, William Irwin, Series Editor (Malden, MA: Blackwell, 2007), p. 1.

15. See Appendix for an annotated list of *The Daily Show's* "correspondents."

16. "Stewart and Colbert Viewers are 'Deep' Study Suggests," *Meet-Press,* January 8, 2012, http://meetpress.ca/2012/01/08/daily-show-viewers/. Retrieved March 9, 2012.

17. "Oprah Talks to Jon Stewart," *O, The Oprah Magazine,* June 2005, http://www.oprah.com/omagazine/Oprah-Interviews-Jon-Stewart/6. Retrieved July 19, 2012.

18. *Committed,* http://www.imdb.com/title/tt0144142/. Retrieved May 1, 2011.

19. *Jay and Silent Bob Strike Back,* http://www.imdb.com/title/tt02 61392/

20. Desson Thomson, "Jay and Silent Bob Strike Back (2001)," *Washington Post,* August 24, 2001, Rotten Tomatoes, http://www.rot tentomatoes.com/m/jay_and_silent_bob_strike_back?nopopup=true. Retrieved August 8, 2012.

21. Brian Kilmeade, "Jon Stewart: Soccer," *The Games Do Count: America's Best and Brightest on the Power of Sports* (New York: Regan Books, 2004), p. 12.

22. In 2012 alone, Jon read all or parts of over 45 books for his discussions with various authors.

23. Quoted in Fretts, "In Jon We Trust," p. 33.

24. "Rally to Restore Sanity and/or Fear," post-rally press conference, August 30, 2010.

25. "We Want Answers!"

26. *The Daily Show with Jon Stewart,* October 28, 2002.

27. *The Daily Show with Jon Stewart,* September 15, 2003.

28. Brad Frazier, "Contingency, Irony, and 'This Week in God,'" *The Daily Show and Philosophy: Moments of Zen in the Art of Fake News,* ed. Jason Holt, The Blackwell Philosophy and Popculture Series, William Irwin, Series Editor (Malden, MA: Blackwell, 2007), p. 188.

29. "An Hour-Long Conversation with Jon Stewart," *Charlie Rose* (WNET), August 15, 2001.

30. Ibid.

31. Robert Koehler, "Peabody Board Casts Wide Net for Excellence," *Variety,* May 21, 2011. http://variety.com/2011/film/news/ peabody-board-casts-wide-net-for-excellence-1118037186/. Retrieved September 2, 2012.

CHAPTER 9

1. Quoted in Marc Peyser, "Red, White & Funny," *Newsweek,* December 29, 2003/January 5, 2004, pp. 70–77.

2. "An Hour-Long Conversation with Jon Stewart," *Charlie Rose,* August 15, 2001.

3. Ibid.

4. Ibid.

5. "America's Best," *Time*, July 10, 2001.

6. *The Daily Show with Jon Stewart*, September 20, 2001.

7. "Jon Stewart," *The Biography Channel*, A & E Television, 2007.

8. Josh Weiner, "Jon Stewart of *the Daily Show* Speaks at the ARCO Forum," Harvard University Institute of Politics, Winter 2003, p. 6.

9. *The Daily Show with Jon Stewart*, April 5, 2001.

10. Weiner, Harvard University Institute of Politics.

11. *The Daily Show with Jon Stewart*, March 3, 2004.

12. Tad Friend, "Is It Funny Yet?" *The New Yorker*, February 11, 2002. http://www.newyorker.com/archive/2002/02/11/020211fa_fact_friend. Retrieved June 30, 2011.

13. *Last Call with Carson Daly*, January 15, 2002.

14. *Live with Regis and Kelly*, February 1, 2002.

15. *The Rosie O'Donnell Show*, February 21, 2002.

16. *The Tonight Show with Jay Leno*, February 26, 2002.

17. *Dennis Miller Live*, March 1, 2002.

18. *Larry King Live*, March 22, 2002.

19. *The Late Show with David Letterman*, March 19, 2002.

20. *The 44th Annual Grammy Awards*, February 27, 2002.

21. May 10, 2002.

22. *Inside Politics*, CNN, May 3, 2002.

23. Tom Roston, "Oscar: The Toughest Room," *Premiere*, March 2006, p. 81.

24. Thomas Goetz, "Reinventing Television: The Wired Interview with Jon Stewart," *Wired*, September 2005, pp. 102–105.

25. *The Daily Show with Jon Stewart*, October 7, 2003.

26. GQ "Men of the Year" Ceremony, New York City, October 21, 2003.

27. Fretts, "In Jon We Trust," pp. 30–37.

28. Ibid.

29. Allison Adato, "Anchor Astray," *George*, May 2000, p. 99.

30. The Daily Show, *Indecision 2002*, November 5, 2002.

31. Fretts, "In Jon We Trust."

32. Ibid.

33. Ibid.

34. "Jon Stewart's ('84) Commencement Address," The College of William and Mary, 2004, http://web.wm.edu/news/archive/index.php?id=3650. Retrieved May 30, 2011.

35. Jon Stewart, Ben Karlin, and David Javerbaum, *America (The Book): A Citizen's Guide to Democracy Inaction* (New York: Warner Books, 2004).

36. Ibid., p. xi.

37. Matt, "Review of *America The Book A Citizen's Guide to Democracy Inaction*," Ruthless Reviews, http://www.ruthlessreviews.com/2063/america-the-book-a-citizen-s-guide-to-democracy-inaction/ Retrieved August 1, 2013.

38. Bruce Fretts, "All the News That's Fit to Rib," *TV Guide*, October 17, 2004, pp. 28–31.

39. Marc Peyser, "Who's Next 2004: Red, White & Funny," *Newsweek*, January 5, 2004, p. 71.

CHAPTER 10

1. Kalbacker, "20 Questions: Jon Stewart," pp. 108–109, 124–125.

2. Quoted in Tom Roston, "The Toughest Room," *Premiere*, March 2006, pp. 80–81.

3. Ibid.

4. Quoted in an appearance on "Jon Stewart," *The Biography Channel*, A & E Television, 2007.

5. *The Daily Show with Jon Stewart*, August 20, 2003.

6. Robert Love, "Before Jon Stewart," *Columbia Journalism Review*, March/April 2007, pp. 1–9.

7. Jason Holt (ed.), *The Daily Show and Philosophy: Moments of Zen in the Art of Fake News*, The Blackwell Philosophy and Popculture Series, William Irwin, Series Editor (Malden, MA: Blackwell, 2007).

8. Gerald J. Erion, Medaille College.

9. Roben Torosyan, Fairfield University.

10. Judith Barad, Indiana State University.

11. Liam P. Dempsey, "The Daily Show's Expose of Political Rhetoric," *The Daily Show and Philosophy: Moments of Zen in the Art of Fake News*, ed. Jason Holt The Blackwell Philosophy and Popculture Series, William Irwin, Series Editor (Malden, MA: Blackwell 2007), p. 121.

12. Maureen Dowd, "America's Anchors," *Rolling Stone* interview with Jon Stewart and Stephen Colbert, October 2006, http://www.roll ingstone.com/news/coverstory/jon_stewart_stephen_colbert_ameri cas_anchors. Retrieved November 9, 2011.

13. "Jon Stewart," *Entertainment Weekly*, December 11, 2009, p. 69. In the article, Stewart is referred to as "America's most trusted news-caster"; later, on the same page, Stewart refers to himself as "the most annoying man on television."

14. Eric Bates, "Jon Stewart: The Rolling Stone Interview," *Rolling Stone*, September 29, 2011, pp. 44–52.

15. Stephen Battaglio, "They've Got Issues," *TV Guide*, October 17–23, p. 33.

16. Fretts, "All the News That's Fit to Rib," p. 31.

17. See for example: Theodore Hamm. *The New Blue Media: How Michael Moore, MoveOn.org, Jon Stewart and Company Are Transform-ing Progressive Politics* (New York: The New Press, 2008).

18. James Poniewozik, "Can These Guys Be Serious?" *Time*, Novem-ber 1, 2010, p. 92.

19. Ibid.

20. Bates, "Jon Stewart: The Rolling Stone Interview."

21. Interview with Bill Moyers, *NOW* (PBS), July 11, 2003, http://www.pbs.org/now/printable/transcript_stewart_print.html.   Retrieved August 1, 2012.

22. *The Daily Show with Jon Stewart*, May 28, 2008.

23. More information at http://comets-asteroids.findthedata.org/q /119951/1102/When-was-the-comet-or-asteroid-116939-Jonstewart-2004-GG39-Jonstewart-first-and-last-observed

24. Appearance on *The Biography Channel.*

25. Review on BN.com (Barnes&Noble), http://www.barnesand noble.com/w/daily-show-with-jon-stewart-presents-earth-jon-stewart/ 1020696004?ean=9780446579223. Retrieved March 2, 2013.

26. Steve Weinberg, "Earth (The Book)" Review, *The Christian Sci-ence Monitor*, September 24, 2010, http://www.csmonitor.com/Books/ Book-Reviews/2010/0924/Earth-The-Book. Retrieved February 17, 2013.

27. Quoted in Lucy Madison, "White House Lauds Jon Stewart for Pushing Passage of 9/11 Health Bill," CBS News.com, December 21,

2010, http://www.cbsnews.com/8301-503544_162-20026333-503544 .html. Retrieved September 3, 2012.

28. Interview with Ted Koppel, *Up Close* (ABC News), November 12, 2002.

29. James Crugnale, "Howard Kurtz on Jon Stewart: Is There Another Program That Has Had More Impact on Politics?" *Media-ite*, December 11, 2011, http://www.mediaite.com/tv/howard-kurtz-and-panel-question-whether-jon-stewart-is-changing-the-political-land scape/. Retrieved December 14, 2011.

30. Jon Stewart's made-up term for the various 24-hour news media, particularly CNN.

31. "Jon Stewart: Rally to Restore Sanity and/or Fear," August 30, 2010.

32. Ibid.

33. All descriptions of events, people, and artifacts from the rally are from firsthand descriptions and photographs by the author's daughter and friends.

CHAPTER 11

1. Jeremy Gillick and Nonna Gorilovskaya, "Meet Jon Stuart Leibowitz (aka) Jon Stewart, the Wildly Zeitgeisty Daily Show Host," *Moment—Independent Journalism from a Jewish Perspective*, November/ December 2008, p. 30.

2. *The Daily Show with Jon Stewart*, September 9, 2009.

3. November 7, 2002, quoted at http://www.imdb.com/name/ nm0829537/bio. Retrieved August 30, 2011.

4. Quoted in Michael Paulson, "How Jewish Is Jon Stewart?" Articles of Faith: Religion News and Ideas from Boston and Beyond, November 28, 2008, http://www.boston.com/news/local/articles_of_ faith/2008/11/how_jewish_is_j.html. Retrieved August 30, 2011.

5. William Novak and Moshe Waldoks, *The Big Book of Jewish Humor—25th Anniversary* (New York: HarperCollins, 2006).

6. Kalbacker, "20 Questions: Jon Stewart," pp. 108–109, 124–125.

7. *The Daily Show with Jon Stewart*, October 6, 2003.

8. *The Daily Show with Jon Stewart*, March 14, 2002.

9. Jacob Silverman, "Culture Kvetch: Jon Stewart's Happily Ignorant Jew Routine Is Getting Stale," *Tablet Magazine*, May 30, 2012, http://

www.jewcy.com/arts-and-culture/culture-kvetch-jon-stewarts-happily-ignorant-jew-routine-is-getting-stale. Retrieved August 9, 2012.

10. Jon Stewart, *Jon Stewart: Unleavened*, Busboy Productions, HBO Downtown Productions, 1996, http://www.imdb.com/title/tt04777021. Retrieved May 11, 2012.

11. Ilan Chaim, "Jon Stewart's Jewish Problem," *The Philadelphia Jewish Voice*, October 12, 2010, http://blog.pjvoice.com/diary/115/jon-stewarts-jewish-problem. Retrieved December 1, 2012.

12. *Savage Nation*, radio program, September 8, 2010.

13. *The Daily Show with Jon Stewart*, August 25, 2010.

14. *The Daily Show with Jon Stewart*, December 8, 2011.

15. Deborah Sontag, "Orthodox Confront U.S. Reform Rabbis at Western Wall," *New York Times*, February 2, 1999, http://www.nytimes.com/1999/02/02/world/orthodox-confront-us-reform-rabbis-at-western-wall.html, Retrieved May 30, 2012.

16. *The Daily Show with Jon Stewart*, February 3, 1999.

17. *The Daily Show with Jon Stewart*, December 8, 2011.

18. David D. Kirkpatrick, "For Evangelicals, Supporting Israel Is 'God's Foreign Policy,'" *The New York Times*, November 14, 2006, http://www.nytimes.com/2006/11/14/washington/14israel.html?pagewanted=all&_r=0. Retrieved July 9, 2009.

19. *The Daily Show with Jon Stewart*, January 13, 2010.

20. Andrew Breitbart wrote that Stewart is "as fearful of an opposing voice as he is his own last name." Breitbart's implication was that the Jewishness of Stewart's real last name, Leibowitz, was a source of discomfort for Jon. (See Donald Lambro, "Breitbart: Jon Stewart & Kumar Go to D.C.," *The Washington Times*, April 13, 2009, http://www.washingtontimes.com/news/2009/apr/13/breitbart-jon-stewart-and-kumar-go-to-white-house/?page=2. Retrieved November 2, 2012.)

21. Danielle Berrin, "Jon Stewart's Version of Judaism," JewishJournal.com, October 15, 2010, http://www.jewishjournal.com/hollywoodjew/item/jon_stewarts_version_of_judaism_20101015. Retrieved December 11, 2011.

22. Danielle Berrin, "Jon Stewart's Version of Judaism," Hollywood Jew: A Blog by Danielle Berrin, October 15, 2010, http://www.jewishjournal.com/hollywoodjew/item/jon_stewarts_version_of_judaism_20101015/. Retrieved January 3, 2012.

23. Saul Austerlitz, "Jon Stewart: Not Your Ordinary Jewish Funny Man (Okay Maybe He Is)," MyJewishLearning.com (undated), http://www.myjewishlearning.com/culture/2/Film/television/television-2000s/Jon_Stewart.shtml. Retrieved December 31, 2011.

24. *The Daily Show with Jon Stewart*, January 9, 2013.

25. *The Daily Show with Jon Stewart*, April 1, 2009.

26. *The Daily show with Jon Stewart*, September 23, 2010.

27. Jon Stewart et al., *Earth (The Book): A Visitor's Guide to the Human Race* (New York: Grand Central Publishing, 2010), p. 162.

28. Ibid., 170.

29. Austerlitz, "Jon Stewart: Not Your Ordinary Jewish Funny Man."

30. Jon Stewart, *Naked Pictures of Famous People* (New York: Perennial, 1998), pp. 41, 47.

31. Mark Oppenheimer, "Jon Stewart: Religion Teacher Extraordinaire," *Religion and Politics*, May 1, 2012, http://religionandpolitics.org/2012/05/01/jon-stewart-religion-teacher-extraordinaire/. Retrieved November 12, 2012.

32. *The Daily Show with Jon Stewart*, November 26, 2012.

33. Roger Waters, Facebook speech on his role on the Fourth Russell Tribunal on Palestine, October 2012, http://www.russelltribunalonpalestine.com/en/sessions/future-sessions/videos/roger-waters-tribunal-epilogue. Retrieved January 12, 2013.

CHAPTER 12

1. "Oprah Talks to Jon Stewart," pp. 186–189, 238–242.

2. *The Daily Show with Jon Stewart*, November 10, 2011.

3. *The Daily Show with Jon Stewart*, May 6, 2013.

4. Quoted in Roben Torosyan, "Public Discourse and the Stewart Model of Critical Thinking," in *The Daily Show and Philosophy: Moments of Zen in the Art of Fake News*, ed. Jason Holt, The Blackwell Philosophy and Popculture Series, William Irwin, Series Editor (Malden, MA: Blackwell, 2007), p. 118.

5. *The Daily Show with Jon Stewart*, November 6, 2012.

6. *The Daily Show with Jon Stewart*, October 17, 2012.

7. "Jon Stewart," *The Biography Channel*, A & E Television, 2007.

8. *The Daily Show with Jon Stewart*, September 18, 2007.

9. "Oprah Talks to Jon Stewart."

APPENDIX

1. Maureen Dowd, "America's Anchors," *Rolling Stone*, October 31, 2006, http://www.rollingstone.com/news/coverstory/jon_stewart_stephen_colbert_americas_anchors. Retrieved June 6, 2012.

2. Michiko Kakutani, "Is Jon Stewart the Most Trusted Man in America?" *New York Times*, August 15, 2008, http://www.nytimes.com/2008/08/17/arts/17iht-17kaku.15357388.html?pagewanted=all&_r=0. Retrieved January 17, 2012.

3. "Jon Stewart," *Entertainment Weekly*, December 11, 2009, p. 70.

4. During his interview of Mrs. Cheney, Stewart asked her about her position on gay marriage as pertaining to her daughter, who is gay. Cheney became visibly irate.

5. *The Daily Show with Jon Stewart*, October 10, 2007.

6. *The Daily Show with Jon Stewart*, March 12, 2009.

7. For a comprehensive list of Jon's guests, e-mail the author: MichaelBlitz@verizon.net.

FURTHER READING

Albert, Al. *William and Mary Men's Soccer*. Chicago, IL: Arcadia Publishing, 2010.

Allen, A. J. *Jon & Me: The Extraordinary True Story of One Man's Obsession to Become a Guest on* The Daily Show. Lexington, KY: CreateSpace Independent Publishing Platform, 2012.

Colbert, Stephen. *I Am America (And So Can You!)*. New York: Hachette Book Group, 2007.

Getlen, Larry, Ed. *The Complete Idiot's Guide to Jokes*. New York: Alpha Books, 2006.

Hamm, Theodore. *The New Blue Media: How Michael Moore, MoveOn. org, Jon Stewart and Company are Transforming Progressive Politics*. New York: The New Press, 2008.

Holt, Jason. *The Daily Show and Philosophy*. Malden, MA: Blackwell, 2007.

Schiller, Allen (ed.). *Stephen Colbert and Philosophy: I Am Philosophy (And So Can You!)*. Vol. 41 in series Popular Culture and Philosophy (George A. Reisch, series editor). Peru, IL: Open Court Publishing Company, 2009.

Stewart, Jon. *America (The Book): A Citizen's Guide to Democracy Inaction*. New York: Warner Books, 2004.

Stewart, Jon, et al. *Earth (The Book): A Visitor's Guide to the Human Race*. New York: Hachette, 2010.

Stewart, Jon. *Naked Pictures of Famous People*. New York: Harper Collins, 1998.

INDEX

Academy Awards, 121–23, 128
The Adjustment Bureau, 147–48
The Adventures of Tom Thumb and Thumbelina, 110
A&E, 44–45
Affleck, Ben, 92
Ahmed, Akbar, 167
Albert, Al, 27, 32
Albright, Madeleine, 167
Alexander, Matthew, 167
Allawi, Alli, 167
Allen, Fred, 41
Allen, Steve, 50
Allen, Woody, 40–41
America (The Book) (Stewart, Jon), 115–16
American Comedy Awards USA, 103
American Idol, 122
Anderson, Gillian, 70–71

Annan, Kofi, 167
Arbabi, Saman, 169
Ashcroft, John, 167
Austerlitz, Saul, 141

Babbin, Jed, 167
Bachman, Michelle, 149
BAFTA. *See* British Academy of Film and Television Arts Awards
Bahari, Maziar, 152
Baker, James, 167
Barkley, Charles, 16
Bar Mitzvah, 17
Barnes, Melody, 6–7, 167
Bartlett, Dan, 167
Baumgartner, Jody, xv
Bayh, Evan, 161, 162
Beah, Ishmael, 167
Beck, Glenn, 99, 132, 150

Begala, Paul, 117–19
Behar, Joy, 44, 165
"Behind the Veil: Minarets of
    Menace," 152
Belzer, Richard, 44, 75, 136, 165
Bernstein, Josh, 167
Berrin, Danielle, 140, 141
Beyer, Lisa, 167
Bezos, Jeff, 167
Biden, Joe, 160
Biels, Jennifer, 59, 61
Big Daddy, 76–77
The Bitter End coffeehouse,
    38–41
Blackwell, Ken, 167
Blackwell Philosophy and
    Popculture Series, 125
Blagojevich, Rod, 162
Blair, Tony, 141
Bloomberg, Michael, 167
Bolton, John R., 167
Bond, Kit, 161
Booker, Cory, 167
The Brady Bunch, 18
British Academy of Film and
    Television Arts (BAFTA)
    Awards, 128
Bruce, Lenny, 30, 37, 39
Burt, Richard, 168
Busboy Productions, 59, 64
Bush, George W., 101, 108

Caesar's Palace, 45
Cain, Herman, 148–49
Caldwell, William B., 163
Cantor, Eric, 161

Captain Noah, 16–17
Carell, Steve, 88
Carlin, George, 92
Carlson, Tucker, 117–19
Caroline's Comedy Hour, 44–45
Carson, Johnny, 50
Carter, Jimmy, 114
Carter, Rosalynn, 168
CBS Broadcasting, Inc.: The
    Late, Late Show with Tom
    Snyder, 67–68, 69; Late Show
    with David Letterman, 51
Celebrity Death Match, 124–25
Chanukah, 144
Chappelle, Dave, 73
Cheney, Lynn, 159
Christie, Chris, 162
Chu, Steven, 168
Clarke, Richard A., 168
Clemons, Clarence, 168
Clinton, Bill, 101, 114, 123
Clinton, Hillary, 127
Clooney, George, 122
Clyburn, James, 161
Colbert, Stephen, 88; election
    results and, 128; Giuliani and,
    108–9; "The Rally to Restore
    Sanity and/or Fear" and, 133;
    UVA valedictory address
    by, 28
Coll, Steve, 164
College of New Jersey (TCNJ), 5
College years, 25–35
Comedian guest appearances,
    165–67
Comedy Cellar, 42–44

Comedy Central. See *The Daily Show*; *Short Attention Span Theater*

Committed, 89–91

Congress persons guest appearances, 161–62

Cornwallis, Charles, 14

Corzine, John, 162

Coulter, Ann, 150

Cramer, Jim, 160

Cross, David, 44, 165

Crossfire, 117–19

Crossword proposal, 89

Crystal, Billy, 122

The Daily Show: "Behind the Veil: Minarets of Menace" segment on, 152; comedians appearing on, 165–67; Congress members appearing on, 161–62; format, 96–97; governors appearing on, 162–63; *Indecision 2000: Election Night-Choose or Lose*, 100–102; *Indecision 2002: Election Night*, 109; *Indecision 2004: Prelude to a Recount*, 114; *Indecision 2008: Election Night—America's Choice*, 127; *Indecision 2012: Mercy Rule Edition*, 148; influence of, xv; Kilborn's tenure on, 70; "The Matzorian Candidate" segment on, 139; "Mess O'Potamia" segment on, 114; military appearing on, 163; muppets appearing on, 164; New York Mets appearing on, 164; Nobel Laureates appearing on, 164; opening segment of, 88–89; other notable guests appearing on, 167–70; premise of, 89; president and vice president guests appearing on, 160–61; prime ministers and kings appearing on, 164; Pulitzer Prize–winning authors appearing on, 164–65; reconfiguration of, 82–83, 88; September 20, 2001, 105–7; Supreme Court justices appearing on, 162; trust and, 99–100; viewer numbers, 157–58. *See also specific topic*

Damon, Matt, 92, 147–48

Darling, Ron, 164

Daschle, Tom, 161

David, Larry, 165

Davis, Tamara, 73

Dean, Howard, 162

Death to Smoochy, 110–11

DeGeneres, Ellen, 124

Dempsey, Liam P., 125

DeVito, Danny, 110

Dick, Andy, 63

Dingell, John, 161

Dominick, Pete, 146

Doogal, 123–24

Dowd, Maureen, xi

Drescher, Fran, 61–62

Dr. Katz, Professional Therapist, 79–82

Dugan, Dennis, 76

Duncan, Arne, 7

Earth: (The Book) (Stewart, Jon), xiv, 129, 143
Easton, Sheena, 45
Edwards, John, 98–99, 113
Election results, 128. See also *Indecision*
Elmopalooza!, 74–76
Emmy Awards, 104, 110, 112, 113, 114, 125, 136

The Faculty, 71–73, 87
Fallon, Jimmy, 124
Feller, Howard, 52
Ferrell, Will, 92, 93
Fey, Tina, 124
Film career, 70–78
The First Wives Club, 61
Flood, Mike, 30
Fox, Michael J., 78–79
Frank, Barney, 161
Frank, Debra, 22
Fundin, Eric, 16
Furlong, Edward, 71–73, 87

Garlin, Jeff, 165
Gbowee, Leymah, 164
Gervais, Ricky, 165
Gibbs, Robert, 131
Gillibrand, Kirsten, 161
Gingrich, Newt, 149, 151
Giuliani, Rudy, 108–9
Goldberg, Whoopee, 122, 124
Goodall, Jane, 168
Goodwin, Doris Kearns, 164
Goolsbee, Austan, 168
Gore, Al, 101

Governor guest appearances, 162–63
Grammy Awards, 107, 110
Grant, Hugh, 158
Greenberg, Hank, 142
Greenspan, Alan, 155–56, 168
Grundfest, Bill, 42

Hagee, John, 140
Hagel, Chuck, 161
Halevy, Efraim, 168
Half Baked, 73–74
Hall, Arsenio, 51
Hand, Edward, 14–15
Hannity, Sean, 150
Hartman, Phil, 63
Helms, Ed, 88
Henson, Jim, 16
Hill, Anita, 168
Hirsch, Caroline, 44
Hoover, Herbert, 2
Hosseini, Kambiz, 169
Huckabee, Mike, 162
Huffington, Arianna, 112
Huntsman, John, 149

Ibrahim, Gigi, 169
Indecision 2000: Election Night— Choose or Lose, 100–102
Indecision 2002: Election Night, 109
Indecision 2004: Prelude to a Recount, 114
Indecision 2008: Election Night— America's Choice, 127
Indecision 2012: Mercy Rule Edition, 148
Isaacson, Walter, 112

Jackson, Lisa P., 169
Jay and Silent Bob Strike Back,
  92–93
Jefferson, Thomas, 29
Jennings, Peter, 112, 113
Jon. *See* Stewart, Jon
Jones, Jason, 152
The Jon Stewart Show,
  52–54
Jon Stewart: Unleavened, 59,
  64–66, 138
Judaism, Jon and, 135–46

Kaine, Tim, 161
Kaling, Mindy, 141
Kamkwamba, William, 169
Karlin, Ben, 35, 115
Katz, Jonathan, 79
Kaufman, Ellen Jin R., 8
Keaton, Diane, 61
Kelly, Mark, 169
Kerry, John, 115
Kid Rock, 133
Kilborn, Craig: *The Daily Show*
  and, 70; interviews of Jon,
  85–87; *The Late, Late Show
  with Tom Snyder* and, 69;
  resume of, 68
Kimmel, Jimmy, 93, 94, 95
King, Larry, xiv
King, Martin Luther, 106–7
King guest appearances,
  164
Klein, Robert, 166
Koppel, Ted, 26, 34, 51, 131
Krakauer, John, 164
Kurtz, Howard, 131

The Larry Sanders Show, 68–69
Laskin, Fannie, 2
Laskin, Marian, 2
Laskin, Nathan, 1, 2
*The Late, Late Show with Tom
  Snyder*, 67–68, 69
Late Night with David Letterman,
  50–51
Late shows formulas, 93–96
Late Show with David Letterman,
  51
Lawrence High School, 21–23
Lawrenceville, New Jersey,
  14–15
Leary, Denis, 52
Leibowitz, Daniel, 5, 10–11
Leibowitz, Donald: background
  about, 3–6; careers of, 4–5;
  death of, 6; education of, 3–4;
  Jon on, 19; psychiatry and, xii;
  religion and, 3; tension with,
  xiii, 6
Leibowitz, Karen, 5
Leibowitz, Larry, 79; background
  about, 8–10; birth of, 4; firing
  of Jon by, 20
Leibowitz, Marian, 38; back-
  ground about, 6–8
Leibowitz, Matthew, 5, 10
Leibowitzs (Jon's grandfathers), 3
Leno, Jay: audience size and, 157;
  Celebrity Deathmatch and, 125;
  show format and, 94, 95; as
  Tonight Show guest host, 50
Letterman, David, 122; audi-
  ence size and, 157; *Celebrity
  Deathmatch* and, 125; *Late*

Night with David Letterman,
50–51; *Late Show with David
Letterman*, 51; show formats
and, 94–95; Snyder and,
67–68; as *Tonight Show* guest
host, 49–50
Lewis, Richard, 166
Limbaugh, Rush, 99
Litowitz, Selma, 22
Locke, Gary, 169

MacMullan, Terrance, xiv
Maddow, Rachel, 97
Madison, James, 30
Mad Money with Jim Cramer,
160
Maher, Bill, 125
Mara, Rooney, 95
Mariano, Connie, 163
Martin, Steve, 54, 122
Matthews, Chris, 99
"The Matzorian Candidate," 139
Mays, Willie, 164
McCain, John, 127
McChrystal, Stanley, 163
McShane, Tracey. *See* Stewart,
Tracey
Merbreier, Carter. *See* Captain
Noah
Merbreier, Patricia, 16
Mercer, Hugh, 20–21
Mercer County Community
College, 18
Mercer Oak, 20–21
"Mess O'Potamia," 114
Meyers, Mike, 166
Military guest appearances, 163

Miramax Films, 55
Mixed Nuts, 54–55
Moment of Zen, 153
Morris, Jonathan S., xv
Moyers, Bill, 112
MTV. *See* Music Television
Muppets, 164
Musharaf, Pervez, 164
Music Television (MTV): *The
Jon Stewart Show*, 52–54; *MTV
Music Awards*, 53; *You Wrote
It, You Watch It*, 46–47
Myers, Richard B., 163

Nagin, Ray, 169
Naked Pictures of Famous People
(Stewart, Jon), 144
The Nanny, 57, 61–63
National Broadcasting Company,
50–51
National Rifle Association
(NRA), 149–50
Navratilova, Martina, 16
NBC. *See* National Broadcasting
Company
Nealon, Kevin, 166
"The New Group," 46
Newman, Randy, 87
Newsradio, 57, 63–64
New York Mets, 164
Nobel Laureate guest appear-
ances, 164
Norquist, Grover G., 169
Norton, Edward, 110, 111
NOW with Bill Moyers, 112
NRA. *See* National Rifle
Association

Obama, Barack, 127, 128; debates and, 151–52; interview with, 129–31, 151–52; Sukkot and, 142
Obama, Michelle, 152
O'Brien, Conan, 54; *Celebrity Deathmatch* and, 125; *Late Show* and, 51; show formats and, 94, 95
O'Connor, Sandra Day, 162
Office Party, 91
Oliver, John, 133, 143
O'Reilly, Bill, 97, 99, 150
Oswalt, Patton, 29

Pan-American Maccabi Games, 32–33
Park, Adam, 61
Parker, Trey, 10
Park 51 project, 138–39
Paul, Ron, 149
Pawlenty, Tim, 163
Peabody Award, 102, 114
Pelosi, Nancy, 149
People magazine, 88
Perdue, Frank, 16
Perry, Rick, 149–50
Petry, Leroy, 163
Philbin, Regis, 78
Phillips, Richard, 163
Pi Kappa Alpha, 26–27
Playing by Heart, 70–71
Plumb, Eve, 18
President and vice president guest appearances, 160–61
Presley, Elvis, 16
Prime minister guest appearances, 164

Princeton Jewish Center, 17
Pulitzer Prize–winning author guest appearances, 164–65

Quaker Bridge Mall, 20
Quinn, Colin, 166

"Race to the Top" initiative, 7
"The Rally to Restore Sanity and/or Fear," 132–33
Ram Report, 11
Rasnic, John, 30
Reagan, Ronald, 30
Reid, Harry, 162
Remnick, David, 165
Republican Jewish Coalition Forum, 139–40
Resnic, John, 31–32
"Restoring Honor" rally, 132
Rice, Condoleezza, 169
Rice, Susan, 169
Rickles, Don, 166
Ridge, Tom, 163
Rivington, James, 2–3
Robbins, Tim, 21
Rock, Chris, 73, 121, 122
Rodriguez, Robert, 71, 73
Rogan, Joe, 63
Rogen, Seth, 142
Romney, Mitt, 151–52
Rosborough, Patty, 46
Rose, Charlie, 101, 103
Rosewater, 152

Saberi, Roxanna, 169
Al Sadat, Jehan, 169
Sanchez, Rick, 146

Sanders, Bernie, 162
Sandler, Adam, 73, 76, 143
Santa Fe Café, 18
Santorum, Rick, 149
Savage, Michael, 138, 139
Schwarzenegger, Arnold, 63, 112, 125
Scott, Tony, 75
Sebelius, Kathleen, 169
Seinfeld, Jerry, 43, 136, 166
September 20, 2001, 105–7
Serleaf, Ellen Johnson, 128
Shamsky, Art, 87, 121
Shandling, Gary, 68–69
Shatner, William, 52
Shelton, Hugh, 163
Short Attention Span Theater, 45–46
Shortz, Will, 89, 123
Schumer, Chuck, 131
Simmons, Gene, 17
Sirleaf, Ellen Johnson, 128
60 Minutes, 114
Snyder, Tom, 50, 67–68
Snyderman, Nancy, 127
Soccer. *See* The Tribe
Specter, Arlen, 163
Spin City, 57, 78–79
Springsteen, Bruce, 37, 154
Starr, Ringo, 170
The State, 46–47, 50–51, 52
Steinberg, David, 124
Stern, Howard, 52, 124
Stewart, Jon: after-school jobs and, 20; Bar Mitzvah of, 17; birth of, 4; The Bitter End coffeehouse and, 38–41; childhood of, 15–21; college years of, 25–35; Comedy Cellar and, 42–44; as contract administrator, 41–42; criticism of, 137–39; crossword proposal and, 89; evasiveness of, xii; film career of, 70–78; insulated personal life of, xiii; intellect of, 98; as intellectual, xiv; Judaism and, 135–46; Kilborn's first interviews, 85–87; Lawrence High School and, 21–23; on Leibowitz, Donald, 19; meeting Tracey, 56–57; move to New York of, 37–38; at *MTV Music Awards*, 53; news media and, 126; September 20, 2001, 105–7. *See also specific topic*
Stewart, Maggie, 121
Stewart, Nathan, 115
Stewart, Tracey, 26; birth of Nathan, 115; crossword proposal and, 89; meeting Jon, 56–57
Stone, Matt, 10
Stuyvesant High School, 3–4
Sukkot (Jewish holiday), 142–43
Sullenberger, Chesley "Sully," 170
Sununu, John, 163
Supreme Court Justice guest appearances, 162
Sykes, Wanda, 80, 167

TCNJ. *See* College of New Jersey
Television Critics Association Awards, 112, 114, 125
Tientsin, 1–2

Tonight Show with Johnny Carson,
    49–50
Tracey. *See* Stewart, Tracey
Trbovich, Tom, 74
The Tribe, 25–26, 31–33
Trillin, Calvin, 41
Tyson, Neil DeGrasse, 170

University of Virginia (UVA),
    27–28
Unleavened. See Jon Stewart:
    Unleavened
UVA. *See* University of Virginia

Waldoks, Moshe, 135
Warren, Elizabeth, 162
Washington, George, 14
Waters, Roger, 145–46
Waxman, Henry, 163
Weiner, Anthony, 30–31
Whitman, Christine Todd, 163

Who Wants to Be a Millionaire, 78,
    102
Wiig, Kristen, 167
William and Mary, College of,
    25–27, 28–29, 31, 115
Williams, Brian, 153
Williams, Robin, 110
Wilson, Luke, 90
Wilson, Rita, 54
Winfrey, Oprah, 4, 6, 56, 147,
    156
Wishful Thinking, 59–61
Wood, Elijah, 71, 72
Wordplay, 123

Yeshiva kindergarten, 136
Yeshiva University, 137
Youssef, Bassem, 97
You Wrote It, You Watch It, 46–47

Zadroga bill, 131

About the Author

MICHAEL BLITZ is professor of English and Interdisciplinary Studies at John Jay College of Criminal Justice, The City University of New York. He is the author or coauthor of more than a dozen books, including *Johnny Depp: A Biography*, *Arnold Schwarzenegger: A Biography*, *Why Arnold Matters: The Rise of a Cultural Icon*, *Five Days in the Electric Chair*, and *Letters for the Living: Teaching Writing in a Violent Age*. Michael and his wife, Mozelle, live in New York and have four children—Daina, Celine, Cory, and Rene.